MEDIEVAL
IN AN ENGLISH LANDSCAPE

Medieval Villages
in an English Landscape

Beginnings and Ends

Richard Jones and Mark Page

WINDgather
PRESS

Medieval Villages in an English Landscape: Beginnings and Ends

Copyright © Richard Jones and Mark Page 2006

Published by: Windgather Press Ltd, 29 Bishop Road, Bollington,
Macclesfield, Cheshire SK10 5NX

Distributed by: Central Books Ltd, 99 Wallis Road, London E9 5LN

British Library Cataloguing-in-Publication Data

A catalogue record for this book is available from the British Library

hardback   ISBN 10 1-905119-08-9
              ISBN 13 978-1-905119-08-0
paperback ISBN 10 1-905119-09-7
              ISBN 13 978-1-905119-09-7

Designed, typeset and originated by Carnegie Publishing Ltd,
Chatsworth Road, Lancaster

Printed and bound by The Cromwell Press, Trowbridge

Contents

List of Figures

Abbreviations

ASC	The Anglo-Saxon Chronicle
BAR	British Archaeological Reports
BL	British Library
BLO	Bodleian Library, Oxford
BRS	Buckinghamshire Record Society
CBA	Council for British Archaeology
CCR	*Calendar of Close Rolls* (45 vols, HMSO, 1892–1954)
CFR	*Calendar of Fine Rolls* (22 vols, HMSO, 1911–62)
CIM	*Calendar of Inquisitions Miscellaneous* (8 vols, HMSO, 1916–2003)
CIPM	*Calendar of Inquisitions Post Mortem* (23 vols, HMSO, 1904–2004)
CLR	*Calendar of Liberate Rolls* (6 vols, HMSO, 1916–64)
CPR	*Calendar of Patent Rolls* (52 vols, HMSO, 1891–1916)
CR	*Close Rolls of the Reign of Henry III* (14 vols, HMSO, 1902–38)
HL	Huntington Library, California
HMSO	Her Majesty's Stationery Office
IHR	Institute of Historical Research
MSRG	Medieval Settlement Research Group
NCO	New College, Oxford
NRO	Northamptonshire Record Office
NRS	Northamptonshire Record Society
RCHME	Royal Commission on Historical Monuments, England
RH	*Rotuli Hundredorum*
TNA:PRO	The National Archives: Public Record Office
VCH	*Victoria County History*
WAM	Westminster Abbey Muniments

Acknowledgements

··

This book presents the results of a five-year research project, 'Medieval Settlements and Landscapes in the Whittlewood Area', funded by the Arts and Humanities Research Council from 2000 to 2005. Additional grants to support archival research, archaeological field-work and photography were received from the Aurelius Trust, the British Academy, the Medieval Settlement Research Group, the Royal Archaeological Institute, the Society of Antiquaries of London and the Society for Medieval Archaeology.

The Whittlewood project was conceived and directed by Professor Christopher Dyer, and was based first at the University of Birmingham, and later at the Centre for English Local History, University of Leicester. Chris was assisted by Dr Mark Gardiner of The Queen's University of Belfast and Dr Stephen Rippon of the University of Exeter. We are indebted to all three for the enormous intellectual and practical contribution they have made to the project and the writing of this book. They have influenced but never dictated its content and we would like to thank them for the freedom they have granted us to generate, explore, and express our own ideas throughout. Of no lesser importance have been the annual peer reviews, which served to both rein us in from our wilder flights of fancy and to identify new research directions for us to investigate. We are grateful to all those who attended and contributed so freely to these meetings.

The project has benefited from the participation of a large group of experts whose knowledge of specialist areas has been fundamental to its success. Dr Paul Barnwell (English Heritage) undertook a detailed survey of the churches of Whittlewood, and secured a large English Heritage grant to enable Paul Woodfield, Anne de Broise and Rod Conlon to undertake a survey of the vernacular buildings of the area. Dr David Parsons and Dr Paul Cullen (University of Nottingham) have provided valuable advice concerning place-names, together with Eleanor Forward whose funded PhD on the place-names of Whittlewood and the surrounding area is due for completion in 2007. Palaeoenvironmental sampling of peat deposits was undertaken by Dr Nick Branch and Dr Gemma Swindle (Archaeoscape, Royal Holloway

University of London). Archaeobotanical remains, and charred and waterlogged wood, were studied by Dr Alys Vaughan-Williams and I. Poole (Archaeoscape). Animal bones from Whittlebury hillfort were assessed by Dr Naomi Sykes (University of Southampton). All pottery from fieldwalking, test-pitting, trenching and excavation was analysed by Paul Blinkhorn. An additional report on the Romano-British pottery was commissioned from Nick Cooper (University of Leicester Archaeological Service). Conor Graham (University of Belfast) undertook the Global Plotting System survey of the manorial site at Lillingstone Lovell, and Graham Brown (English Heritage) produced the earthwork survey at Lamport. Dr Jeremy Taylor and Dr Mark Gillings (University of Leicester) carried out the magnetometry and resistivity surveys of Whittlebury hillfort.

The project has made use of large numbers of documents preserved in a variety of libraries and archives. Thanks are due to the staff of the Bodleian Library, Oxford; the British Library; Buckinghamshire Record Office; the Huntington Library, California; Lincolnshire Archives; Caroline Dalton at New College, Oxford; Northamptonshire Record Office; the Public Record Office (now rebranded as The National Archives); and Westminster Abbey. Kate Felus and Richard Wheeler of the National Trust assisted in our work on Stowe. Philip Riden, former county editor of the Victoria County History of Northamptonshire, allowed access to the parish histories of Cleley Hundred prior to publication. Professor Bruce Campbell of The Queen's University of Belfast has been a good friend of the project, and hosted a useful meeting with the Irish Discovery Programme's medieval rural settlement project. Peter Kitson (University of Birmingham) resolved our difficulties over the 'Deanshanger' charter, and Keith Bailey has shared his knowledge of Buckinghamshire place-names. David Griffiths (University of Oxford Department of Continuing Education) has helped in a number of ways, not least in hosting our Oxford meetings. Harold Fox (University of Leicester) has always been at hand to offer friendly advice and encouragement.

There would have been no project or book, of course, were it not for the access we were able to gain to fields and gardens. We would like to thank all those farmers who allowed us to walk their fields and on occasion dig the odd hole. We would also like to express our sincere gratitude to over 200 house owners who allowed test-pits to be dug in their private gardens. Paving the way was a small but vital team of local 'fixers' – Stan Bennett (Akeley), David Moore (Lillingstone Lovell), Nigel Reed (Silverstone), Brian and Denise Gayle, and Ray Pearson (Whittlebury), and Mike Parsons (Wicken) – whose negotiation and diplomacy on our behalf provided us with such unprecedented

Acknowledgements

access. Especial thanks must go to Leo and Cassandra McNeir and the Appleby family for permission to excavate more extensive parts of their respective paddocks. We are also grateful to Mr Richmond-Watson for permission to survey woodland on the Wakefield Lodge Estate, to Oliver Jessop and Gary Marshall (National Trust) who allowed us to work at Stowe, and to Sir James Wilson for authorisation to survey the site at Heybarne. For much practical help and advice, we thank Sandy Kidd and Julia Wise (Buckinghamshire County Council), Graham Cadnam (Northamptonshire County Council), David Hall and Glenn Foard.

It is impossible to name individually almost 300 students from the universities of Sheffield, Leicester and Southampton, and an army of volunteers drawn from across the country, who participated in excavation and other field survey over the five years of the project. We hope that this book stands as a testament to the efforts they all put in to recover the data on which it is based. But we would like to thank personally David Jackson, Gerry Mico and Lyn Robinson who together, on our reckoning, walked nearly half of the 1,400 miles of transects during the fieldwalking campaign. We would also like to single out those who supervised the fieldwork so expertly and with such good humour: Ben Pears (Northampton Archaeology), who directed excavations at Whittlebury hillfort and Wicken, and for numerous other contributions; Colin Merrony (University of Sheffield), for overseeing many of the earthwork and geophysical surveys; and Ed King, Leonie Pett, Chris Harrison and David Knight for supervising trial trenches and test-pitting.

Our families have offered constant support and encouragement, and occasional distraction. To Naomi and Susanna, and to our children – Ione, Emilia and Tobias – all of whom arrived during the course of the project, we offer grateful thanks.

Finally, long-term projects of this sort need a local home. We have had three unofficial headquarters during the last five years and we would like to thank those who have made the brief time we have spent in the area so comfortable. First, there is Willows Farm, where Bernard Fox has constructed one of the best-appointed archaeological campsites to be found anywhere in the country. Secondly, the Bull and Butcher, Akeley, where the student and authors' pound has been so ruthlessly extracted (by Bernard again). And finally, Dolly's Cottage, Whittlebury, where Pat Clapp, Alan Beeden and their much-missed goat, Blossom, have been such gracious hosts to project staff and visitors alike. If after reading this book, you are inclined to visit the area, and we hope you do, you will find that both Dolly's Cottage and the Bull and Butcher provide perfect bases from which to strike out and investigate the villages, woods and fields of Whittlewood for yourselves.

Preface

Christopher Dyer

This book has its roots in the investigation into medieval villages that began with the collaboration of Maurice Beresford and John Hurst in the late 1940s. They set up the Deserted Medieval Village Research Group, and edited a book summing up the Group's findings in *Deserted Medieval Villages* in 1971. The study of deserted villages inspired the initial research, but by the 1970s it was realised that this focus was too restraining, and that the majority of villages which still survived were of equal importance. The excavations of Wharram Percy, which went on for 40 years, reflected in their changing agenda for research the general shifts in interpretation and enquiry. The original focus of the project was to reveal evidence for the desertion of the village, and to recover insights into peasant life from the remains of the abandoned houses. Attention shifted to village origins and village planning, and these themes became a preoccupation in the last quarter of the twentieth century for those working on medieval settlements and landscape history everywhere. It was during that period that it was realised and generally accepted that nucleated villages were formed towards the end of the first millennium AD (after AD 850 was the common view), and that the development of the villages was connected with landscape changes, such as the laying out of the open fields. Thinking about village origins shifted attention to the regions in which nucleated villages were either scarce or non-existent, and this encouraged research on dispersed settlements (farmsteads and hamlets) in the south-west, the west midlands, and parts of the east midlands and East Anglia.

In 1987 the Medieval Settlement Research Group was formed to inherit and advance the work of the former groups concerned with villages and moated sites. The MSRG had great success in attracting members and enthusiasm, but with the imminent end of the Wharram Percy excavation it might have lacked a focal point. As the Group's secretary, sensing the need for a push forward, I proposed that a research project should make its aim to identify an area, perhaps as large as a group of parishes, in the east midland region where dating evidence in the form of pottery made it possible to discover and investigate settlements of the period AD 400–1100. The area should have the potential for making comparisons between dispersed and nucleated settlements. The research would not just be focused on settlement origins, but also on their subsequent development, through to their survival or desertion at the end of the Middle Ages.

The Leverhulme Trust supported a study of four east midland counties, and through the zeal of Carenza Lewis and Patrick Mitchell-Fox we achieved both a study of the landscape, society and settlements of the region, published as *Village, Hamlet and Field* in 1997, and a list of places which seemed to offer the best opportunities for research. The list gave numerical scores for such characteristics as the modern use of land, which would enable earthworks to be surveyed and ploughed fields to be walked. The ideal area would have informative documents, and include both nucleated and dispersed settlements. The dozen parishes which can loosely be named Whittlewood figured among the leading three areas.

No progress was made for some months after the publication of *Village, Hamlet and Field*, perhaps through temporary exhaustion. In the main square of Bruges in October 1997, during the archaeological conference called *Medieval Europe*, Mark Gardiner asked me pointedly why the list of suitable places had been left in the air. This precipitated two years of activity, guided by a working party sponsored by the MSRG (of which I was then president), culminating in a successful application to the Arts and Humanities Research Board for funds. The authors of this book, Richard Jones and Mark Page, were appointed as researchers in the spring of 2000, initially for two years, and a second application kept them at work until the summer of 2005. I was the 'principal applicant' for this research, with two co-applicants: Mark Gardiner from Belfast and Stephen Rippon from Exeter. It was officially entitled 'Medieval Settlements and Landscapes in the Whittlewood Area', but quickly became universally known as 'The Whittlewood Project'.

The five-year span of the project was one of intense activity on many fronts. Our working routine was for myself and the two researchers to keep in regular contact, with project board meetings every two months, attended by the two co-applicants. Each year a review was held by the MSRG, to which a panel of experts came to hear reports and to offer criticism and encouragement (mostly the latter). In addition to the many days of fieldwalking in the winter, every summer for four years a period of fieldwork was organised, with the digging of test-pits as a major activity. Labour was provided by students from a number of university archaeology departments, together with volunteers from Whittlewood and beyond.

Much else was going on at the time: we all had commitments to other research programmes, and had to find time for them. I and both researchers relocated our jobs from Birmingham University to Leicester in 2001, after which we all moved houses. I lived in Oxford temporarily in 2000–1. Mark Page and Richard Jones faced additional responsibilities thanks to the successive births of Emilia, Ione and Toby. We were still able to write a dozen articles and essays arising from the Whittlewood work, and in order to spread the news about the project we reported our results in many lectures, both to local groups and to learned societies, and took part in a number of conferences. It would be wrong to suppose that we were all in a permanent state of hyperactivity, as many working lunches were consumed in pubs all over England, but especially at the Bull and Butcher at Akeley, the Fox and Hounds at Whittlebury and the White Lion at Wicken. We were welcomed and entertained by local people, and we learned much about the villages, including their gossip. We had a series of encounters, many informal, with academics of every kind, whose conversations have helped to mould the ideas in this book. The students provided constant stimulus and entertainment, including end-of-excavation theatricals, and we hope that they will carry with them good memories of summer fieldwork that was both pleasurable and academically purposeful.

This book was written jointly by Richard Jones and Mark Page (in alphabetical order). Some research projects result in a multi-authored work, and among the authors are those who contributed to the project as applicants for funds or as advisers, but did not write much of the text. We decided at an early stage that the names on the project's publications would reflect the actual authorship. The title caused much discussion, and was the result of a collective decision by myself, the two co-applicants and the two researchers. We were anxious to show in the main title that this study of one small group of villages could be applied more widely: hence *Medieval Villages*.

We believe that many English landscapes and settlements followed similar paths of development, so the evidence used, the methods of research, and the interpretation have significance beyond the boundaries of Whittlewood. The subtitle, *Beginnings and Ends*, emphasises the diversity of experience that we found – settlements came into existence at different times between about AD 500 and 1200, and they began in a variety of ways. They also followed divergent paths in later centuries: some expanded and flourished like Silverstone, others remained small in size or shrank, and others were completely abandoned. *Ends* refers to a place-name much used in Whittlewood to identify the constituent parts of the larger villages, from West End in Silverstone to Limes End in Leckhampstead; the ends provide evidence of the piecemeal growth of villages and describe a type of dispersed settlement; the word also refers to the ultimate fate of a number of the deserted villages and hamlets.

This book does not mean the end of the Whittlewood Project, but marks a stage in its progress. There will be many lunches, test-pits and seminars still to come, as we seek to answer the still unresolved questions thrown up by the research.

CHAPTER ONE

Studying Medieval Villages and Landscapes

....

The village has a powerful hold on the English imagination. Generations of writers and artists have celebrated and idealised the visual charm and traditional social rhythms of village life. A common perception of the village, inspired by the apparent antiquity of its buildings, lanes and fields, is of an unchanging place, a constant and comforting presence in a rapidly changing world (Figure 1). This picture is not entirely false; elements of continuity can be identified in the countryside over long periods of time. But in recent years, the emphasis of much writing on the English village has been on change, even if the precise nature of that change is disputed. The study of villages and landscapes, especially in medieval England, offers ample scope for controversy and debate. A contemporary account describing the formation of a medieval village does not survive, and one was probably never written. But even if such a document existed, doubts about its representativeness would almost certainly be expressed, as in the accounts that survive from the twelfth century of the reorganisation of field systems.[1] Similarly, the complete excavation of a village would not yield all of the necessary archaeological evidence, and again would be open to interpretation.[2] To understand rural settlements and landscapes we need to combine the efforts of different disciplines, including the work of historians, archaeologists, geographers, landscape historians, place-names scholars, palaeoenvironmental scientists, and students of vernacular and church architecture. Our ideas about where, when, how and why different patterns of settlement and landscape emerged in England are thus dependent on the interpretation of a wide range of documentary, material and scientific evidence, the complexity of which allows divergent conclusions to be drawn.

Particular disagreement surrounds the definition of settlements. The rural settlements of medieval England are conventionally divided into villages, hamlets, and farmsteads. The classification adopted here – which is by no means universal – is based largely on differences in size. A farmstead refers to a single dwelling house, together with

FIGURE I.
An English village: church,
rectory and medieval
manorial earthworks in
Lillingstone Lovell.
RICHARD JONES

its associated agricultural buildings, which may have been occupied by one or more families. A hamlet is a small group of farmsteads – of no more than a dozen – the buildings of which either lie close together in the form of a cluster or row, or follow a more winding course along lanes, usually separated from their neighbours by small arable or pasture fields. A countryside in which most people live in hamlets or farmsteads is said to have a dispersed pattern of settlement. A village has more than a dozen farmsteads, which may be arranged in a cluster or regular rows, in which case it is described as nucleated. In some places, the houses may be more widely and irregularly spaced, perhaps forming a number of distinct parts or 'ends', which can lead to the village being called 'polyfocal'.[3] The dividing lines between these categories can be unclear, so that it is difficult to draw distinctions between small villages and large hamlets, and regularity of plan is not always clear-cut. Some villages are so fragmented that they can be perceived as a form of dispersal. But, we suggest, the classification of settlements based on differences in status or function are even less satisfactory than those expressed in terms of size.[4]

After more than a century of scholarship, a measure of agreement has been reached on some aspects of the study of rural settlements and landscapes in medieval England, while others continue to arouse debate. In this chapter we attempt to outline the current state of knowledge about where, when, how and why different patterns of settlement and landscape emerged. Particular problems and issues raised by our case-study of a small part of midland England are highlighted. The authors of this book are, respectively, an archaeologist and a historian, and the evidence from archaeological fieldwork and documentary research forms the basis of many of our conclusions. However, experts in other disciplines have made important contributions, and short discussions are provided about the significance for settlement studies of an understanding of historical geography, place-names, palaeoenvironmental science, and secular and church architecture.

Regional variation

Writing towards the end of the nineteenth century, F. W. Maitland observed the basic division of rural England into 'a land of villages' and 'a land of hamlets'. In some parts of the country, he noted, nucleated villages made up of clusters and rows were distributed at regular intervals across the landscape, surrounded by large fields in which few isolated farmsteads were built. By contrast, in other areas, farmsteads and hamlets – often of no more than three or four houses – were scattered across the countryside, interspersed with small irregular fields, and connected to one another by a multitude of lanes and paths.[5] Maitland provided sections of the Ordnance Survey maps of the border between Oxfordshire and Berkshire (dominated by nucleated villages) and that between Somerset and Devon (where hamlets and farmsteads are the characteristic settlement form). More recently, an attempt has been made to map the settlement pattern of England as a whole. Based on mid-nineteenth-century Ordnance Survey maps, and plotting towns, villages, hamlets and farmsteads by using subjectively size-graded dot symbols, Roberts and Wrathmell have created a comprehensive atlas of rural settlement, which may be employed in studies of settlement patterns both in the nineteenth century and in earlier times.[6]

On the basis of the atlas, Roberts and Wrathmell have argued that England may be divided into three main settlement zones (Figure 2): firstly, a 'Central Province', dominated by a dense pattern of nucleated villages; secondly, a 'South-eastern Province', characterised by more widely spaced nucleated villages, hamlets and market towns; and thirdly, a 'Northern and Western Province', comprising a variety of settlement forms, but which may be distinguished from the Central Province by a consistently higher level of dispersion – that is, more

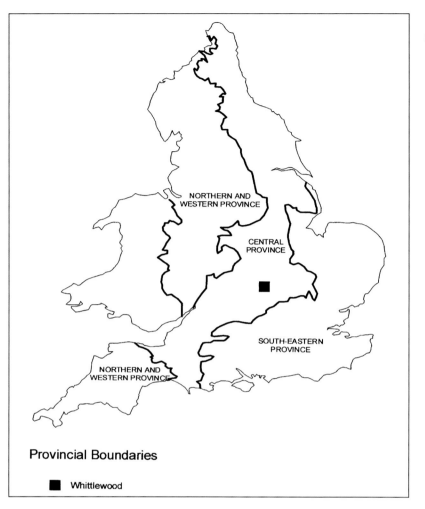

NORTHERN AND
WESTERN PROVINCE

CENTRAL
PROVINCE

SOUTH-EASTERN
PROVINCE

NORTHERN AND
WESTERN PROVINCE

Provincial Boundaries

■ Whittlewood

FIGURE 2.
Rural settlement provinces
in England, from Roberts
and Wrathmell 2000.

hamlets and farmsteads. The identification of a Central Province
dominated by nucleated villages has rapidly gained acceptance, partly
because it corroborates much earlier work. For example, a broadly
similar map of rural settlement types was published by Thorpe in
1964, and has been frequently reproduced.[7] Likewise, a map depicting
deserted medieval (nucleated) villages, published in 1968, revealed
that these too were largely restricted to a belt of central England,
stretching from Hampshire and Dorset in the south to the counties
of the north-east.[8] But if the principle of a Central Province has been
accepted, the precise location of its boundaries, as drawn by Roberts
and Wrathmell, has kindled dissent; for example, the exclusion from
the Central Province of the Wiltshire and Hampshire downlands, an
area of mainly nucleated settlement, has been criticised.[9]

4

The identification of contrasting regions of rural settlement has been accompanied by, and related to, similar divisions of England according to observed differences in landscape. The Central Province, for example, has been broadly equated with the area of 'champion' countryside, a term first coined in the sixteenth century, which referred to the large open fields (Fr. *champagne*) in which the land of the villagers was divided into numerous small and unhedged strips.[10] More recently, this countryside has been described as 'planned', because it was initially laid out according to a coherent scheme of villages and open fields, and then transformed by large-scale, planned enclosure, often by parliamentary act in the eighteenth and nineteenth centuries. By contrast, the dispersed settlements of hamlet and farmstead lay mainly in zones of 'ancient' countryside, which in general have not been subject to such sweeping changes as those brought about by the enclosure movement. In these areas, such as on the Somerset–Devon border, the pattern of fields, hedgerows, and roads is much more intricate and irregular than is usually found in the planned countryside. Much land lay in hedged fields dating to long before parliamentary enclosure.[11]

Such broad distinctions are useful at a national level, but often lack the subtlety needed for more localised studies. Some landscape characterisations have thus sought to take more account of small-scale local variations. One scheme, for example, divided England into categories of countryside or *pays*. These were defined principally by their physical characteristics, such as champion, down, fen, forest, heath, marsh, moor and wold.[12] However, it was also recognised that these landscapes supported a unique combination of settlement patterns, agricultural and industrial economies, social groupings, and cultural affinities. In other words, the character of a place was determined not only by the physical environment but also by the responses to it, over many generations, of individual communities; such insights have given rise to the idea of the cultural province.[13] The boundaries of each *pays* (or province) are in some cases sharply defined, but more frequently diffuse, grading in and out of each other almost imperceptibly on the ground, but understood by those who inhabited them. Some *pays* might be relatively self-contained, while others interacted more fully with their neighbours. The precise mapping of *pays* is often problematic, but acknowledgement of their existence offers a more nuanced understanding of the English landscape than a simple bipartite or tripartite division. Roberts and Wrathmell have also divided their three provinces into a larger number of sub-provinces.[14]

Within the Central Province of mainly nucleated villages, pockets of more dispersed settlement may be found. In some places, this was the result of opportunities in the Middle Ages to colonise areas of woodland and waste, which were cleared for agricultural use and farmed from newly established villages, hamlets, and farmsteads. In other places, new settlements were established by freeholders who were granted, sold or leased land by the lord of the manor.[15] One such area may be found on the border between Buckinghamshire and Northamptonshire, which was formerly part of Whittlewood Forest. Surrounded by large tracts of champion countryside, the open fields of which were farmed by the inhabitants of nucleated villages – usually the only settlement within the parish or township – the landscape and settlement pattern of medieval Whittlewood presented a different picture. Not only was there a great deal more woodland and waste in Whittlewood than in surrounding areas, but also some agricultural land lay outside the open fields, in closes farmed in severalty (not communally); the inhabitants of hamlets and farmsteads, of which there might be a number in each parish, often held land which was separate from that of the villagers; and some of the villages had a distinctly dispersed appearance. The Whittlewood area provides the focus for the case-studies presented in this book; its character and the reasons behind its choice as a suitable area for investigation are discussed more fully in the following chapter.

There is, therefore, broad agreement about where different patterns of settlement and landscape emerged in medieval England, even if the boundaries of individual provinces, *pays*, or smaller areas of countryside continue to be queried, refined and debated. The main contributors to this work have been archaeologists, geographers and historians, although the findings of other disciplines have sometimes also been invoked in support of a particular interpretation. For example, Roberts and Wrathmell make use of the distribution of place-name elements which denote a particular type of settlement, such as 'green' and 'worth', to demonstrate the character of their three provinces.[16] Not all place-names may be used in this way, but some indicate whether a settlement was likely to have formed in a wooded or more open landscape, or close to an area of common waste.[17]

Continuity and change

Early studies of medieval rural settlement identified a period of profound change in the immediate post-Roman period. The Romano-British settlement pattern of hamlets, villas and farmsteads was, it was claimed, replaced in the fifth and sixth centuries by fully formed nucleated villages, imported from the continent by Germanic invaders who imposed them on the English countryside with little regard for what had gone before. Across much of lowland England, the colonists planted their villages, forcing the indigenous British population to flee to the north and west, where settlement continued to be based on the hamlet and farmstead. At the same time, open fields were laid out around the nucleated villages, which were farmed in common by all the inhabitants, the observed differences in their structure reflecting, it was argued, the geographical distribution of the various newly-settled ethnic groups. According to this interpretation, much of midland England underwent a 'thorough Germanization' during the fifth century.[18] These ideas have now been largely rejected, as we discuss more fully in Chapter Five, and replaced by a number of hypotheses which stress the importance of the three or four centuries after AD 800 as the key period of village and open-field formation. Particularly influential in this process of revision was Thirsk's evolutionary explanation of the origins of the open fields, impelled by population growth, which was published in 1964.[19] However, although it is generally agreed that the period AD 800–1200 represents the broad time frame within which nucleated villages and open fields superseded an earlier pattern of dispersed settlements and ancient fields, there remains dispute about a more precise timetable. Villages formed at different times in different places; in some cases the process was rapid, while in others it was more protracted; open fields might be laid out at the same time or later; subsequent phases of reorganisation may mask earlier developments; and the surviving evidence is often patchy and difficult to interpret. The question of when villages and open fields formed is thus far from straightforward; the chronology presented in this book falls within the broad range AD 800–1200, but differs from most previous studies (see below, page 101).

Although there is now agreement that the Saxon invasions of the fifth and sixth centuries did not herald the arrival of widespread nucleated villages and open fields, debate persists about the extent to which the end of the Roman era marked a decisive break in the settlement pattern, and in the management and ownership of land. The most recent survey of the period identified elements both of continuity and discontinuity, but concluded that 'overall, the landscapes of post-Roman Britain remain in use' and that 'there was no catastrophe here, just a slight increase in the rate of change in constantly evolving landscapes'.[20] Many local studies, too, emphasise continuity over change.[21]

There has been a particular focus recently on the survival and reuse of ancient field systems and boundaries. These are well known in areas of 'ancient' countryside, where midland-type open fields were not introduced in the Middle Ages: for example, the 'Scole-Dickleburgh field system' in south Norfolk, the evidence for which has recently been challenged and restated.[22] But now evidence has emerged from within the Central Province demonstrating a similar pattern of survival. At Caxton in Cambridgeshire, for example, Oosthuizen has shown that a fragmentary coaxial field system survived into the modern period: 'the relationship between these ancient field boundaries and medieval cultivation remains … appears to show that these earlier fields were straightforwardly incorporated into the open-field layout'.[23] Further work on the open fields of Cambridgeshire has also suggested the antiquity of linear features, which may have served as routes for seasonal transhumance or as land divisions, before being incorporated into medieval field boundaries.[24] The survival of prehistoric and Romano-British field systems implies that the land remained in some sort of agricultural use throughout their existence. Nevertheless, this does not mean that patterns of ownership and farming persisted. There may have been considerable tenurial disruption in the fifth and sixth centuries, as farmsteads were abandoned and taken over, and new estate structures imposed on an existing pattern of fields and roads. Likewise, there may have been a retreat of arable farming and an increased emphasis on pastoralism.[25] Elements of both continuity and discontinuity could coexist in the post-Roman landscape.

The retention of the physical boundaries of earlier fields may have important implications for our understanding of the creation of the open fields in the late Saxon period. At Caxton most of the land was held by sokemen before the Norman Conquest. According to Oosthuizen, 'the implication may be that the introduction of the midland system in those parishes which were largely or wholly held by sokemen was achieved by consensus. This consensus may have received physical expression in the retention of the underlying layout of the original field system through the use of some earlier boundaries as furlong boundaries'.[26] Further work is needed to test this hypothesis, but it is possible that the reuse of ancient field boundaries was related to late Saxon social hierarchies. Thus, in areas where lordship was strong, the opportunities for more radical reorganisation of the countryside may have been more widely pursued. For example, in Northamptonshire, where sokemen were less numerous than in Cambridgeshire, 'the pattern of medieval fields generally bears no relationship to the underlying Iron Age and Roman field systems revealed as crop marks by aerial photography'.[27] Even in Northamptonshire, however, Roman field boundaries may have survived in a few places, especially in areas of heavy soils, which were difficult to cultivate and hence less likely to experience innovation and reorganisation.[28]

The survival of ancient field boundaries does not necessarily imply continuity in patterns of rural settlement. At Catholme in Staffordshire, for instance, a Romano-British ditch continued to form the eastern boundary of the Anglo-Saxon settlement. But even in this area, where the impact of Anglo-Saxon cultural influence was limited and mostly late, continuity of settlement is hard to prove. Thus, although the distinctive layout of the settlement at Catholme has prompted speculation that this was 'what a "Dark Age" British (or a hybrid Anglo-British) settlement looked like', the evidence does not suggest a simple model of continuity. Reoccupation of the site probably began several generations after the end of Roman rule in Britain, while the presence of *grubenhäuser* and 'Anglo-Saxon'-style burials of the late fifth or sixth centuries 'are likely to be due both to acculturation and a limited movement of people'.[29] In many cases, problems of dating mean that we do not know whether the earliest phases of Saxon occupation were contemporary with or later than the final phases of Romano-British occupation. Some settlements, such as Catholme, or Quarrington in Lincolnshire, may have been abandoned and later reoccupied; in the interval, they probably ceased to be functioning agricultural units.[30] Nevertheless, as Rippon observes, 'post-Roman native settlement is notoriously difficult to identify', and in counties such as Essex, 'it may have been far more common for Romano-British settlements to have still been occupied in the fifth or even sixth century than has previously been thought'.[31]

But settlement was not sustainable everywhere in the post-Roman period, such as in the fenland or on the claylands.[32] In Northamptonshire there seems to have been 'a fundamental change in the rural settlement pattern, and presumably also in land use, during the late fourth or the earlier fifth century'.[33] In particular, there was probably a retreat of settlement from the claylands in favour of lighter soils.[34] Moreover, as population declined and agricultural land fell out of use, the conditions were created for woodland regeneration. The extent to which woodland colonised former open land in the post-Roman period has been questioned.[35] Many pollen sequences, indeed, suggest continuity or even increased clearance of land in the period AD 400–800.[36] Nevertheless, in parts of Britain, such as eastern Hertfordshire, woodland probably regenerated on a significant scale.[37] The scientific analysis of the early medieval environment has the potential to revolutionise our understanding of landscape and settlement development in the post-Roman era; to date, however, the available information is too limited and widely scattered to allow a convincing general picture to be drawn. Cores of peat have been extracted from the Whittlewood area, the pollen in which points to woodland regeneration in the period AD 400–600 (see below, pages

56, 106).[38] Unlike the emphasis in much recent writing, therefore, the palaeoenvironmental evidence from Whittlewood indicates a period of discontinuity in land use in the centuries following the Roman era, a view supported, for the most part, by the data derived from archaeological fieldwork. Some Romano-British settlements remained occupied for a time, but in general little continuity of field systems or settlement sites can be demonstrated between the Roman and early medieval periods (see below, pages 85–7).

Settlement and open-field formation

There are four principal ways in which a nucleated village might have developed during the Middle Ages: by steady growth from a single place; by the agglomeration or growing together of a number of initially separate farmsteads or hamlets; by the abandonment of individual farmsteads and hamlets in favour of a larger nucleation; and by deliberate planning of a new settlement.[39] Of these four possibilities, the third has been particularly influential in explaining how nucleated villages developed in the Central Province. Systematic fieldwalking, especially in Northamptonshire, has revealed that in parishes now containing a single nucleated village, the fields of the village territory were formerly occupied by a number of early medieval farmsteads. These all appeared to have been abandoned by the mid ninth century, their inhabitants apparently moving to a single site which formed a village (see below, pages 81–2).[40] According to some interpretations, this process of nucleation was followed at a later date by the replanning of the settlement, which involved the laying-out of tenements along a street or in a grid, possibly in accordance with an ideal of what a village ought to look like.[41] The reorganisation of the village plan may have been accompanied by changes in the landscape; principally the formation of the open fields and the equitable distribution of arable strips and pasture rights among the inhabitants. Together these changes to village and field system have been described as the 'great replanning' of the late Saxon period.[42]

Phrases such as the 'great replanning' imply that there was a guiding hand at work in the formation (or reorganisation) of nucleated villages. This is possible. Lords may well have either commanded or influenced the development of new, compact settlements on their estates. For example, at Shapwick and other places in Somerset, the monks of Glastonbury Abbey appear to have been able to reorder both landscape and settlement 'on an impressive scale, probably to increase revenue'.[43] Other studies have also stressed the role of lordship in the formation of nucleated villages. At Barrington in Cambridgeshire, Oosthuizen has suggested that a former community of free tenants living in at least eight separate settlement foci was reduced to villeinage by the new Norman lord and moved to a planned village laid out alongside a green.[44] Evidence has also been found in Cambridgeshire of the 'great replanning', albeit later than that posited for Northamptonshire. Again, it is argued, Norman lords were responsible for laying out the villages, in this case over former arable land, and reducing the sokemen to villeinage. The earlier settlements were emptied and it is not known whether they were nucleated or dispersed.[45]

Despite the focus in many studies on lordship, however, it is likely that the local community also had an influence over how villages evolved and developed.[46] For example, the old church site at Shapwick was left marooned to the east of the village, 'perhaps because the move was unpopular locally'.[47] A combination of seigneurial and peasant decision-making can be suggested at Roel in Gloucestershire, where many tenants apparently chose to remain in Roelside next to the village of Hawling rather than relocate to a new settlement and manorial site further north.[48] In a number of places before the Norman Conquest, the population was made up largely of sokemen, privileged peasants who were better able than others to exercise choice in the location and form of their villages, hamlets and fields, as in Cambridgeshire.[49]

The idea and the initiative for change to the village plan or field system may thus have come from the lord, or the local community, or a combination of the two; as Paul Harvey has commented, 'mostly that is anyone's guess', because a lack of evidence obscures our view in all but a few, exceptional, cases.[50] But whatever agency was responsible, it is generally accepted that settlements and landscapes were subject to constant redevelopment, and sometimes large-scale replanning, throughout the Middle Ages and beyond. Much more contentious is the proposition that there was a 'great replanning', affecting large swathes of countryside, as a result of political developments in the tenth century.[51] Certainly it has not yet been demonstrated that such a change took place over a wide area. On the basis of the studies undertaken for this book, the laying-out of the open fields in the tenth century was a quite separate process from the replanning of settlements, which for the most part occurred in the centuries after the Norman Conquest (see below, pages 91–5).

According to Christopher Taylor, 'steady growth from an initial farmstead is perhaps the most obvious and widely accepted reason invoked for the appearance of a nucleated village', but that 'while continuous growth from a single farmstead is theoretically likely, given the undoubted rise in population in late Saxon and early medieval times, it remains very difficult to pinpoint specific examples with any confidence'.[52] The lack of evidence is certainly a problem, but in recent years there may also have been a reluctance to accept an explanation that conflicts with the widely held notion of settlement mobility or shift; this has dominated much recent writing on the subject of village origins, and forms a central tenet of the hypothesis that the inhabitants of isolated farmsteads or hamlets abandoned their homes and relocated to a single site which expanded to form a village.[53] While not wishing to deny that the position of settlements might change over time, or that some may have been abandoned in favour of alternative sites, evidence from the Whittlewood area indicates that many settlements demonstrated remarkable stability in their location in the centuries after AD 400, and that both nucleated villages and dispersed settlements grew after AD 850 from small nuclei, gaining their population either from natural increase or migration (see below, pages 101–3).

Nucleated villages and dispersed settlements

The basic division of England into a land of villages and a land of hamlets is very striking. Why did nucleated villages form in some places and not in others, sometimes only a short distance away? Recent attempts to answer this question have focused on the eastern boundary of the Central Province. In a major study of eastern and central England, Williamson has argued that the overriding determinants of settlement formation were agricultural and environmental (Figure 3). Nucleated villages developed in those places where there were practical farming reasons for the inhabitants to live close together. For example, in some areas variation in rainfall and the presence of particular types of clay soil meant that there were relatively limited opportunities to plough and harrow the fields, especially in the period of spring sowing. 'Where cultivations needed to be carefully timed, and where full advantage had to be taken of every hour in which the soils were suitable for ploughing or harrowing, ploughteams needed to be assembled with particular rapidity; and this was obviously much easier to achieve where farms were in close proximity, rather than scattered across the landscape'.[54] Likewise, in areas in which meadowland was abundant and concentrated in large parcels, the need to mobilise labour rapidly on the few days of the year suitable for haymaking encouraged the nucleation of settlement. By contrast, in other places, where meadowland was widely distributed in small pockets, a more dispersed pattern of settlement developed.[55] Furthermore, in nucleated villages, the sense of cohesion

and cooperation which communal farming engendered was likely to have promoted the formation of open fields, in which the land was divided among the villagers in the form of intermingled and unhedged strips, ensuring that each landholder received an equal share of both good and bad soil, some land situated near to their homes and some at a distance.[56] The conclusion drawn is that different patterns of settlement and field system were 'the outcome of rational adjustments to complex environmental circumstances'.[57]

Williamson's emphasis on environmental factors contrasts with that of Christopher Taylor, who has made a close study of the settlement pattern in Cambridgeshire, through which the boundary of the Central Province passes. According to Taylor, influences such as environment, population or social organisation appear to show no significant relationship to the pattern of nucleated and dispersed settlement. Instead, the frontier 'seems to be *just there*, as if by chance'. He goes on to pose the question: 'could not the frontier have no real significance at all except in marking an arbitrary line where the spread of the process of nucleation stopped at some time'?[58] The idea that nucleated villages, and their associated open fields, were a cultural phenomenon which spread by emulation for a limited time across the Central Province has been likened to a successful evolutionary adaptation, or to a fashion which was duplicated without a great deal of reasoning, except for status or imitation.[59] And then, in the thirteenth century, the vogue for nucleation faded away; villages and open fields were regarded as passé; they were no longer seen to be a useful adaptation. Thus, when dispersed settlements expanded, or new settlements proliferated, in the period after 1200 the inhabitants did not adopt nucleation, even in areas in which environmental conditions may have made such a change beneficial.[60] In this view, the reasons why different patterns of settlement and landscape emerged have as much to do with the conflicting human ideals of conformity, change, innovation and style, as with more rational responses to environment and farming.

The spread of nucleated villages and open fields has been compared to the development of the British railway network in the nineteenth century. According to Taylor, 'there the combination of topography, economic value, commercial speculation, technological advance, and status and fashion, all within a rapidly changing society, produced a pattern which is inexplicable in monocausal terms'.[61] Others, too, have argued that no single factor will adequately explain the variations in the pattern of medieval settlement and landscape that emerged between the ninth and thirteenth centuries, another formative period in European history. For example, although it can be demonstrated that the role of lordship, or local communities, or population density, was influential in determining the formation of particular types of settlement or field system in certain places, the relationship between them is not straightforward and exceptions can always be found.[62] Clarity and certainty remain elusive, and recent explanations offer little room for complacency. Even Williamson's bold statement of the environmental hypothesis, though compelling and attractive, cannot be considered conclusive; as he himself recognises, it is likely to be criticised as its arguments are tested, and found wanting, in individual localities (see below, pages 95–9).[63]

The variations in the rural settlement pattern are generally linked to human decision-making; whether the settlements were nucleated or dispersed, initiatives were taken by lords or communities in response to a variety of factors.[64] There can be little doubt that most settlements, to a greater or lesser extent, were planned: lords and tenants had to decide where to locate new buildings, taking into account existing tenements, manor house and church, and the alignments of roads and fields. The location of the church may have been particularly influential, and studies of parish churches are often revealing about settlement development (see below, pages 185–9).[65] Few settlements can be considered to be wholly random collections of buildings, and in some places a decision has clearly been taken to reorganise and replan the settlement and its fields at one point in time.[66]

In areas such as Whittlewood Forest, nucleated villages and dispersed settlements lie side by side, often no more than a few miles from each other. Their juxtaposition might be explained by differences in the extent to which they were deliberately planned or reorganised. But it is far from certain that the layout of a nucleated village was subject to a greater degree of control and coordination than that of a dispersed settlement. As Taylor has argued, decisions may have been taken to encourage or allow dispersion, while nucleation was not necessarily the outcome of careful design.[67] The formation and development of settlements in the centuries after AD 800 was not a random process, but it was complex and diverse. The decisions taken by lords and communities, influenced by environment, culture and other factors, had broadly similar, but not identical, effects in particular regions. Subtle differences in topography, both natural and man-made, combined with the idiosyncrasies of human behaviour, produced settlement plans that were, in each case, unique. In some places, differences in topography and decision-making were so slight that settlements resembled one another; in others, of which Whittlewood Forest is just one example, the variations were sufficient to produce a more diverse mix of dispersed and nucleated plans.

CHAPTER TWO

Whittlewood:
An Introduction

W. G. Hoskins described the English landscape as 'the richest historical record'.[1] Those who follow in Hoskins's footsteps agree: the study of past landscapes begins with that of the present day and the search – with map and on foot – for the clues it holds of earlier patterns and developments. This chapter provides an introduction to the Whittlewood area by examining its present appearance and cultural background; the modern settlement pattern is described and recent landscape changes discussed. In addition, we explain why Whittlewood was chosen as a test-bed for exploring general questions about rural settlement and landscape in medieval England, and outline the principal methods used in the investigation. Finally, we assess the results of earlier work undertaken in the project area, and discuss some of the research techniques employed.

The present landscape

The study area comprises a dozen parishes, covering about 97 sq km (37 square miles) of countryside, on either side of the Buckinghamshire–Northamptonshire boundary (Figure 4). Characterised by a gently rolling landscape, which is wooded in parts, the area is unexceptional, without extremes, providing an unobtrusive backdrop to our investigation. The twelve parishes under consideration possess no administrative or cultural cohesion. In the last millennium, they have not been subject to any single authority, nor have they developed distinct economic or social characteristics. Diversity, not uniformity, has been their experience; that variety is reflected in the conclusions offered in this book. The area shared one aspect of identity, however. All twelve parishes were once, briefly, part of Whittlewood Forest: hence the name of our project.

Today, the villages of the study area receive relatively few visitors, having failed to develop as a tourist destination, although the area includes two well-known attractions: the motor-racing circuit at

Location Map

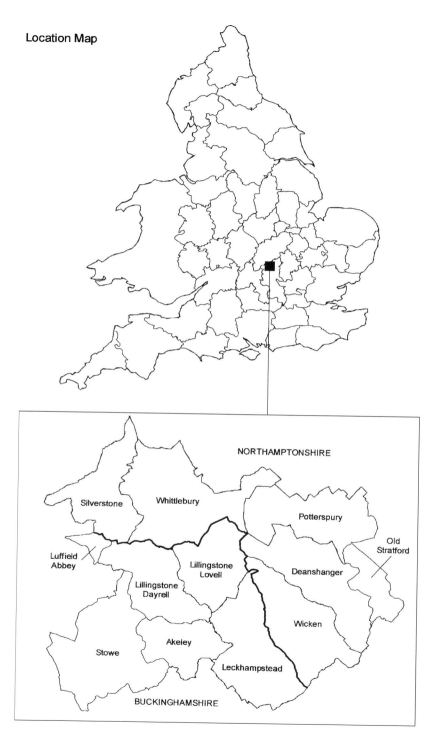

FIGURE 4.
Location map of the
Whittlewood Project study
area.

Silverstone, and the landscape gardens at Stowe. Many more people travel through the area along the region's busy roads. On the north-western edge of the project area, the A43 passes between the villages of Silverstone and Whittlebury, linking the M40 and the M1. To the north-east, traffic thunders along the A5, the Roman Watling Street, passing the village of Potterspury and the Wakefield estate, the heart of the former forest. Other roads are less heavily used, except by members of the project team, and most of the villages of the study area may be described as lying off the beaten track.

The present appearance of the villages is mixed. Some have a regular shape, taking the form of a cluster of houses, as at Akeley and Wicken, or a row of houses along a street, as at Lillingstone Lovell and Whittlebury. These places may be described as nucleated villages. Other villages are more dispersed, comprising a number of different parts, often known in this area as 'ends': examples include Leckhampstead, made up of Church End, Middle End, South End, Barretts End and Limes End (Figure 5); and Silverstone, which includes West End and Cattle End. The shape of a village today is not necessarily a reliable guide to its form in the Middle Ages: modern growth and infilling may disguise its earlier appearance. Nevertheless, the variety of settlement forms in the project area is a principal feature of the diversity which this book aims to explain.

There is no town in the project area. However, to the south-east lies the urban sprawl of Milton Keynes, a mid to late twentieth-century development, which has brought new prosperity to a region formerly marked by poverty, under-employment, poor housing and falling population. The influx of urban wealth has changed the appearance of many of the surrounding villages, in some ways enhancing, in others diminishing, their rural charm. The amenities offered by Milton Keynes have drawn custom away from the smaller market towns which surround the project area. Brackley, Buckingham, Stony Stratford and Towcester were significant centres of local trade in the Middle Ages; limited redevelopment in recent decades has allowed them to retain something of their historic character.

The varied landscape of the project area contains a considerable

FIGURE 5.
A dispersed village: pointing the way in Leckhampstead.
FRAN HALSALL

acreage under crops, and the ploughed fields are a necessary require-
ment for the archaeologist who seeks to recover sherds of pottery from
the topsoil. Likewise, there are large areas of permanent pasture, in
many cases preserving medieval earthworks, which may be surveyed
both above and below ground. Deciduous woodland also survives in
considerable quantities, in parts of which have been found the remains
of medieval coppice banks and ditches. The area escaped the worst
excesses of industrialisation in the nineteenth century and was not
subject to large-scale redevelopment in the twentieth. The surviving
estate, enclosure and tithe maps of the seventeenth to nineteenth
centuries thus depict a landscape that is easily recognisable today.

Our earliest map was drawn *c.* 1608, possibly in connection with
a survey of Whittlewood Forest in that year, although it survives as
an eighteenth-century copy (Figures 6, 42, 45, 53).[2] Its chief purpose
was presumably to depict the extent of the forest, and the individual
coppices into which the woodland was divided. Happily, however,
the mapmaker also illustrated some of the surrounding villages, fields
and enclosures. In glorious colour, the map allows us to view the
villages of Silverstone, Whittlebury, Passenham and Deanshanger as
they appeared 400 years ago. Moreover, archaeological investigation
suggests that the map is accurate in its location of individual buildings
(and the spaces between them), thereby providing us with a fixed point
of departure from which to reconstruct earlier patterns of settlement.

The landscape of the project area was subject to two extensive
changes in the eighteenth and nineteenth centuries: parliamentary
enclosure of the open fields, and disafforestation. The map of *c.* 1608
(referred to hereafter as the Forest Map), and other later maps and
surveys, reveal considerable areas of ancient enclosure consisting of
parcels of former woodland which were converted to arable or pasture
and fenced by their owners. However, they also depict the expanse of
the open fields, the cultivation of which occupied the inhabitants of
all of our villages for varying times from the tenth century until the
nineteenth. A flurry of enclosure acts, beginning with Deanshanger in
1772, resulted in the transformation of this landscape in Potterspury
(1776), Akeley (1794), Whittlebury (1797) and Silverstone (1824).
Elsewhere, enclosure occurred by agreement, as in Wicken in 1757, or
by compulsion, of which the most startling examples are Lillingstone
Dayrell at the end of the fifteenth century and Stowe in the mid
seventeenth. The patchwork of irregular-shaped fields we see today
was in many cases the result of this drawn-out process of enclosure.
The preservation of this hedged landscape in recent decades owes
much to the pursuits of fox-hunting and pheasant-shooting.[3]

Further changes to the landscape followed the disafforestation of

Whittlewood Forest in 1853. The project area was included within the royal forest after the Norman Conquest: the imposition of forest law restricted the right of landowners to hunt and fell trees on their own land. Part of the area was disafforested in the Middle Ages, but the remainder was subject to crown control until 1853. Following disafforestation, large numbers of trees were felled, the land was cleared and divided into regular blocks, and new dispersed settlements, such as Victoria Cottage, now called Forest Farm, were created (Figure 7). The long straight roads providing access to such farms also date to the period after disafforestation, adding to a network of roads and paths that linked an already complex pattern of nucleated and dispersed settlements. Much of the woodland depicted on the Forest Map has thus vanished, to be replaced either by farmland or by leisure facilities, such as the golf course at Whittlebury and the motor-racing circuit (formerly a Second World War airfield) in Silverstone. Remarkably, however, a significant number of the coppices named on the Forest Map have been preserved, especially around Wakefield Lawn, a former royal hunting ground.

Contemporary writers viewed the destruction of the forest with alarm, reckoning the woodland to have 'found food for hundreds of families, where the cleared land now scarcely furnishes employment for thirty or forty people'.[4] Historians, too, have argued that the loss of common rights led to a decline in the number of smallholding and landless peasants who made their living in the forest from grazing, poaching, gathering nuts, berries, flowers and fuel, and woodworking.[5] After disafforestation, most people in the project area continued to work on the land, although the numbers employed in agriculture gradually fell, especially with the onset of depression in the last quarter of the nineteenth century. Nor was there a compensating growth of industry, except in Deanshanger, where an iron foundry and engineering works employed about 100 men and boys in 1900.[6] Thus, the increase in population in the study area between 1801 and 1851 did not continue, with numbers

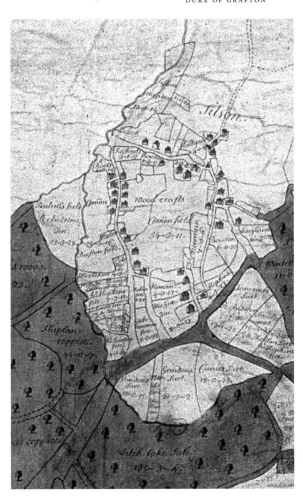

FIGURE 6.
Detail of the *c.* 1608 map of Whittlewood Forest, showing the village of Silverstone, and the surrounding fields, closes and woods.

NORTHAMPTONSHIRE RECORD OFFICE AND HIS GRACE, THE DUKE OF GRAFTON

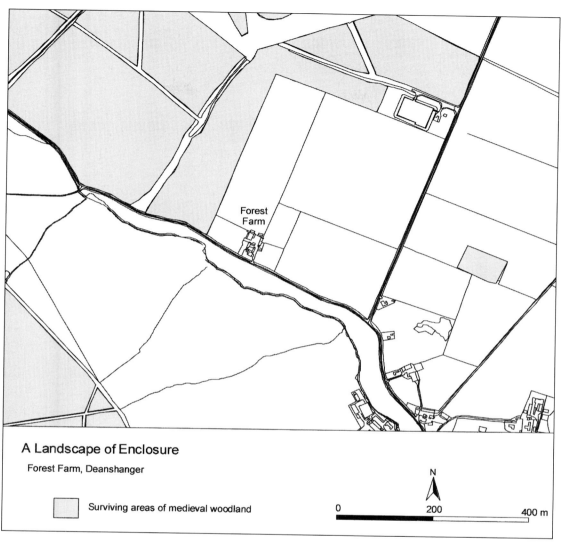

A Landscape of Enclosure

Forest Farm, Deanshanger

Surviving areas of medieval woodland

N

0   200   400 m

falling slightly until 1891 before declining more sharply; not until 1951 did the population begin to climb once more (Figure 8).

The first half of the twentieth century was marked not only by the migration of villagers in search of factory jobs in the expanding towns of the region; it also witnessed the loss of some of the aristocratic and gentry families associated with the project area. Of these, the most notable was the Temple-Grenville family, dukes of Buckingham, owners of the great house at Stowe, which was sold in 1921 and its contents dispersed. Other families also sold up at about this time. Crippling death duties following the demise of the seventh Duke of Grafton in 1918 compelled his successor to sell Wakefield Lodge, the contents of which were auctioned in 1921. The long association of the Banastre family with the manor of Passenham was ended in 1918. Several of the area's mansions became private schools, most famously Stowe, but also the seventeenth-century Potterspury Lodge, the former lodge in Wicken Park, enlarged in 1716, and houses in Akeley and Lillingstone Dayrell.[7] The area has few architectural gems: apart from Stowe, a spectacular expression of the power of its owners, the most notable house is Wakefield Lodge, which though not beautiful, according to Pevsner, has 'power and a strange primeval attraction'.[8]

In the villages, a considerable number of houses built with crucks have been identified. Dating from the fifteenth and sixteenth centuries, these buildings provide evidence of some prosperity in the study area at the end of the Middle Ages. Many more houses survive from the seventeenth and eighteenth centuries, a period of rebuilding and infilling following earlier contraction. In the twentieth century, efforts to close unfit accommodation before the Second World War, such as two 'defective' cottages in Leckhampstead (Figure 9), were followed after 1945 by private and local authority housing developments and the renovation of much of the older housing stock by middle-class incomers.[9] A number of villages, such as Deanshanger and Silverstone, have expanded markedly as a result. In others, a variety of constraints has ensured that development has been more limited.

Employment opportunities within the study area are few. Apart from motor racing at Silverstone, which generates considerable revenue, and the extraction of sand and gravel on the Great Ouse, the area lacks economic vibrancy. Most villagers work outside the area, in Milton Keynes, Northampton, or further afield. Nevertheless, a tangible sense of community and village sociability persists. An interest in the past is sustained by local history societies and preservation groups. Several

FIGURE 8.
Population in the Whittlewood Project study area, 1801–1981.

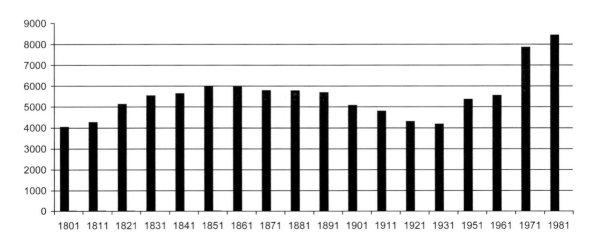

FIGURE 9.
Thatched cottages in
Leckhampstead in 1938.
BUCKINGHAMSHIRE COUNTY
COUNCIL

village histories were published to mark the millennium.[10] Above all, members of the project team have been welcomed with generous hospitality. Without access to private farmland and gardens, this book could not have been written.

Why Whittlewood?

The Whittlewood project arose directly out of earlier work on the four east midland counties of Bedfordshire, Buckinghamshire, Leicestershire and Northamptonshire, the results of which were first published in 1997.[11] The purpose of this study was to demonstrate the distribution of different settlement forms, and offer some preliminary hypotheses about their development. In addition, it was intended to identify a smaller block of territory suitable for more detailed investigation. Whittlewood was one of fourteen groups of parishes initially selected and given scores on the basis of the following criteria: topography; archaeology; pottery; documentation; maps; palaeobotanical evidence; location; and accessibility. The highest marks were awarded to Chalgrave in Bedfordshire, Horwood in Buckinghamshire, and Whittlewood. The final choice was made following a more detailed assessment of the archaeology, land use and landownership of the three areas. An important consideration was the knowledge that

Whittlewood lay within an area where we could expect to find pottery dateable to the period AD 400–1100, during which nucleated villages began to develop.[12]

The choice of study area was thus determined by the questions we wished to ask. The twelve parishes of the Whittlewood area afforded a suitable focus for developing new ideas about medieval rural settlement for a number of reasons. First, the pattern of settlement in the area was mixed, comprising both nucleated villages and dispersed settlements. We need to understand why nucleated villages formed in some places and not in others, sometimes only a short distance apart. Secondly, the settlement pattern must be viewed within the context of the wider landscape. Rural communities depended for their livelihoods on the territories surrounding their settlements. In the Whittlewood area comparison between different geographical conditions was unnecessary, as the landscape had a broadly uniform character. Thirdly, the Whittlewood area comprised a range of deserted, shrunken and surviving settlements. By exploring why some settlements fared better than others over the course of the later Middle Ages, we may be able to learn more about their beginnings, as well as (in some cases) their ends.

In many ways the Whittlewood area has exceeded the expectations of the selection procedure. Not only has it provided a rich array of archaeological finds from excavation, fieldwalking and survey, but the documentary and map evidence has proved to be fuller than initially thought. Nothing was known initially of the area's potential for environmental evidence (such as pollen), but subsequent searches have produced some very rewarding sites. Nevertheless, the study of individual parishes has not been without its complications. For example, our understanding of Potterspury has been hindered by the impracticality of excavating in a village which was the centre of a long-lived pottery industry, because we presumed that we would be overwhelmed with an abundance of finds. Cosgrove shared a field system with Potterspury and Furtho in the Middle Ages and held detached portions of land within the study area, but this parish has not been thoroughly investigated. In the light of knowledge that we gathered during the project, the area of study might have been extended to the west of Silverstone to include the royal park of Handley and the deserted settlement of Charlock, but by the time the merits of such a change became apparent it was too late to put it into effect.

Even for a five-year project, the size of the area to be investigated was large. An ambitious target to fieldwalk 10 per cent of the study area was met (just); this represents some 1,000 ha (2,470 acres), or about 25 per cent of the available arable. A total of 386 test-pits were excavated within areas of medieval settlement over four six-week campaigns of fieldwork; yet several villages and numerous dispersed settlements (in all about two-thirds of the total) were not explored due to lack of time and resources. Much has been achieved, but we cannot claim to have exhausted the area's archaeological potential. Nor can we hope to incorporate fully within the pages of this book the vast range of evidence we have collected. A number of specialised reports have been published elsewhere; others are in preparation. Large quantities of additional information may be found in our digital archive, available via the Archaeology Data Service. The following chapters offer instead a synthesis of our principal ideas, and at this stage we emphasise these four: firstly, in the Whittlewood area nucleated villages evolved from pre-existing settlements (which we call 'pre-village nuclei'), rather than from the abandonment of outlying hamlets and farmsteads; secondly, the origins of dispersed settlements lay in the same process of expansion that produced nucleations, the differences between them a consequence of subtle variations in morphology; thirdly, the medieval settlement pattern of Whittlewood demonstrated a greater degree of stability than shift; and, lastly, in a dynamic and constantly changing landscape, institutions such as the royal forest were culturally rather than physically determined.

From the outset, the Whittlewood project was designed to be interdisciplinary. Archaeologists and historians have worked closely together, contributing evidence and ideas at every stage of the research. Experts have been called upon to provide specialist knowledge. A study of the place-names of the Whittlewood area has been funded by the University of Nottingham. A survey of the vernacular architecture of our parishes was commissioned by English Heritage, while examination of the churches was carried out by Paul Barnwell. Palaeoenvironmentalists from Royal Holloway University of London have undertaken pollen analysis on peat cores taken from in and around the study area. This work has important implications for our understanding of medieval settlement and landscape and has informed the writing of the chapters that follow.

In terms of the archaeological fieldwork, a range of techniques has been employed. Fieldwalking – the systematic recovery of ceramic evidence and other artefacts from ploughed fields – has been conducted on the basis of a 15 m line interval and 20 m stint collection, ensuring that 10 per cent of each field was intensively surveyed. Attention has also been paid to the effects of different walkers and environmental conditions.[13] Finds have been analysed by a pottery specialist (Paul Blinkhorn), before being plotted on Ordnance Survey base maps using a Geographic Information System. Test-pits (one square metre in size) have been excavated by spit (generally 100 mm) unless archaeological stratification or features were identified, in which case they were excavated sequentially. Wherever possible test-pits were excavated to natural. All spoil was sieved (through graded mesh), all artefacts were recorded by spit or feature, and all features were recorded in plan. After excavation all four faces of the test-pit were recorded in section.

Occasional opportunities to undertake more extensive excavations have produced exciting results; for example, at Whittlebury churchyard and a manorial site in Wicken, which have produced both material and organic remains. Four trial trenches have also been excavated across headlands. Earthworks in a number of parishes have been surveyed, both above and below ground, using traditional survey methods, geophysical survey and, in one case, Global Plotting System analysis. Aerial photographs have provided additional information; for instance, in mapping ridge and furrow, much of which has been destroyed in recent decades by modern deep ploughing. Archival research has been conducted in parallel with the archaeology, ensuring an integrated approach. Surprisingly, perhaps, archaeologist and historian have rarely been in dispute.

Earlier surveys and techniques

The Whittlewood project area lies on either side of a county boundary. Inevitably, previous studies of the archaeology and history of the two counties vary considerably in their quality and scope. In many respects, our Northamptonshire parishes have fared better than those in Buckinghamshire. This section examines firstly, previous archaeological surveys and techniques; secondly, historical studies; and thirdly, the range of surviving documents.

Archaeology

Northamptonshire has been the focus for much recent discussion about the origins of the nucleated village and the creation of the open fields; in some ways the county is regarded as midland England in microcosm. The work of Brown, Foard and Hall has been particularly influential in raising Northamptonshire's profile, although for the most part they have not worked in the Whittlewood area.[14] Nevertheless, our methods of fieldwalking and understanding of settlement and landscape development have been informed by their research, even if our conclusions are different.[15] Studies of the county have been aided by the work of the Royal Commission on Historical Monuments (now sadly subsumed within English Heritage), which conducted detailed surveys of earthworks and cultivation and

CHAPTER THREE

Inherited Landscapes

....

The medieval rural landscape comprised three principal components: farmsteads, the basic economic unit; settlements combining farmsteads together; and settlement territories.[1] Physical and legal boundaries divided the communal spaces, which were further subdivided into areas of different land use and landholding, while roads and trackways linked them together. It is now widely accepted that the ordering of these elements – the 'patterns of the peasant landscape' – may be recognised in, and grew out of, physical, socio-economic, political and cultural frameworks established in the landscape at much earlier periods.[2] A long series of developments, going back before AD 400, lie behind the division of England into three provinces by Roberts and Wrathmell, and it is a commonplace of recent local studies, beginning with Finberg's work on the parish of Withington (Glos.), that prehistoric and Roman settlements and territories influenced the arrangements in later periods.[3]

Early structural arrangements survive, not because the landscape remained unaltered, but because it tended to evolve slowly. In particular, boundaries, as conservative features, might outlive other changes. Older landscapes were adapted and subtly reorganised to meet contemporary needs. Even when landscapes were the subject of more rapid and revolutionary change, as at parliamentary enclosure, this rarely led to the total erasure of what had gone before. Cultural and administrative territories might be redrawn, but the economic base, and thus the physical face of the landscape on which new polities were founded, could remain the same. Settlements might shift, their forms might be modified, field systems might be redesigned, but these changes could be effected within established boundaries. Despite being the creation of the decision-making of others, the landscape thus remained one of the most influential and restricting controls upon the use and division of space for later generations. Those that chose to adopt a new form of rural community, the village, did so within an inherited landscape which already possessed structure and form from earlier periods, and offered opportunities or imposed limitations. The reconstruction of this landscape, therefore, is a vital prerequisite if village formation is to be fully understood, because the origins of different forms of medieval settlement could lie in long-established frameworks, predisposing some areas to nucleation and others to dispersion.

The natural inheritance

The richest, and perhaps most problematic, of all inheritances was that provided by nature. It only requires the briefest of acquaintance with Whittlewood to appreciate that clay dominates: walk a mile along one of the area's many footpaths in autumn and feel the weight of your boots (Figure 11). Clay soils continue to dictate the timing of the agricultural year: dry springs and summers hold back crop growth, leading to very late harvests; occasional wet autumns render the fields unworkable even with modern machinery, forcing them to be left fallow and untilled until spring, and denying farmers the opportunity to sow winter cereals or legumes. Waterlogging has been a perennial problem, tackled by medieval farmers by forming and maintaining furrows between their ridges, orienting the strips with fine attention to the drainage possibilities that even the slightest slopes offered. These clayey soils formed from the underlying parent material, a layer of boulder clay or till around 15–50 m (50–165 feet) thick, dating to the advance of the ice sheet 470,000 to 350,000 years ago, in an episode known as the 'Anglian glaciation'. Composed largely of Jurassic and Lower Cretaceous mudstone picked up by the advancing ice sheet north-east of Whittlewood, this clay till, also containing much chalk and flint, was deposited over a local solid geology of cornbrash and limestone. As the glaciers retreated, other materials stored within the ice, notably gravels and sands, were washed out and deposited in the channels of streams created by the passage of the glaciers, or collected in depressions formed by the melting of the blocks of ice caught in the earth. A complex geological record in fact identifies not one but two advances of the ice sheet over Whittlewood, brought about by its proximity to the ice front, no more than 32 km (20 miles) further south at its greatest extent. So near to the edge of the sheet, the area was released for a time from the grip of the ice in a period of warming, the so-called 'Swanscombe' interglacial.[4]

This glacial reworking of the landscape of southern Northamptonshire and north-western Buckinghamshire has given it the unexceptional character of low hills and shallow valleys, lacking in extremes, already described: it left little impression on earlier observers, such as Leland.[5] Its uniformity, however, is deceptive. The indiscriminate collection, mixing and deposition of different geologies by the ice sheet has created infinite largely uncharted and highly-localised variety in the properties of the parent material from which the cultivated soils have

FIGURE 11.
The geology of the Whittlewood area.

been created. The excavation of archaeological test-pits has shown that the boulder clay can change in nature within the space of a few metres, while a single field may contain heavy intractable clays together with pockets of more freely-draining sands and gravels. This diversity has been further magnified by the erosion of the till over-burden by post-glacial watercourses, notably the Great Ouse together with its tributaries, and the feeder streams of the Tove. These have

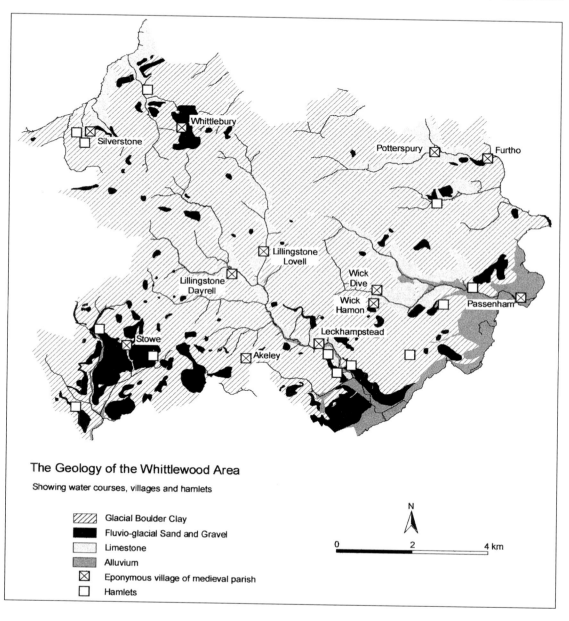

The Geology of the Whittlewood Area

Showing water courses, villages and hamlets

- ▨ Glacial Boulder Clay
- ■ Fluvio-glacial Sand and Gravel
- ☐ Limestone
- ▨ Alluvium
- ⊠ Eponymous village of medieval parish
- ☐ Hamlets

0   2   4 km

exposed the underlying solid geology in some places, and in others led to its reburial under gravel terraces or alluvium (material brought along by rivers) and colluvium (material washed from surrounding hillsides). Lighter, more easily worked soils have developed in these areas. Moreover, it is these rivers which have created the local topography, moulding the flat table of glacial till so that it now shelves down from a high point on the principal watershed on the county boundary between Whittlebury and Lillingstone Lovell, north and east to the broad curve of the Tove, and south to the Great Ouse. The action of the tributary streams, most prominent amongst which are Silverstone Brook, the rivers Alder and Leck, and Dogsmouth Brook, have further dissected this shallow dome of boulder clay, and have given it its gently rolling appearance (Figure 12).

Just as farmers struggled to tame the clays for cultivation, so it would seem on first inspection that these heavy soils were avoided as settlement sites in favour of the better-draining soils. The villages which formed in the Middle Ages, most of which still survive, at Leckhampstead, Lillingstone Dayrell, Lillingstone Lovell, Potterspury, Silverstone and Wicken, were all located on limestone exposures on the tributary streams; Passenham developed on one of the gravel terraces of the Great Ouse; while Akeley, Deanshanger, Stowe and Whittlebury all exploited islands of glacial sand and gravel within the boulder clay. But we should not be too dogmatic about this preference in the placing of settlement. Even during times of low population, such as the early Middle Ages, some communities clearly chose to settle on clay, ignoring available patches of sand, gravel and limestone. The founders of Romano-British farmsteads seem to have preferred high sites, with wide views, and therefore sought uplands even when these meant settling on the clay. Clay soils, which retained water, were also attractive to settlers over many centuries, from the Iron Age to the Middle Ages, who wanted to surround their houses with ditched enclosures and moats (Figure 13). However, at times of settlement contraction, such as at the end of the Roman period, or in the fifteenth century, sites established on clay soils were often the first to be abandoned. Geology and soils, therefore, might be said to have had a stronger influence on the survival and failure of sites – their ends – than on their original locations – their beginnings (see below, pages 56, 213–14).

The clay-dominated but varied geologies of the Whittlewood area offered many opportunities to those who lived and worked with them. If heavy to plough, the alkalinity of the chalk content balanced the acidity of the boulder clay to provide a chemically-neutral and fertile seedbed; its impermeability meant that the nutrients held in the soil,

FIGURE 12.
The topography and watercourses of the Whittlewood area.

or which were purposefully added to it, were not easily leached out. Where well-managed, properly drained and manured, clay soils were thus able to produce higher yields than those which developed on the sands and gravels. Beyond agriculture, clay was the raw material for Roman and medieval pottery industries, and eighteenth- and nineteenth-century brick and tile-making. These all made use of the pockets of sand within the boulder clay as a source of temper. In the seventeenth century, and before being usurped by brick in the late eighteenth century, limestone was the principal vernacular building

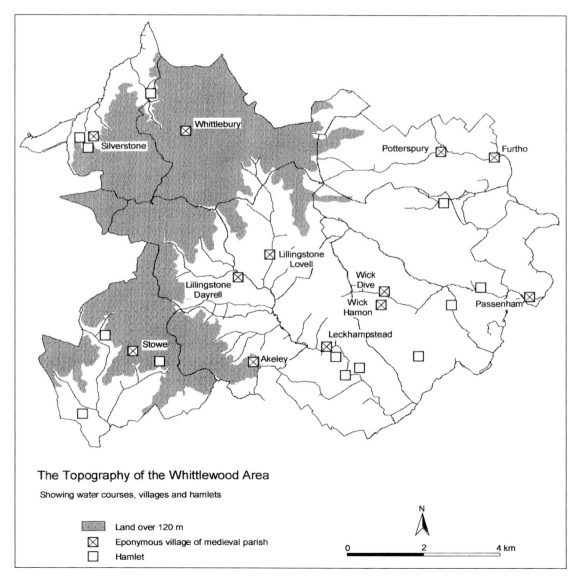

The Topography of the Whittlewood Area

Showing water courses, villages and hamlets

- Land over 120 m
- Eponymous village of medieval parish
- Hamlet

N

0   2   4 km

material of the area, although by this period it had long been exploited, used notably in the construction of high-status Roman buildings and medieval churches, but also to provide the masonry foundations for more lowly medieval dwellings and ancillary buildings. Geological resources are exploited locally today, at limestone quarries such as that at Pury End, Paulerspury, and at gravel pits along the Great Ouse. The river gravels contain the workable flint which perhaps first attracted groups of prehistoric gatherers.

FIGURE 13.
Settlement on clay: the map shows likely settlements, not all finds recovered from the clay.

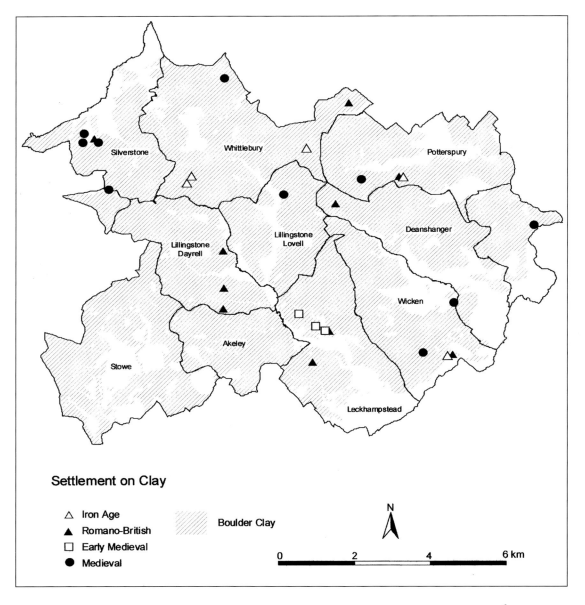

Settlement on Clay

△ Iron Age

▲ Romano-British

☐ Early Medieval

● Medieval

▨ Boulder Clay

N

0   2   4   6 km

Wildscape to landscape

The earliest human activity in Whittlewood can be dated to the Mesolithic period, 12,000–5,500 years ago. Flint flakes, cores, projectile points, blades and bladelets have been recovered across the whole area in low numbers (Figure 14). None of these finds occur together in sufficiently dense concentrations to indicate flint-working sites, or temporary or seasonal shelters. Instead, the finds of worked flint suggest that small bands of people moved through the area, stopping occasionally to hunt animals, and to gather fruits and edible plants. In general, Mesolithic people preferred to live on freely draining soils, especially when these gave them views across the landscape, or were located close to wetland areas. They consciously avoided claylands, so their principal settlement zones ringed Whittlewood.[6]

The distribution of Mesolithic activity might reflect uneven modern fieldwork rather than past reality. When a band stayed for a short time, it may have left a small scatter of flints, which in the modern ploughsoil might be no more than 2–5 m (6–16.5 feet) in diameter, and would be easily missed if the field was not intensively surveyed. Other sites, like that found close to the river Tove at Towcester, may have been covered by alluvium,[7] or lie buried under modern settlement, or have been removed in gravel extraction. That the Mesolithic flint scatters recovered from Whittlewood underestimate the level of human occupancy of the area and its impact on the natural environment is perhaps hinted at by a peat core taken from one of Whittlewood's neighbouring parishes, Syresham.[8] This contained charcoal in deposits dated to 7070–6690 BC. If the charcoal originated from the managed clearance of woodland through burning, this represents the first stage in human manipulation of the natural environment. Charcoal remains present in the next 5,000 years' worth of peat build-up, representing a prolonged period when vegetation was burned, and demonstrating that a man-made landscape was already in formation. After the Ice Age, woodland was cleared very slowly, as the pollen samples were dominated by tree species such as pine (*pinus*) and alder (*alnus*). But the presence of grass pollens (*poaceae*) in the radiocarbon-dated deposit could only have originated from more open land and demonstrate that by this period the coverage of trees was interrupted by patches of grass.

The basic timing of these events on the edge of Whittlewood fit with the general chronology of woodland clearance by fire and other means seen in other parts of the country. At Thatcham (Berks.), for instance, there is evidence for the opening-up of woodland between 7500–6000 BC,[9] broadly consistent with clearance episodes identified on the North York Moors and Dartmoor.[10] But the Whittlewood clearance appears to pre-date significantly that observed in the Exe valley (Devon), dated to around 5000 BC.[11] Pollen samples more than 9,000 years old have been recovered from the Nene valley which show no signs of woodland clearance, while a core taken at Burton Latimer (Northants.) suggests clearance by human hand around 4904–4714 BC.[12]

The first woodland clearance, therefore, appears to have been the work of groups of hunter-gatherers. This must have had three immediate benefits. First, by creating a diversity of habitats, a larger range of animals could be enticed into any given area, broadening the types of quarry to be hunted and the period over which these would be available. Secondly, by maintaining small pockets of grassland amongst the more general tree cover, the movement and location of grazing herds could be manipulated, and hunting made more efficient.[13] Thirdly, by improving grazing and browsing conditions, perhaps by restoring soil fertility through periodic firing, greater numbers of animals might be supported, providing richer potential killings.[14] At the same time, woodland clearance also promoted greater numbers of plant species,

FIGURE 14.
Mesolithic flint projectile points, blades and bladelets. Scale 1:1.

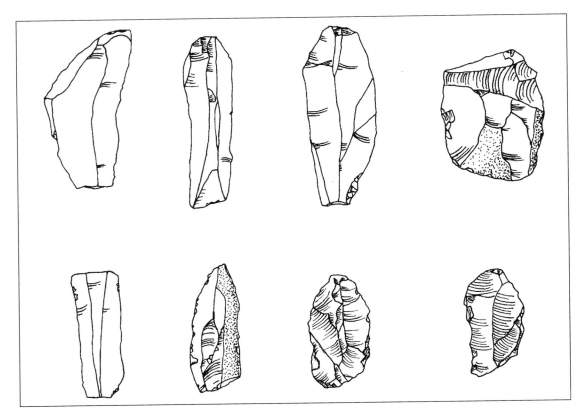

improving yields to be gained from gathering.[15] This was only the first man-made hunting landscape in the history of Whittlewood, which would continue with the formation of the royal forest after the Norman Conquest, when the various deer parks were enclosed later in the Middle Ages, and in the last 200 years as the countryside was managed for fox-hunting and pheasant-shooting (see above, page 19; see below, pages 110–17).

A landscape cleared, colonised and divided

By the beginning of the Neolithic period (*c.* 4000 BC), people were moulding the landscape by more complex and intensive methods than an occasional firing of the woods. Changes in this landscape during the fourth and first half of the third millennium BC are as difficult to trace as those of the Mesolithic, but that they occurred is demonstrated by the Syresham peat core.[16] A layer of mineral-rich deposits within the sequence, associated with a destabilisation of surrounding slopes and increased soil erosion, has been dated to 2580–2270 BC. Within this has been preserved the pollen of hazel (*corylus*), alder, pine, elm (*ulmus*) and birch (*betula*). This indicates more open deciduous woodland on the drier ground, with alder occupying wetter areas. Pollen of ferns (*dryopteris* type and *polypodium*) and sedge (*cyperaceae*) show that these damp-loving plants grew around the mire where the peat accumulated. Unmanaged and drier open ground close by is implied by the presence of grass pollens and chickweed (*caryophyllaceae*), although the latter is also known to colonise disturbed ground. Of these, pollen deriving from plants other than trees are found in the majority in the samples, indicating that the decline in tree cover begun in the Mesolithic continued. One consequence of this clearance appears to have been a change in soil quality. This is seen on the surface of the flints: those discarded during the Mesolithic tend to exhibit signs of patination caused by the alkaline soils, while those dropped during the Neolithic are unpatinated, suggesting more acidic conditions caused by leaching of the soil in the more open environment.[17]

The cleared woodland was evidently replaced by grassland rather than arable fields, as the peat core fails to produce cereal pollens at this date. In this respect, Whittlewood was no different from many other parts of central-southern England where the Neolithic agricultural revolution was late in arriving. In the river valleys of southern England around 6,000 years ago, relatively little alluvium can be found, which means that the soil on the river-banks and on the sides of the streams running into the rivers was relatively stable, under grass and woodland. Extensive ploughing beside the rivers and streams would lead to soil being carried into the watercourses and the accumulation of alluvium downstream.[18] Indeed, evidence for crop cultivation of any kind in Whittlewood only appears in the late Iron Age, nearly 2,500 years later.

By the late Neolithic/early Bronze Age transition (*c.* 2000 BC), the landscape of Whittlewood was characterised by broken woodland and open tracts of grassland. Whether this had been achieved through extensive or piecemeal clearance, slowly or rapidly, continuously or episodically, cannot be learnt from the samples of pollen. The possibility that some cleared land might have reverted back to woodland cannot be dismissed, as suggested by pollen preserved in a former river channel in the Nene valley.[19] In Whittlewood, what is certain from the presence of charcoal in the peat sequences, and the absence of specific woodworking tools, with the exception of a single chisel, amongst the thousands of flints collected from the area, is that fire remained the principal method of clearance. Such an undertaking required labour; even after burning, stumps would still have to be dug out individually. The number of objects which can be dated to the later Neolithic and early Bronze Age suggests an increase in people who were living in the Whittlewood area. Worked flints appear to have been dropped in ever greater numbers over more extensive parts of the area from around 3000 BC. Many are waste flakes, found in association with cores, indicating the fabrication of utensils on site. An incomplete range of tools, which includes blades, burins, chisels and scrapers, but which lacks larger axeheads and other heavy implements, has been recovered (Figure 15). Flint scatters of this date have been plotted over more than 976 ha (2,410 acres) of the 993 ha (2,450 acres) of modern ploughed field surface systematically fieldwalked in Whittlewood (Figure 16). Three dense concentrations of finds from this period have been found in the parishes of Deanshanger, Leckhampstead and Lillingstone Lovell: all lie close to streams, but are located respectively on clay soils, sand and gravel. We cannot be sure that they were settlement sites, but this seems likely. Certainly a permanent population and sustained agricultural production is suggested by the pollen samples on the western edge of the study area, which show management of the landscape in this period with no revival in the growth of trees.

The concentration of Bronze Age flints at Leckhampstead seems to be related to a group of ring ditches lying on the gravel terraces of the Great Ouse. Further ring ditches have been discovered on the north side of the river valley in neighbouring Wicken and in Cosgrove,[20] while the largest group, located by geophysics, lies immediately south of Passenham in Calverton parish.[21] Two further ring ditches have been found on the north side of Dogsmouth Brook in Potterspury.[22] Without excavation these monuments cannot be closely dated or understood. Traditionally, ring ditches have been associated with barrows, the burial sites of a social elite. But excavations at Warren Farm between Wolverton and Stony Stratford, a few miles downstream of Passenham, and Stacey Bushes, Milton Keynes, have also linked these sites with settlement centres of the Neolithic and Bronze Age.[23] The people who lived at these sites, it has been argued, could have been keeping animals which spent their winters by the permanent settlements in the river valley, but which were driven on to the summer pastures on the claylands. Further down the Great Ouse were other groups of ring ditches, associated with larger religious monuments, including long barrows, large ditched enclosures resembling henges, and cursuses consisting of parallel ditches used for rituals.[24] Their regular spatial distribution, separated by a distance of about 6 km (4 miles), has not been dictated by geology or topography, but appears to relate to a territorial division of the valley. A study by Green identified eighteen such groups on the Great Ouse, and comparable clusters have been found along many of the east-draining rivers, including the Nene and Welland.[25] Whether they lay peripheral to a territory,

FIGURE 15.
Bronze Age scrapers.
Scale 1:1.

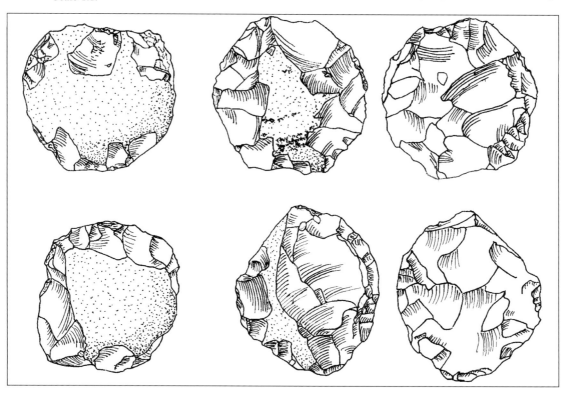

marking its boundaries or providing meeting-places for more than one community, or whether they lay at its centre, cannot currently be established. It is generally accepted, however, that they represent ritual or sacred landscapes, and are the first indication that we have of a subdivision of our area into territories with borders.[26] One of these almost certainly accompanies the ring ditch group at Passenham, with another perhaps centred on the Leckhampstead cluster.

While the valleys appear to have been favoured as settlement centres, the claylands too had been populated and divided by 1000 BC, an

FIGURE 16.
The distribution of worked flint finds and prehistoric sites in Whittlewood.

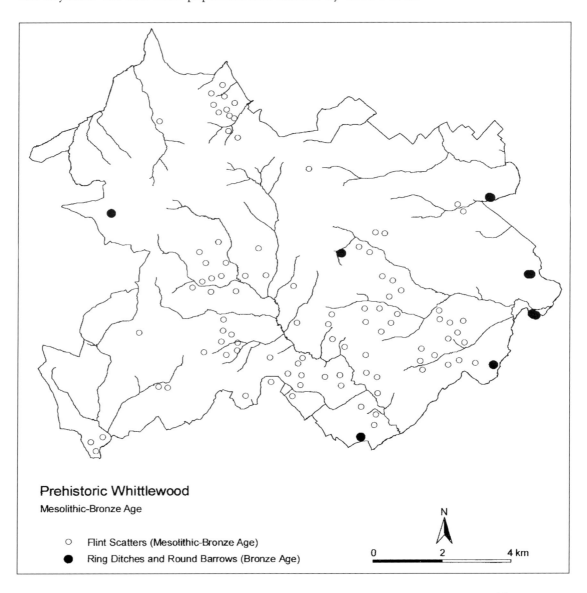

Prehistoric Whittlewood

Mesolithic-Bronze Age

○ Flint Scatters (Mesolithic-Bronze Age)

● Ring Ditches and Round Barrows (Bronze Age)

N

0   2   4 km

impression supported by the high density of flint scatters and concentrations found across our area, and a single round barrow excavated on the high ground between Lillingstone Dayrell and Silverstone.[27] In a broader survey of late Bronze Age and Iron Age settlements in the catchments of the rivers Nene and Great Ouse, Knight also noted such early expansion on to the clays, contrasting this with other parts of southern England where the move away from lighter and on to the heavier soils appears to have occurred later during the first millennium BC.[28] Clay only proved troublesome to those early farmers who sought to cultivate crops and were thus required to till the soil. No such barrier faced pastoralists, whose grassland could be managed and maintained through regular herding of livestock. People were certainly living in the Whittlewood area between 2000 and 500 BC, but there is no certain evidence that they cultivated the soil: pastoral farming may have been their mainstay. An economic reliance upon animals rather than the plough might begin to explain this precocious colonisation of Whittlewood's clay soils.

People, place and plough

The uncertainty created by the thinness of the archaeological evidence from the earlier prehistoric period begins to lift with an explosion in the quality and type of evidence from the second half of the first millennium BC surviving above ground, or retrievable through excavation, fieldwalking and metal-detecting. For the first time it is possible to have some confidence in the nature of settlement and its distribution across our area, and to detect changes in the way that the land was exploited. Total reconstruction of the Iron Age landscape, however, remains an elusive ambition. More information becomes available not because of the accident of preservation of evidence, nor because of biases in the methods of fieldwork, but because life changed dramatically in the area around 600 BC. The background to these developments was an improvement in climatic conditions, with an increase in average summer temperatures and lower rainfall, and an 'exponential' rise in population.[29] In combination, these led to greater use being made of the lowland clays. Drier conditions and longer growing seasons meant that the clays could be more easily worked, while population levels began to exceed the carrying capacity of the lighter, more freely draining soils, further encouraging colonisation on to heavier soils. These trends, observed across southern Britain, were mirrored in Whittlewood.

In this period we begin to find remains of houses for the first time: that is, circular structures built of timber with wattle and daub walls

and thatched roofs, known to us as 'roundhouses'. Sometimes when
the remains of the walls have been removed, the site of the house is
marked by the circular ditch which ran round the outside of the house
to drain rainwater from the roof. Settlements in some places were
particularly dense (Figure 17). In northern Silverstone, for example,
three sites within 650 m (710 yards) of each other were identified in
advance of recent road building.[30] All were very similar in layout:
the first comprised three roundhouses with associated pit alignments
and gullies contained within a ditched enclosure; the second, a single

FIGURE 17.
The distribution of Iron
Age sites in Whittlewood,
showing settlement within
a 3 km radius of
Whittlebury hillfort.

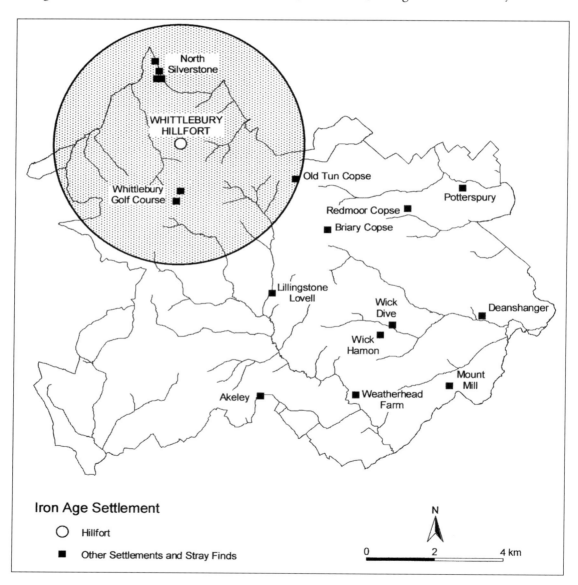

roundhouse within a large rectangular enclosure measuring 70 × 50 m (230 × 165 feet); the third, a group of three or four roundhouses with a group of 80 pits, surrounded by a 75 × 50 m (245 × 165 feet) trapezoidal enclosure. It remains unclear, however, whether these represent three contemporary and separate farmsteads, or three phases of settlement shift of a single unit. Whatever the circumstances, none of the enclosures is likely to have housed more than one extended family group.[31] Two further enclosures, surviving as earthworks until recently, and of approximately the same dimensions and shape, are considered on typological grounds also to belong to the Iron Age. These lay only 300 m (985 feet) apart, in the northern and western part of what is now Whittlebury golf course.[32] Another sub-rectangular enclosure with a ring gully has also been recorded adjacent to Watling Street in the western part of Potterspury.[33]

Elsewhere, an unenclosed group of three roundhouse gullies has been excavated east of Redmoor Copse,[34] while a single roundhouse was found at Deanshanger.[35] In both instances, the Iron Age structures lay beneath or next to later Roman buildings. This same association was made during the excavation of a Romano-British settlement revealed by woodland clearance east of Briary Copse, again high on the watershed.[36] About 1 km (0.5 miles) south-east of this, the recovery of a large quantity of Iron Age pottery from ploughsoil probably identifies another site,[37] while 2 km (1.25 miles) to the north another concentration of pottery of early and middle Iron Age date marks one more. A small pottery cluster has been found in the eastern part of Potterspury village,[38] but by far the largest, comprised of several discrete concentrations, but covering over 20 ha (50 acres), has been recovered from Old Tun Copse in eastern Whittlebury.[39] This may represent a form of more nucleated or 'agglomerated' settlement, occupied by several households, a category of settlement now being recognised elsewhere, as at Crick, and Wilby Way, Wellingborough (Northants.).[40]

Later land use has clearly played some part in the preservation of sites of this date. Of those already mentioned, the vast majority lay in areas of medieval woodland and were thus not subject to prolonged plough attrition, or the sites lay beneath Romano-British settlements, which again protected them from immediate ploughing. In those areas which were cultivated, evidence of Iron Age activity is restricted to stray finds of pottery, with no dense or large concentrations. The fragility of Iron Age pottery means that it does not survive in any quantity in plough soil that has been repeatedly cultivated. These individual or low-density scatters of finds may, however, be highly significant. Often they can be associated with later settlement, such as the sherds recovered from Roman sites at Mount Mill Farm, Wicken, and 500 m (550 yards) west of Cattleford Bridge in Leckhampstead. These coincidences bear the hallmark of those other sites – Redmoor Copse, Briary Copse and Deanshanger – revealed through excavation to have continued in use throughout the two periods. Other finds made beneath medieval settlements – for instance, in the southern part of Akeley; at Weatherhead Farm, Leckhampstead; in the south-western part of Wick Hamon; in southern Wick Dive; or beneath plough headlands at Lillingstone Lovell – may again represent settlement sites.

Sites of the Iron Age could therefore have been numerous, and if occupied at about the same time, a complex society can be presumed, no doubt with roads linking settlements for the exchange of goods. Knight identified such integrated systems in other parts of Northamptonshire, and argued that they fall into two types.[41] The first, based on sites within the Wellingborough area, termed 'dispersed', comprised single farmsteads, whose inhabitants were chiefly occupied by subsistence activities and small-scale craft production. More specialised sites were engaged in such industries as metal-working. The second, a 'centralised' system, was characterised by a central place such as the hillfort at Hunsbury, in which there was physical evidence for non-subsistence activities and long-distance exchange networks, with such objects as quernstones for hand mills.[42] Surrounding the hillfort, but firmly within its orbit, a similar pattern of interconnected dispersed settlement existed, but whose links with the central place were much stronger than those between farmstead and farmstead. In all cases, the individual farmstead or specialised site looked to the hillfort, its presence seemingly encouraging a greater density of settlement in its immediate hinterland than beyond.[43] Distinct and discrete distributions of various forms of decoration on pottery also point not only to the cultural affinities which existed between these sites, but to the division of territory into defined blocks, perhaps based on a small number of central places.[44] Presumably the hillfort had political functions, and tribute was collected there.

A hillfort stood on the rising ground in the north of Whittlebury, the existence of which had not been realised before our research began. We can suppose that the settlement system most likely to have operated in our area in the Iron Age was of the 'centralised' type. The hillfort, oval in shape with an interior measuring 3.5 ha (8.5 acres), occupies the western end of a high spur of land to the north-west of the village (Figure 18). Following the natural contours of the hill, the southern alignment of the surrounding bank and ditch can be traced on aerial photographs, and has been precisely fixed by geophysical survey. To the north, the line of the Silverstone road, looping around the parish church which stands within the enclosure, also appears

FIGURE 18.
The Iron Age hillfort at Whittlebury, from the south west. The farm on the left-hand-edge of the photograph was on the north side of the hillfort. The line of the eastern rampart is marked by the curving modern road, the western rampart by parchmarks in the pasture field. The medieval church lies near the centre of the hillfort.

NATIONAL MONUMENTS RECORD, SP 6843/1

to follow the original ditch. Situated almost equidistant from the four closest known hillforts – Rainsborough to the south-west (21 km or 13 miles), Arbury Hill to the north-west (21 km or 13 miles), Hunsbury to the north-east (16 km or 10 miles) and Padbury to the south (13 km or 8 miles) – Whittlebury thus slots neatly into what appears to be a careful and largely equitable division of the landscape. The high density of smaller sites found within a 3-kilometre (2-mile) radius of it, within which fall sites in Paulerspury,[45] in addition to those already described in Silverstone and Whittlebury itself, exhibits remarkable similarity with the cluster around Hunsbury and to a lesser extent with that around Rainsborough.[46] The complex of sites based on Whittlebury may have been independent of its neighbour to the north-east, as no pottery of the types associated with the Hunsbury fort has been found. The Hunsbury wares have distinctive decorations, with multiple dots impressed into the clay before firing, and rosettes within a running scroll, and if there were contacts one would expect these to be represented among the hundreds of pieces of pottery from the Whittlebury excavations. On these grounds, then, it seems safe to presume that by the middle Iron Age (*c.* 400 BC) large parts of our area lay within a single political entity based on Whittlebury. This territorial division must have encouraged social cohesion and economic cooperation among its members, and must have provided the framework within which decisions concerning settlement and land use were made.

Within Whittlebury hillfort, the footprints of at least twelve round-houses have been pinpointed, all with eastern entrances, all located immediately behind the southern and eastern ramparts (Figure 19). Within the unoccupied central area, partial sections of gullies, pits and other features containing quantities of undecorated pottery have also been observed in test-pits. The hillfort thus appears to have been an important part of the settlement pattern and not simply an episodically used refuge, entrepot, corral or meeting-place. North of the church, the remains of three grain storage pits, truncated by medieval burials, were found within the churchyard. The carbonised grains of emmer and spelt wheat, together with seeds of weeds such as brome, recovered from these silos, represent the earliest evidence for arable cultivation in Whittlewood.[47] The fields within which these cereals were grown remain archaeologically invisible: their boundaries cannot be identified from the air since neither crop marks nor soil marks survive on the boulder clay; while pot sherds are not found regularly in the plough soil to indicate areas that were manured. Evidence for extensive regular and irregular field systems of Iron Age date have been found nearby both on the permeable geologies and on the claylands.[48] There is little reason to doubt that these would have extended over Whittlewood, presumably stretching out from the settlements. Even small-scale field systems must have led to a degree of landscape formalisation which had not previously existed. A once open and uncompartmentalised landscape would now contain areas where access was restricted, particularly during the growing season. Routes to and from the settlements would be dictated by permanent boundaries. Unable to drift from these lines, such communication

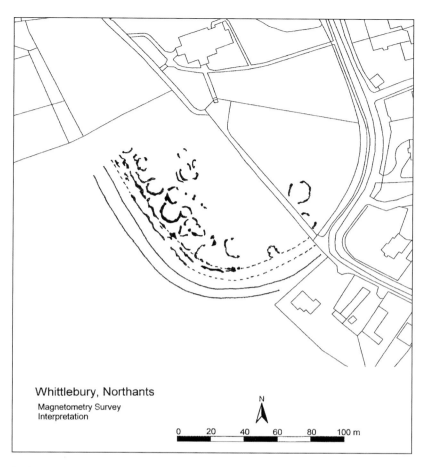

Whittlebury, Northants
Magnetometry Survey
Interpretation

N

| 0 | 20 | 40 | 60 | 80 | 100 m |

links would quickly become embedded in, and difficult to eradicate from, the landscape. In combination, the establishment of these Iron Age settlements, field systems and routeways provided Whittlewood with its first physical structure, and a landscape grammar so tenacious that it continued to exert influence on all subsequent developments.

Roman countrymen

The landscape framework created in the Iron Age can be discerned in the Roman settlement pattern. The vast majority of recently excavated villas in Northamptonshire and Buckinghamshire appear to have late Iron Age antecedents.[49] In this respect Whittlewood is no different. If early unscientific excavations on villas located at Foxcote, The Gullet, Whittlebury, and under the artificial lake at Wakefield Lodge have deprived us of the evidence of this association, those undertaken at Deanshanger villa revealed at least one Iron Age roundhouse.[50] The cultural debris of high-status Romano-British occupation recovered by fieldwalking at Mount Mill Farm, Wicken, and in Leckhampstead, was associated with late prehistoric pottery. Of the non-villa sites, those at Redmoor Copse and Briary Copse have produced evidence of occupation on both sides of the late Iron Age/early Roman transition. These examples all highlight a certain stability of settlement pattern across the two periods and imply continuity of occupation at a number of favoured locales. This is not to deny, however, that virgin sites were colonised: few of the twenty-six dispersed settlement locations of the Romano-British period known within the twelve Whittlewood parishes or just beyond, each representing no more than a single farmstead, have produced any evidence for earlier occupation. It would seem, therefore, that the basic Iron Age settlement pattern was retained, and perhaps also elements of the territorial divisions with which they were associated. This was extended during the Roman period, in response to a growing rural population and an intensification of farming, with new sites developed from the principal centres and perhaps located within their estates.

Eleven high-status Romano-British sites, identified by their use of roofing tiles, underground heating and significant quantities of imported pottery, have been located within our area. These exhibit no preference for soil type, five being found on the gravels or limestone exposures, six conspicuously located on the clay (Figure 20). Away from the valley bottoms, however, elevation appears to have played some part in the choice of site, as all are positioned on prominences which afforded broad vistas of the surrounding countryside. Their even spacing across the area argues for a largely equitable division of the available land, at least in terms of estate size if not the resources that these landholdings contained. The estates cannot be reconstructed with any certitude. Hypothetical boundaries might be suggested by using Thiessen polygons centred on the known sites and those, like Cosgrove, Foxcote, Mile Oak and Paulerspury, which lie outside our limits.[51] The Great Ouse might be thought to have formed a natural boundary. On this basis, our twelve parishes may have been divided between thirteen whole or part units. The largest of these exceeded 1,200 ha (2,965 acres), the smallest just over 500 ha (1,235 acres), with a mean of 920 ha (2,275 acres), though a figure below 800 ha (1,975 acres) is likely in view of the settlements that have not yet been discovered. If this is the case, then the size of villa estates in Whittlewood is comparable with those identified in other parts of the country.[52]

The nineteen known small single farmsteads lying within Whittlewood, and the additional seven within 1 km (0.5 miles) of

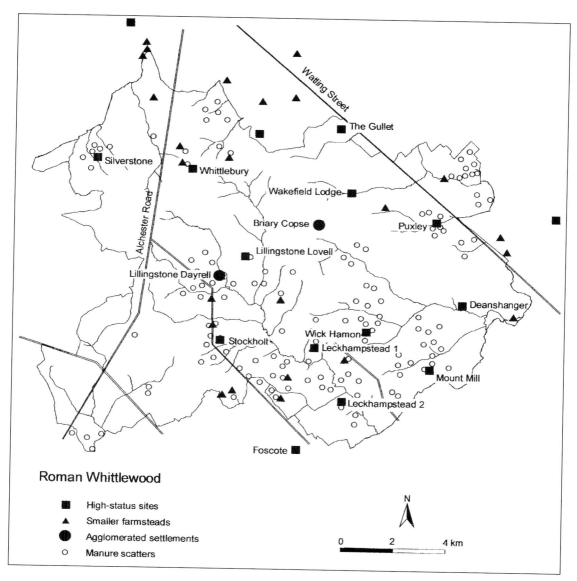

FIGURE 20.
Location of Romano-British
sites, Roman roads and
manure scatters.

it, must also grossly underestimate the former density of these sites. Most have been located within the 993 ha (2,450 acres) covered by fieldwalking, only 10 per cent of the total area, and others have been located by test-pits. Since these demonstrate that soil type, elevation, access to water and aspect were no barrier to the choice of site, it might be conservatively estimated that the area actually contained upwards of 75 such farmsteads, at a site density of one every 1.25 sq km (0.5 square miles), figures slightly lower than those found at Raunds, to the north-east of the project area, where densities were

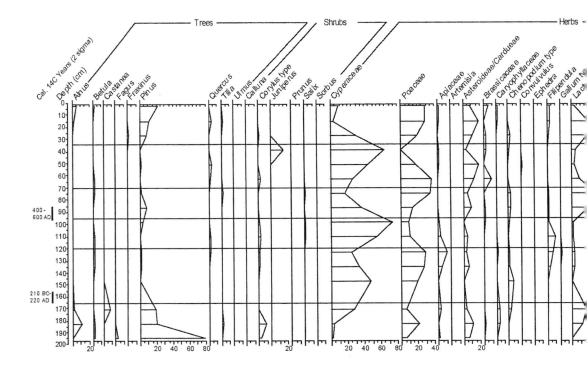

estimated at every 1 sq km (0.33 square mile) in the early to middle Roman period, and one every 0.75 sq km (0.25 square miles) in the late Roman period.[53]

These farmsteads were set, at least by the end of the second century AD, within a largely open landscape of arable fields and grassland, containing few stands of trees. Consistency across three types of evidence means that this mixed but arable-dominated economy of both the villas and farmsteads of Whittlewood can be confidently assumed. The first is the pollen evidence: a peat core taken from Biddlesden shows that the environment of the first and second centuries AD contained extensive areas of meadow and pasture, together with cultivated fields producing both wheat (*triticum* type) and barley (*hordeum* type) (Figure 21). Surfaces of bare earth, encouraging accelerated erosion and increased surface run-off, may also have been responsible for a build-up of mineral deposits here at about this period.[54] Secondly, evidence for cereal processing was found in the excavation at Redmoor Copse, where a greater variety of cereals have been found; its assemblage is dominated by spelt (*triticum spelta*) with a little emmer (*triticum dicoccum*), together with a few grains of oats (*avena sativa*) and barley.[55] Corn driers have also been found at the Deanshanger villa.[56] But it is fieldwalking which provides the clearest

FIGURE 21.
Percentage pollen diagram of a peat core taken at Biddlesden. Dates are shown on the extreme left, so that the Roman period is represented by the peat between 90 and 160 cm deep. The shaded part of the diagram towards the right hand side shows the decline and rise in the proportion of pollen from trees and shrubs.

ARCHAEOSCAPE, ROYAL HOLLOWAY UNIVERSITY OF LONDON

52

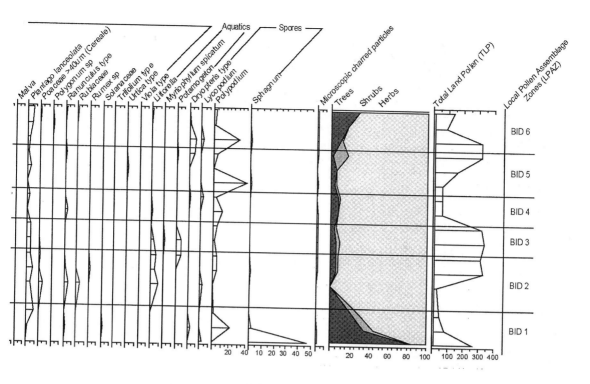

impression of the extent of arable cultivation. Over 960 ha (2,370 acres) of the 993 ha (2,450 acres) surveyed have produced low-density Romano-British pottery scatters, resulting from the manuring of fields with farmyard dung which also contained domestic refuse. This represents an area of tillage far in excess even of the medieval open fields at their greatest extent, which was the high tide of arable cultivation in the post-Roman period. No more than half of this vast area is likely to have been cultivated at any one time. Kron has shown that a regime of ley-farming, characterised by extended periods of permanent cultivation (10–15 years) followed by periods of equivalent length during which the former arable land was laid down to pasture, was favoured by Roman agronomists and practised by farmers.[57] Such a system might explain the extensive ceramic manure scatter coverage, spread while the fields were in cultivation, and the high ratio of grass pollens present in the Biddlesden core, produced while the fields were rested and grazed. As for trees, the few surveyed hectares which have failed to produce Roman pottery scatters, notably high on the clays in southern Whittlebury and north-west Akeley, which were known to have been tree-covered in later periods, might mark the location of small blocks of woodland. Indeed, sweet chestnut (*castanea sativa*) pollen in the Biddlesden peat attests to both the Roman introduction of new tree species and their careful management. Certainly wood was required, not only as building material and for domestic use, but as a fuel to sustain small-scale industries such as the pottery manufactory at Stowe.[58]

The likely preservation of earlier tribal territories in the Roman administrative system ensured that local forces drove agricultural and environmental change in Whittlewood. Where once Whittlewood had lain on the boundary of areas controlled by the Corieltauvi and the Catuvellauni, so it remained on the edge of *civitates* based on Leicester (*Ratae Coritanorum*) and St Albans (*Verulamium*) (Figure 22). Far

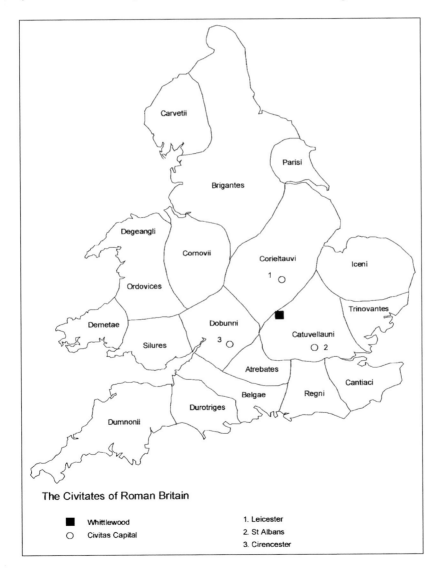

The Civitates of Roman Britain

■ Whittlewood
○ Civitas Capital

1. Leicester
2. St Albans
3. Cirencester

FIGURE 22.
The Roman *civitates* and their Iron Age territorial antecedents.

between AD 400 and 1100. Elements of continuity can be identified from the prehistoric and Roman periods, but there was, too, considerable innovation in the adaptation of territories and boundaries to suit the requirements of a new age.

Central places and dependent settlements

After the collapse of Roman state power in Britain, urban centres declined, the market economy failed, and political authority was fragmented. From the fifth century, dominant families emerged to exercise control over a multitude of territories, variously labelled by historians as kingdoms, *scirs*, *regiones* and provinces. Authority over these territories was based not on the ownership of land but on the power to command goods and services from the population of the area. The tribute exacted from subject peoples may have been collected at central places where the dominant families were based. Following the conversion of the English kingdoms to Christianity, churches were established at many estate centres, from which priests ministered to the surrounding territory. The land was worked both by dependent tenants, including slaves, directly subject to a lord, and by a self-sufficient peasantry, practising varied forms of agriculture in small scattered settlements.[1]

The boundaries of these early territories can rarely be recovered. Indeed, it may be questioned whether precise lines of demarcation existed at all. In post-Roman Gaul, Merovingian *villae* appear to have consisted of scattered estates whose limits were so poorly drawn that even proprietors were uncertain of their exact extent.[2] On a larger scale, similar problems have been encountered in determining the size of the territories controlled by the Anglo-Saxon folk groupings named in the late seventh-century Tribal Hidage. In part this may be explained by the apparent division of these territories between a settled and heavily exploited heartland, and one or more underdeveloped but no less important marginal areas used for pastoral and hunting activities, which may have been shared between neighbouring groups of people.[3] Despite the limited evidence, we will suggest that the study area comprised one such marginal area in the early Middle Ages, the internal organisation and boundaries of which are rarely clear, but which were based both on long-standing arrangements and more recent innovations.

On the strength of the ceramic and environmental evidence, we would argue that the claylands of the Whittlewood area were lightly settled between the fifth and ninth centuries, a result of population retreat from the fourth century onwards (see above, pages 55–6;

see below, pages 85–7). A few sherds of handmade pottery dated to AD 400–850, indicative of settlement, have been found in several of our villages and in a handful of places outside the later village cores (Figure 23). A cemetery at Passenham, comprising more than fifty burials, was associated with pottery and metalwork of the fifth century.[4] Roman settlements in Leckhampstead and at Mount Mill in Wicken continued to be occupied on a small scale until the ninth or tenth centuries. But there is no evidence in the study area of the dense dispersed settlement pattern which has been identified in other parts of Northamptonshire.[5] Land which had been farmed during the Roman era ceased to be cultivated thereafter, and pollen analysis indicates woodland regeneration. The Roman town of Towcester, which probably received supplies of grain and livestock from the Whittlewood area before AD 400, was not a major centre afterwards (see below, pages 85–7, 106–8).[6]

The inhabitants of Whittlewood between the fifth and ninth centuries almost certainly practised mixed arable and livestock farming, albeit on a limited scale. Pollen analysis reveals both the cultivation of crops and the presence of grass and woodland, indicating areas of wood pasture.[7] The extraction of produce as rent, tax and tribute by those with political and economic power may have been organised through landholdings known to historians as multiple estates. These estates were controlled by kings, bishops, monasteries and nobles, and consisted of a central manor and a number of dependent settlements, which may each have specialised in the production of grain, cattle, sheep, dairy products, honey and wood.[8] Some of these dependencies might be located at a considerable distance from the central manor; for example, areas of woodland or wold were sometimes many miles from the principal manor, and survived as detached holdings following the break-up of the multiple estates and the creation of shires, hundreds and parishes.[9]

A number of settlements in the Whittlewood area were, at a later date, dependent on a central place. For example, Silverstone and Whittlebury were part of a multiple estate based on the royal manor of Greens Norton. Relics of their links endured throughout the Middle Ages. Both parishes were chapelries of the mother church at Greens Norton and formed a detached part of Greens Norton (or Foxley) Hundred. Greens Norton provides an example of a minster church, which are thought to have provided pastoral care to the laity in the era before parish churches. An argument has been made that a network of local churches existed in England before the break-up of minster parishes in the ninth to eleventh centuries, but no evidence from Whittlewood has been found to support this claim.[10] An account roll

FIGURE 23.
Distribution of pre-1000 pottery at Lillingstone Dayrell, showing the small size of the settlement compared to the later medieval village.

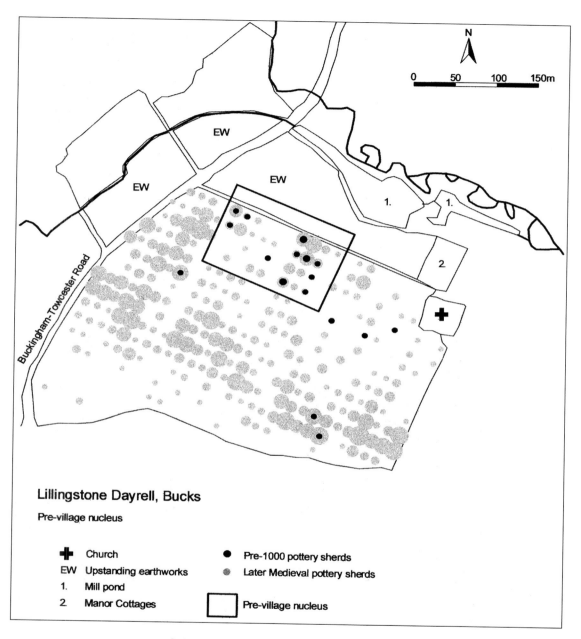

Lillingstone Dayrell, Bucks

Pre-village nucleus

✚	Church	●	Pre-1000 pottery sherds
EW	Upstanding earthworks	●	Later Medieval pottery sherds
1.	Mill pond		
2.	Manor Cottages	☐	Pre-village nucleus

of Greens Norton in 1536 records that Silverstone and Whittlebury paid an annual due called *aberyes rent* to the lord there, a reminder of a time when tribute was rendered.[11] The likelihood is that both settlements were valued as an area of wood pasture, for grazing cattle and pigs, felling timber for building and wood for fuel, and hunting. A council was held at Whittlebury by King Athelstan in about AD 930;

we may speculate that the assembled nobles took the opportunity to hunt after their business was concluded.[12] There was still a Norton wood in Whittlebury in the thirteenth century, by which time the area formed part of a royal forest (see below, page 108). Whittlewood's status as a hunting ground may well have been a legacy of its Anglo-Saxon past.

Another royal manor also held dependent settlements in the Whittlewood project area. Boycott in Stowe parish and Lillingstone Lovell were both detached portions of the Oxfordshire hundred of Ploughley, probably as the result of a dependency upon the manor of Kirtlington, about 32 km (20 miles) to the south-west.[13] Like Silverstone and Whittlebury, they were presumably valued as a source of wood pasture. The settlements of Wick Dive and Wick Hamon (modern Wicken) may have been dependent too. The place-name element *wic* means 'specialised farm', although we do not know to which central place the *wic* belonged.[14] One possibility is Passenham, which is likely to have been the centre of a larger territory than that encompassed by the medieval parish. In 1086 the jurisdiction ('soke') of part of neighbouring Cosgrove was vested in the manor, which at this time was a royal possession. Indeed, in AD 921 Edward the Elder chose to station his West Saxon army at Passenham while the stronghold at Towcester was being fortified.[15] The king would have found it useful on his visits, and especially on that occasion, to call on the produce of a multiple estate.

In the early tenth century, therefore, the Whittlewood area appears to have been largely subject to royal control, divided between at least three estate centres, one of which – Passenham – lay within the study area (Figure 24). A fourth royal manor – Buckingham – might be expected to have enjoyed rights in the south of the project area, although clear evidence is lacking. The outlying settlements of a multiple estate were probably not exploited with great intensity. The Whittlewood area may have been chiefly used as a source of wood pasture, to which animals were brought on a seasonal basis and from which wood and timber was gathered when it was needed. In some of our settlements, such as Lillingstone Lovell, no evidence of habitation has been found before the late tenth century. In others the evidence is so slight that we cannot be sure that the settlements were occupied for a long period. In any case, ceramic evidence and the figures recorded in Domesday Book suggest that the population of the area was small; before the creation of the open fields in the tenth century, the inhabitants may have comprised mainly cowherds and swineherds who also cultivated a few acres, and possibly, too, some woodworkers and smiths (there were smiths recorded under the Domesday entry for Greens Norton

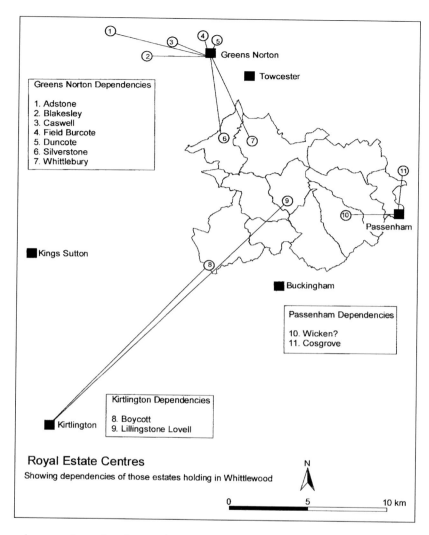

Greens Norton Dependencies

1. Adstone
2. Blakesley
3. Caswell
4. Field Burcote
5. Duncote
6. Silverstone
7. Whittlebury

Passenham Dependencies

10. Wicken?
11. Cosgrove

Kirtlington Dependencies

8. Boycott
9. Lillingstone Lovell

Royal Estate Centres
Showing dependencies of those estates holding in Whittlewood

N

0   5   10 km

FIGURE 24.
Early estate centres
and their links to the
Whittlewood area as
revealed in later documents.

who may have lived in Whittlewood, or visited there to gather wood, for which they paid £7 in 1066) (see below, page 125).[16] Nevertheless, there is the possibility of agricultural specialisation (at Wicken) and the development of an infrastructure to support royal gatherings at Passenham and Whittlebury. Further clues to the internal organisation of the study area might also be suggested.

A network of roads existed, allowing people to travel to the area to trade in woodland produce and the livestock which grazed there. Watling Street provided a direct link to London as well as to a number of smaller urban centres; another Roman road lay close to Lamport, which was perhaps a trading venue (the name means 'long market-place') before the foundation of Buckingham in the early tenth century. Stowe, too, may have been a meeting-place, as the name signifies; according to later tradition, it was the moot-place for the hundred of Stodfold. Another hundred meeting-place was located in open countryside at Cleley Well in Potterspury, at which even now several footpaths meet. At the heart of the later forest lay Wakefield, which, judging from the place-name, may have been a clearing in the woods used for festivities.[17] The Whittlewood area was evidently visited and exploited in the fifth to tenth centuries, and some places developed clearly defined functions. More generally, Domesday Book suggests that the area was used as a feeding ground for pigs, which were likely to have been driven in large numbers from a wide region to browse for acorns and other food in autumn. Lillingstone Dayrell alone had sufficient woodland to support 1,200 pigs, far more than would have been kept by the resident population.

Multiple estates were not fixed entities: they might suddenly fragment as pieces were granted to followers and family; equally they might gain territory through the annexation of additional land. In the Danelaw, Hadley has shown how fluid large estates might be, growing and contracting, fragmenting and reforming over time.[18] This fluidity makes it difficult to establish the date at which the estate centres we have identified – Greens Norton, Kirtlington, Passenham, Buckingham – began to exercise authority over the dependent settlements in the study area. Similarly, we cannot be sure whether different patterns of estate organisation existed at other times, or whether parts of the project area were independent of a central place. Nor do we fully understand the relationship between the multiple estates and wider political and administrative structures. In the seventh century Whittlewood presumably belonged to one or more of the middle Angle 'tribes' listed in the Tribal Hidage, which were absorbed into the kingdom of Mercia before AD 653. One suggestion is that the project area, or part of it, formed part of the territory of the *Hendrica*.[19] Another is that Whittlewood lay within a provincial territory comprising much of north-western Buckinghamshire, south-western Northamptonshire and north-eastern Oxfordshire, with an administrative centre at Kings Sutton.[20] Evidence from the study area is insufficient either to prove or disprove these hypotheses. However, we would emphasise the tradition of authority over the area which was likely to have developed at Whittlebury, now positively identified as an Iron Age hillfort.

In Chapter Three we suggested that in the Iron Age large parts of the project area formed a unified territory based on Whittlebury. In the Roman period, authority over the area seems to have passed to the town of Towcester, the political, administrative and economic hinterland of which may have included much, if not all, of the hill-fort's territory (see above, pages 46–9, 55). What, if any, significance did these early authoritative landscapes have for patterns of power in the early Middle Ages? There is a general consensus that many early medieval territories were based on prehistoric or Roman arrangements. For example, it has been proposed that the kingdom of Essex recreated the Iron Age Trinovantian territory.[21] In parts of the country, Roman town-based territories, or *pagi*, are thought to underlie medieval administrative groupings.[22] In Northamptonshire, Iron Age origins have been proposed for the royal estate at Kings Sutton, based on the fact that the hillfort at Rainsborough and small Roman town at Blacklands both lie within 2 km (1.25 miles) of the estate centre. According to Brown and Taylor, 'could not this fort have been the *caput*, citadel, or "manor house" of an Iron Age estate and its component parts arranged in much the same way as the later Roman, Saxon, and medieval ones?'[23] A similar juxtaposition has been noted around Northampton, where the hillfort at Hunsbury and Roman town of Duston are similarly disposed.[24] On the edge of the project area, a comparable pattern of Iron Age hillfort, Roman town, and medieval royal estate centre can also be found, in this case at Whittlebury, Towcester and Greens Norton (Figure 25).

An argument has been made that centres of local power and authority survived in the landscape over long periods of time. Traditions of power continued in particular localities; these places were taken over by the newcomers in order to legitimise their position. The foundation of central places close to those of an earlier age is thus of significance.[25] In the Whittlewood area, the establishment of an estate centre at Greens Norton may have been intended to assume the authority formerly exercised at Towcester, just as the Roman town apparently took over the position once occupied by Whittlebury. The territories controlled by each of these places were not necessarily identical, but we may suppose that they all encompassed at least part of the project area. Greens Norton was evidently the centre of a large multiple estate and minster parish, which included both Towcester (before the creation of Towcester Hundred in the tenth century) and Whittlebury. The memory of Whittlebury's former power, as well as its proximity to a hunting landscape, may have made it an appropriate place for the meeting of Athelstan's *witan*, to be preferred over a royal residence. Furthermore, it has been suggested that both Whittlebury and Whittlewood were named after a mythical or legendary figure – Witela – possibly as a result of stories told by the Saxons about the area's past.[26] The association of other royal manors with Whittlewood – Kirtlington, Passenham, Buckingham – ensured the king's exclusive

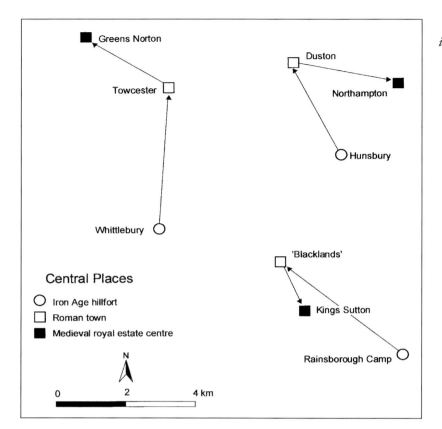

Central Places

○ Iron Age hillfort
□ Roman town
■ Medieval royal estate centre

N

0   2   4 km

FIGURE 25.
Central places of the
Iron Age, Roman period,
and Middle Ages are
found in close proximity
at several locations in
Northamptonshire.

connection with the tradition, as well as satisfying his need for timber, fuel, grazing and hunting.

The apparent domination of the study area by the king in the early Middle Ages, and its likely use as a hunting ground, prompts us to ask whether the royal interest would have extended to attempting to preserve the character of the landscape, for example, by limiting woodland clearance, arable cultivation and settlement. In other words, was a form of 'forest law' imposed before the Norman creation of the forest after 1066? A notable feature of Whittlewood's place-names is the paucity of settlements with the element -*tun* (meaning farmstead), in contrast to the surrounding area, which may indicate some restrictions on settlement in the woodland (Figure 26). Whittlewood may thus already have possessed a particular status as an area of hunting and grazing which encouraged the Norman kings to create a forest there. In other parts of England, Saxon kings maintained hunting grounds; as Young has observed, 'there were Saxon precedents that were transformed by the Conquest to create the royal forest as an institution'.[27]

Finally, a word about settlement. There are grounds for supposing that the nucleation of settlement around the 'pre-village nuclei' of the Whittlewood area did not take place within the multiple estate structure. At Akeley, for example, the pre-850 settlement zone beneath the later medieval village was no more extensive in area than many of the small scatters of pottery identified as hamlets or farmsteads elsewhere in Northamptonshire. Likewise, at Whittlebury, activity before the ninth century appears to have been confined to one part

FIGURE 26.
Place-names in *-tun* and
-feld.

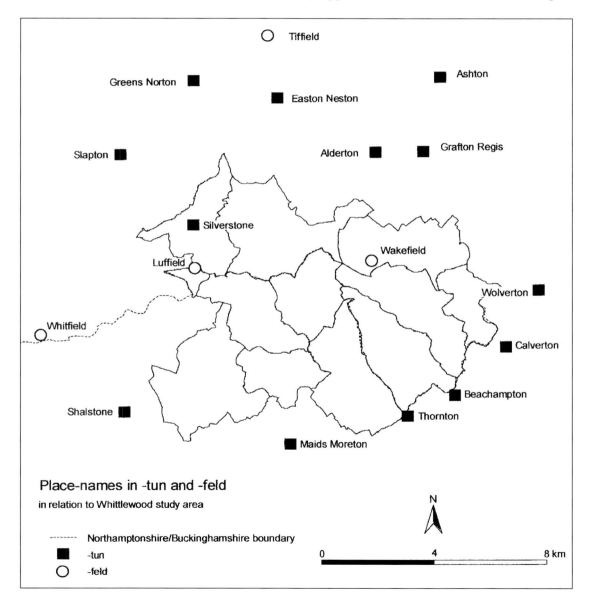

Place-names in -tun and -feld

in relation to Whittlewood study area

-------- Northamptonshire/Buckinghamshire boundary

■ -tun

○ -feld

N

0   4   8 km

of the Iron Age hillfort and, at Silverstone, there is little evidence of any permanent settlement before the end of the first millennium. The relatively light exploitation of dependent settlements from a central place and the lack of a resident lord were not factors likely to have encouraged the growth or reorganisation of the settlement pattern. Instead, the individual farmsteads and hamlets already established within the landscape were brought under the control of the estate centre, without an apparent effort to change their location or extent. In short, multiple estates were not agents of village nucleation, and the pattern of settlement was more likely to have been influenced by the decisions of the inhabitants than those made by lords.

Manors and parishes

In many parts of England, the period from the ninth to the eleventh centuries marked the final fragmentation of the multiple estates and the permanent creation of smaller units of landholding. In the Whittlewood area, the decision to break up the multiple estates was probably taken by the king. There is no evidence, for instance in Domesday Book, to suggest that any other lord possessed a large block of territory which could be dispersed. By contrast, in 1086 the king held the important manors of Buckingham, Greens Norton, Towcester and Passenham. In the ninth to eleventh centuries, therefore, new patterns of authority and landownership were created as the number of manors proliferated.

We have suggested that the pre-Conquest kings valued the woodland of the Whittlewood area and may have sought to preserve its character. This impression is reinforced by the apparently careful decisions taken during the break-up of the multiple estates. For example, at Silverstone only a quarter of the woodland recorded in Domesday Book belonged to the manor held by Godwin of Giles, brother of Ansculf. The remainder may have been retained as a condition of the grant by the king as lord of Greens Norton. Likewise, the Saxon kings retained control of Whittlebury and Wakefield, places with large amounts of woodland which later became the centre of the royal forest. No manor of Whittlebury appears in Domesday Book, possibly because it remained embedded in the estate of Greens Norton, while at Wakefield the manor was probably newly created by William the Conqueror. No Saxon holder of Wakefield is recorded in the Domesday survey, and the Norman manor did not survive long, being absorbed into the royal forest and probably converted into a royal hunting lodge (see below, pages 211–12).

At Passenham, too, the king retained control of the extensive woodland, while at the same time carving out new manors for his followers and servants: half a hide for his almsman, Reginald, another half-hide for a sokeman at Puxley; Saxon holders are not recorded for either of these holdings, suggesting that they were probably created after the Conquest. Nevertheless, the Conqueror was following Saxon precedents: a smallholding in Puxley, again without any wood attached, was held by Almær in 1066. In the Buckinghamshire parishes of the study area, the king held no manor in demesne, although Boycott and Lillingstone Lovell, former dependencies of Kirtlington, were held directly from him. In the other Buckinghamshire manors no trace of royal interest can be found, suggesting that, if they were once part of a multiple estate based on Buckingham, the links were severed at a relatively early date. Significantly, the king held no demesne woodland in north Buckinghamshire: the extension of the royal forest to encompass this area occurred only during the reign of Henry II and was to last only about 100 years.[28] The Buckinghamshire manors were thus less subject to royal oversight than those in Northamptonshire.

In general, the lords of the Whittlewood area recorded in Domesday Book each held only one or two properties, which would lead us to expect that they were resident on their estates. In some cases, their predecessors gave their name to the place: Akeley means 'Aca's clearing'; Deanshanger is 'Dynne's wooded slope'; Passenham is 'Passa's meadow'; Silverstone is 'Sæwulf's farmstead'. The creation of manors, often quite small in size, was far advanced by the end of the eleventh century: in the study area there were thirteen in Buckinghamshire and fourteen in Northamptonshire in 1086, and only slightly fewer in 1066. We cannot be sure whether this proliferation was due to the action of the land market, partible inheritance or deliberate subdivision. Between the Conquest and the compilation of Domesday Book, however, there appears to have been both consolidation and fragmentation of holdings in the study area: at Furtho, for example, five manors became three, while at Lillingstone Lovell an additional manor was created.

A lord might build a manor house in which to reside and from which he could direct the management of his lands. Certainly a lord with few properties required his estate to supply his daily needs. There could be no question of living on occasional renders of tribute. Instead, an area of land was developed as a home farm which was under the lord's direct supervision and became the main source of produce for his household.[29] Mills, too, might be constructed to grind the neighbourhood's grain, providing a service to the tenants and yielding both profit and prestige for the lord.[30] In the project area, Domesday Book records mills at Leckhampstead, Passenham and

Potterspury. The demesne was worked mainly by full-time servants or slaves, supplemented at busy times of the year by the labour services of peasant tenants. Domesday Book and pottery evidence reveals that arable farming was widely practised in the study area, albeit on a more limited scale than in some neighbouring districts.[31] Most manors possessed meadow to feed the plough beasts and woodland to graze the pigs. The recorded population of the project area in 1086 was low: about five people per square mile (1.9 per sq km), compared with more than sixteen per square mile (6.2 per sq km) in other parts of the region.[32] But it is likely that the ninth to eleventh centuries witnessed a growth of population as new manors were created and the land was more intensively farmed to supply resident lords.

The eleventh-century lords of Whittlewood were mostly minor secular lords. Only a few magnates are named in Domesday Book, such as Earl Leofwine, lord of Leckhampstead in 1066, or Alan, count of Brittany, lord of Wakefield in 1086. Those lords with few properties, such as Almær, at Puxley before the Norman Conquest, or Berner, at Lamport afterwards, who were likely to have resided on their manors, may be expected to have played an important role in shaping the pattern of landscape and settlement to accommodate the more intensive exploitation of their estates. For instance, on some manors, such as Wick Dive, a substantial proportion of the recorded population was made up of slaves, for whom the lord might be expected to provide food and shelter, perhaps in a group of houses close to the demesne. Likewise, lords may have encouraged the laying-out of the open fields, which in the Whittlewood area can be dated to the tenth century (see below, pages 92–5).[33] Minor lords, however, may not have possessed either sufficient power or influence to direct these changes alone, especially in areas of multiple ownership. They were probably obliged to cooperate with neighbouring lords and the village community, who would have been equally concerned to manage their holdings more effectively in order to pay the increased rents and taxes which lords and kings were beginning to impose during this period.[34]

Archaeological evidence reveals that the settlements of the study area expanded during the ninth to eleventh centuries. Indeed, it is in this period that the 'pre-village nuclei' grew to a sufficient size to be described, for the first time, as nucleated villages: for example, those at Leckhampstead (Church End), Lillingstone Dayrell, Wick Dive and Whittlebury. New elements in the settlement pattern also formed during this time, as at Dagnall in Wicken and Middle End in Leckhampstead. Evidence of systematic planning in the early medieval period is generally lacking. But even at those places where growth appears to be haphazard, decisions about the siting of tenements had to be made, either by the lord or the inhabitants themselves (see below, pages 89–92).

As well as residences, mills and other manorial buildings, lords often also built churches, as an act of piety, or as a sign of their status and proprietorship, or for the convenience of themselves and their tenants. The ninth to eleventh centuries were a period which witnessed the break-up of the large minster parishes and their replacement by the parish system which has survived to this day.[35] Minsters were often located at central places, such as Greens Norton, and some local churches remained dependent upon these 'mother churches' throughout the Middle Ages, as was the case at Silverstone and Whittlebury. Many parish churches, however, secured their independence from the minsters at an early date, and no evidence survives of their former attachment: for example, we cannot be sure whether Passenham was a minster church in the early Middle Ages and, if it was, the extent of its territory is unclear.[36] A hierarchy of churches developed as the subdivision of the minster parishes proceeded. For example, Leckhampstead originally held precedence over the church at Akeley, which was acknowledged in the twelfth century by the payment of an annual rent.[37] At Lillingstone Lovell (called *Magna* in the later Middle Ages), evidence of an eleventh-century porticus has been identified, which likewise indicates an ecclesiastical site of some importance, perhaps with authority over the neighbouring church at Lillingstone Dayrell (called *Parva*).[38]

The rector of the parish church was entitled to support himself by receiving a tenth part or tithe of the agricultural produce of his parishioners, together with other customary dues. As a result, parish boundaries began to form, to delineate the rights of neighbouring priests.[39] Since many parish churches were founded and endowed by local lords, the boundaries of parish and manor may originally have been the same. However, in the Whittlewood area, as elsewhere, the fragmentation of landownership in subsequent generations meant that by the later Middle Ages most parishes included more than one manor. Some parish churches were positioned on already sacred or pagan sites in order to ensure continuity of worship; possible examples include Stowe, which may mean 'holy place', and Whittlebury, where the church lies within the hillfort in which ritual depositions were made.[40] In a number of our settlements, the church probably lay next to the medieval manor house, indicating seigneurial involvement either in the foundation and location of the church or in the subsequent reorganisation of the settlement pattern. Elsewhere the community may have played a greater role; for example, the settlement at Akeley may have been colonised by inhabitants of Leckhampstead, who

FIGURE 27.
Furtho parish church.
FRAN HALSALL

founded a church initially dependent on that of their home village (see below, pages 199–200).[41] New churches were rarely built after the mid twelfth century: hence the absence of a parish church in the large late medieval village of Deanshanger, the inhabitants of which had to travel to Passenham. At Furtho, a small settlement formerly dependent on Cosgrove, a church was constructed in the eleventh century, but its limited territory meant that the parish measured less than 280 ha (700 acres) and was squeezed awkwardly between those of its larger neighbours (Figure 27).[42]

The break-up of the multiple estates and minster parishes fundamentally altered the landscape of authority in the Whittlewood area. Local power no longer resided with the king or his officials but with lesser landowners. The capacity of these lords to determine the lives of their subordinates and, conversely, the community's ability to regulate its own affairs (both secular and religious), was restricted to much smaller territorial units: the parish, the manor and the vill. The more extensive horizons offered by the large estates, in which separate groups of people had cooperated, interacted, serviced and supported the needs of a broader community, were now severely narrowed. These new individual communities demanded levels of self-sufficiency and autonomy previously unrequired. In order to secure such autonomy, we can envisage the reorganisation of the physical landscape so that the more limited natural and agricultural resources of these small units might have been more efficiently exploited; and the renegotiation of social relationships between lord and peasant, within the peasantry itself and between neighbouring lords in reaction to their new, more insular worlds. Likewise, alterations to the socio-economic base of these communities may have contributed to changes in the settlement pattern, as new ways of cooperative living and working were found within the boundaries of these new manors. As we shall see in the following chapter, the origins of some of the Whittlewood villages appear to be found in this period of change in the structure of authority, although how this was related to village formation remains uncertain.

Shires and hundreds

The independence of the new manors and parishes created in the study area in the ninth to eleventh centuries should not be exaggerated. Economically they were tied into wider trading networks and subject to changing market forces; ecclesiastically they were united under the diocesan jurisdiction of a bishop based eventually at Lincoln; and politically they were subject to the competing claims of rival kingdoms. The late ninth- and early tenth-century history of Whittlewood is especially complex. In AD 874, the expulsion of the Mercian king Burghred by the Viking 'Great Army' brought our area into the orbit of Danish influence.[43] Their impact, however, appears to have been slight. Few place-names contain Scandinavian elements west of Watling Street, an exception being Turweston near Brackley, a 'Grimston hybrid' (Scandinavian personal name *Thurulf* + Old English *tun*).[44] In part this can be explained by the rapid restoration of English control. Only four years after the Viking usurpation of AD 874, King Alfred's victory over the Danes at Edington checked the Scandinavian advance. According to an interpretation based on the subsequent peace treaty between Alfred and Guthrum, conventionally dated to AD 886x890 but possibly earlier, the boundary of the Danelaw was fixed on the line of Watling Street running north-westwards from its bridging point over the Great Ouse at Stony Stratford.[45] Most of our area was thus restored to English hands, only those parts of Furtho, Passenham and Potterspury east of the Roman road remaining within Danish jurisdiction. As a frontier zone, the area may have continued to suffer raids; its strategic importance and vulnerability led to the refortification of the *burh* at Towcester in the autumn of AD 921. However, the submission of the Viking army garrisoned at Northampton in the same year pushed the boundary of the Danelaw far to the east, ensuring that Whittlewood became firmly incorporated within the English kingdom.[46] Administratively too, by the beginning of the eleventh century if not earlier, our manors and parishes formed part of larger units, the shires and hundreds.

The creation of Buckinghamshire, Northamptonshire and Oxfordshire led to an untidy division of the study area between the three
shires, as a result of the inclusion of Boycott and Lillingstone
Lovell within the hundred of Ploughley. The date of the creation
of the midland shires has been particularly controversial. There is
general agreement, however, that the political backdrop to these new
arrangements was the tenth-century reconquest of the Danelaw and
its absorption into a united England under West Saxon control.[47]
This is not to deny the possibility that earlier territorial divisions
may have provided the framework for some later shires. A territory equating to Northamptonshire, for instance, may have existed
within the Danelaw.[48] However, the new midland shires appear to
have been designed as military and taxation units, based around
fortified towns, which provided these urban centres with a territory
from which they might draw men and victuals. As such, they were
created with direct reference to the prevailing political situation and
often owed little to administrative structures that had gone before.
Certainly Buckinghamshire seems to have had no antecedent, the
boundaries of which cut across older, long-established political groupings.[49] Although probably created in the tenth century, the three
shires are mentioned by name only at the beginning of the eleventh:
Buckinghamshire and Oxfordshire in 1010, and Northamptonshire
a year later. As a result, there are some who would argue that the
whole system was reorganised in one phase under Ealdorman Eadric
Streona in 1007.[50]

In the project area, the boundary separating Buckinghamshire
and Northamptonshire pursues an irregular course: it leaves what
appears to be its natural line along the river Great Ouse and loops
to the north around Buckingham, passing through what was almost
certainly dense woodland in the early Middle Ages, before joining the
river again a few miles north-east of Brackley. The Ouse flows through
the centre of Buckingham and before the creation of the town may
have acted as an important frontier. Certainly to the east and west
of Buckingham, the river serves as a convenient boundary for shire,
hundred and parish. The construction of a fortress at Buckingham
by Edward the Elder in AD 917, to combat the threat posed by the
Danes, necessitated the creation of a hinterland to the north of
the *burh*.[51] The extent of this territory may not at first have been
precisely defined, but was intended to lie on the watershed between
Ouse and Tove about midway between Buckingham and Towcester.
Watersheds, like rivers, were often important natural boundaries in
the early Middle Ages.[52] As the tenth century progressed, the formation of new manors and parishes from the fragments of the multiple

FIGURE 28.
The county boundary of
Buckinghamshire and
Northamptonshire. The
boundaries of a number
of parishes converge in
the woodland, meeting at
a point formerly known
as Westmead Dike. The
hachured area represents
presumed royal woodland
in the tenth/eleventh
centuries.

estates created the need for additional boundaries, some of which may have been determined by the division between estates of the valuable woods of Whittlewood, and which were subsequently adopted as the boundary between the shires. In places the position of the county boundary may have been influenced by the location of Bronze Age barrows, which were sometimes used to mark the edge of prehistoric as well as medieval territories (Figure 28).[53] This raises the possibility that parts of the county boundary were older than the shires themselves, and of the hundreds into which they were divided.

In southern England it is far from clear whether the shires were divided into hundreds or were constituted from them. The first document explicitly to mention English hundreds, the so-called Hundred

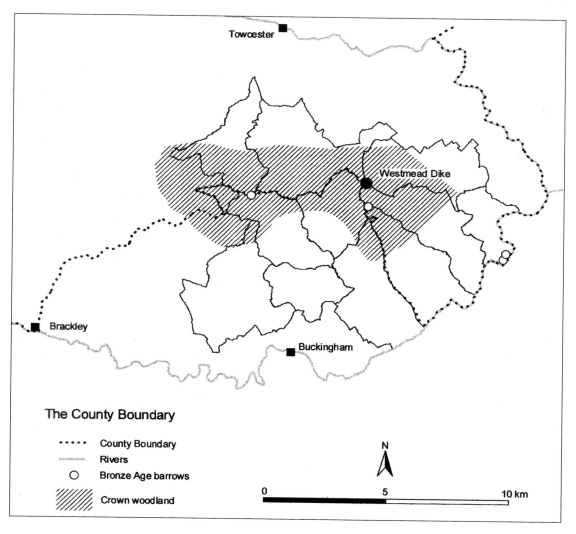

The County Boundary

· · · · · County Boundary

∼∼∼∼∼ Rivers

○ Bronze Age barrows

▨ Crown woodland

N

0   5   10 km

Ordinance, dates to the mid tenth century.[54] The Whittlewood hundreds are named for the first time in the Northamptonshire geld roll of *c.* 1075.[55] Nevertheless, we will argue that it was the shire and not the hundred which was the last administrative layer to be draped over the landscape. The importance of the hundred in the administration of the late eleventh century is made clear by the arrangement of manorial entries under their respective hundredal headings in Domesday Book. By this stage the hundred had long been the basic unit for the administration of financial, military, judicial and political matters, centred upon the hundred court.[56] The antiquity of the hundreds, moreover, is implied both by their place-names and by their geographic disposition in the landscape.

The four hundreds included in the Whittlewood project area were Cleley, Foxley (later Greens Norton), Stodfold and Ploughley, the meeting-places of which (except Stodfold at Stowe) lay in open countryside, remote from areas of settlement.[57] Two of the hundreds contain the element *leah* (clearing), indicating open ground within a more wooded environment (the second element in Ploughley is *hlaw*, meaning tumulus). Hundreds named after meeting-places in the countryside are generally agreed to represent an early phase of hundredal creation and are certainly considered to be older than those which take their name from the hundredal manor.[58] This observation reminds us that the division of the administrative landscape, and the grouping of individual manors and parishes into these larger territories, was part of an evolutionary process and not a single event which can be fixed in space and time. Hundreds, like the multiple estates before them, and the manors and parishes from which they were formed, were not monoliths. Once created, their shape, form and internal structure might all be subject to change. There are strong indications, for instance, that the hundred of Foxley was greatly reduced in size by the later creation of the hundred of Towcester (taking its name from the hundredal manor), and that formerly these two hundreds once constituted a single entity.[59]

The geographical layout of the hundreds may be significant. Cleley Hundred, with its southern boundary following the Great Ouse, took in the western bank of the lower reaches of the river Tove, and east of Towcester encompassed the whole of the river basin. For large stretches, its outer bounds appear to follow the Tove's watershed faithfully (Figure 29). Stodfold Hundred, too, uses strong topographic features to identify its limits, notably the Great Ouse to the south and west, while to the north and east its extent follows the Great Ouse/Tove watershed. Both bear many of the hallmarks of the valley-based estates identified by Klingelhöfer in Hampshire,

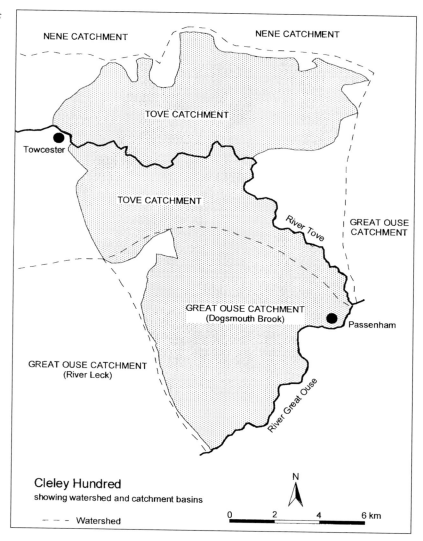

NENE CATCHMENT   NENE CATCHMENT

TOVE CATCHMENT

Towcester

TOVE CATCHMENT

River Tove

GREAT OUSE
CATCHMENT

GREAT OUSE CATCHMENT
(Dogsmouth Brook)

Passenham

GREAT OUSE CATCHMENT
(River Leck)

River Great Ouse

Cleley Hundred
showing watershed and catchment basins

– – – Watershed

N

0   2   4   6 km

FIGURE 29.
Cleley Hundred,
showing the coincidence
of the northern and
western boundaries of
the administrative unit
with watersheds, and
the southern boundary
following the river
Great Ouse.

which he termed 'archaic hundreds', while Gelling has argued that in
Stodfold 'the other parishes are arranged round Stowe in a manner
which suggests that some of them have been carved out of a larger
unit to which it was central'.[60] If the hundreds of Greens Norton
and Towcester are taken together to represent the full extent of an
earlier Foxley Hundred, similar geographic traits can be seen. This
unit would appear to include the whole of the river catchment of the
upper Tove, its southern boundary following the Great Ouse watershed, its western boundary located on the Cherwell watershed, and
its northern boundary encroaching only slightly upon the river Nene
basin. It too may have its origins in a multiple estate, the break-up of

which created the administrative anomaly of detached holdings which, in some cases, were not swept away until the nineteenth century.

Conclusions

Early medieval Whittlewood, it has been argued, was a marginal landscape, authority over which resided largely outside the study area at a number of royal estate centres. Of these, the most important was probably Greens Norton, the Saxon lords of which may have assumed the tradition of power in the locality formerly exercised from the Iron Age hillfort at Whittlebury. The Whittlewood area was valued for its reserves of timber, grazing and game, and attempts were likely to have been made to preserve its character, even during the break-up of the multiple estates. Between AD 400 and 850, the boundaries of the various territories which made up the project area are often unclear and may not have been closely defined. With the creation of shire, hundred and parish, new boundaries were formed or old ones reused: some followed the natural courses of river and watershed; others converged in the woodlands, ensuring that each estate enjoyed a share of this valuable resource; a few lay close to prehistoric barrows and other features.

By 1100, the landscape of Whittlewood was divided in a variety of ways, some of them new, others inherited from earlier times, but which were adapted to meet the needs of an era of fragmented lordship and small estates. The creation of new manors, held mostly by resident lords, led to a more intensive exploitation of the landscape. Arable farming became widespread; settlements expanded; manor houses, churches, mills and a variety of other buildings were constructed. By the time of Domesday Book, Whittlewood can no longer be described as a marginal area, exploited by outsiders on an irregular or seasonal basis. Authority had become more localised, exercised in manorial, hundred and shire courts. Links between former dependencies and estate centres were either broken or survived as anomalous relics of a previous age. Available resources were reorganised and exploited more efficiently to ensure the survival and growth of small, largely self-sufficient communities. The ways in which this reorganisation occurred are complex, varied geographically and over time, and have been the subject of long-running debate. In the following chapter, we explore these changes in the Whittlewood area, and outline the beginnings of open-field farming and the origins of the medieval village.

CHAPTER FIVE

Beginnings:
The Origins of the Village

The period between the ninth and thirteenth centuries is generally regarded as one of change. Across Europe, states emerged, towns grew and the economy expanded. New ideas flourished, affecting property, agriculture and social relationships. England experienced its own version of these transformations.[1] A unified kingdom was created in the tenth century. A number of settlements developed urban characteristics and, henceforth, towns — net consumers, not producers, of agricultural produce, administrative, judicial, military, ecclesiastical, manufacturing and market centres — formed a significant part of the settlement hierarchy. In many parts of the countryside, a dispersed pattern of hamlets and farmsteads was replaced by a more regular pattern of nucleated villages; field systems were reorganised, and open-field farming was adopted in place of the cultivation of smaller parcels; woodland was more intensively managed and areas formerly perceived as marginal, such as uplands, wetlands and forest, were brought into more systematic exploitation and were settled.[2]

There can be little doubt that many of these changes, both rural and urban, were linked, and that common pressures, such as population growth and the opportunities stemming from technological change or improved climatic conditions, either lay behind or help to explain these widespread and contemporary developments. In trying to characterise this period, and in particular the origins of villages and open-field systems, earlier writers were drawn to the idea of discontinuity. However, more recent discussions have stressed the idea that the late medieval landscape and settlement pattern formed out of evolutionary rather than revolutionary processes.[3] This chapter addresses these themes of continuity and discontinuity, and examines how they have been used specifically to explain the appearance of nucleated villages and open fields in the Central Province, within which Whittlewood is situated. We begin with a brief review of the various hypotheses that have been proposed, before turning to the evidence from the study area. Since the results of our work fail to conform closely with any previous explanation, we offer an alternative model that accounts not only for the development of villages and their fields in the Whittlewood area, but which may also be applied to other parts of England.

Explanations of the village and open fields

The social and economic history of the village has attracted much scholarly attention over the last 100 years, revealing the complex social hierarchies that might exist, and the collaborative and divisive tendencies among the inhabitants.[4] In the study of village plans, historical geographers have grouped the variety of layouts recorded on modern maps into a small number of categories sharing common characteristics, at the same time acknowledging the diversity that such archetypes might contain.[5] Many approaches have been taken to the subject of the medieval village; nevertheless, common traits in the historiography can be observed. Few studies, for instance, fail to set their observations against a broader physical, social, economic and political backdrop: the village landscape. In addition, almost all accept that establishing the chronology of formation is an essential prerequisite to village interpretation. By dating the origins of a village, a context is provided to explain the processes by which it formed and the agencies that lay behind these changes; moreover, from this base all subsequent developments may be traced.[6]

Early attempts to explain the origins of the village and open-field system emphasised the role played by different ethnic groups of Germanic invaders in the fifth and sixth centuries.[7] In the absence of dating evidence, the 'introduction hypothesis', that villages were brought fully formed to England during the period of Anglo-Saxon settlement, became the orthodoxy and proved a tenacious and attractive thesis. For example, Gray, using evidence mainly from the thirteenth to the seventeenth centuries, distinguished five subcategories of open-field system categorised by subtle structural variation and broadly defined by their geographical extent. The distribution of these farming systems and their associated settlement types, it was argued, strengthened the case for their introduction by different ethnic groups.[8] Foreign introduction remained the cornerstone of further studies, such as those by Homans, who was the first to recognise a similarity in the physical layout of thirteenth-century village and field, in particular the regular and sequential order of peasant tofts and their strips, paralleled by the Scandinavian system of *solskifte*.[9]

From the 1960s, the identification of even greater variation in field layout and management cast doubt on the direct link that could be made between particular systems of the later Middle Ages and the ethnic groups of the fifth and sixth centuries. The emphasis shifted to drawn-out processes rather than single events.[10] Thirsk argued that regular open fields developed from more irregular systems over time, and that regional variation might simply represent the fossilisation of a changing landscape at different stages in its development. Consequently, it was suggested that the midland system, the most regular of all the regional archetypes, with its associated nucleated villages, was the latest to develop, and may not have been in existence until the thirteenth century or later.[11] These objections proved convincing, but they lacked clear-cut dating evidence. Eventually, archaeology provided the first definitive dating evidence for village origins, from the recovery of pottery through archaeological survey and the identification of the first phases of occupation in later village cores. There is now a consensus that this evidence offers a solid foundation for discussing the origins of the village; nevertheless, three opposing models of village development have replaced the 'introduction hypothesis'.

The first model to be proposed on the basis of the new data placed the moment of village formation in the ninth century. Based largely, but not exclusively, on evidence gathered in Northamptonshire, it was argued that villages formed in a process of nucleation which saw the abandonment of an earlier settlement pattern of dispersed farmsteads in favour of a single communal centre. Systematic fieldwalking suggested that these farmsteads, marked by small scatters of pottery, were largely deserted by the mid ninth century because new pottery types, such as St Neots ware, which were introduced into the region at this time, were not found. Importantly, excavation within the cores of later nucleated villages demonstrated that these were occupied at the same time as the farmsteads. Moreover, the spreads of pottery in the villages were more extensive than those encountered on the farmstead sites. When the farmsteads were abandoned, therefore, the population seems to have moved to one settlement in the territory, which may have been larger than the surrounding farmsteads and was perhaps of higher status; as a result, the settlement grew still further to become a village (see above, page 10).[12] Administrative and economic reforms, it was proposed, lay behind these developments. The chronology of nucleation was seen to be intimately linked with the breakdown of the multiple estate structure and the development of more localised manorial holdings. Where large royal estates persisted, dispersed settlements could survive, accommodated within their extensive territories and insulated against change by them. But where these estates were carved into smaller units, nucleation was an inevitable consequence, providing the means by which the now limited resources within a territory could be most efficiently exploited.[13]

In the associated open fields, the identification of long furlongs running over several hundred metres, in some places the whole length of the farming territory, appeared to indicate that the open fields were laid out with little regard for preceding land arrangements.[14] This was likely to have been undertaken only if the landscape was unencumbered by the existence of individual farmsteads which would have disrupted the system. Since those farmsteads which formerly occupied parts of the later fields could be demonstrated to have been deserted before AD 850, and since there was evidence to suggest that nucleation had occurred by this date too, it followed that the open fields were in existence and 'substantially completed' by the end of the ninth century.[15] Archaeological evidence suggested that the open fields were replanned in the late Saxon period, when the long furlongs were split into shorter lengths by balks and headlands.[16] This reorganisation was seen to be contemporary with the replanning of their associated settlements. In the late ninth and tenth centuries, irregular house plots were replaced by more regular rows of tenements. The context for these changes, it was argued, was the continued fragmentation of multiple estates and the parcelling-out of land to lords who exercised more control over their tenants than previously. Such changes required significant capital investment, which was dependent on the growth of the market economy. But the implication is that the village plan had been formalised by the time of the Norman Conquest.[17]

The second model to emerge from the integration of the historical and archaeological evidence took a more evolutionary approach. Villages were born out of a complex interplay of social, economic and cultural circumstances that prevailed over a period of 400 years from the mid ninth to the mid thirteenth century, an era labelled the 'village moment'.[18] The model identified particular stresses which came to be imposed on existing patterns of land use and settlement during these centuries, which could only be countered through the radical reorganisation of the countryside. A growing population, for example, required accommodation. In an already crowded landscape, opportunities for expansion were limited as small farming units around individual farmsteads became interlocked. This intricate pattern of landholding increasingly became a barrier to movement across the landscape, making access to woodland and pasture problematic. At the same time, the produce needed to feed a burgeoning population necessitated the expansion of the arable zone at the expense of these vital non-arable resources. Village nucleation and the open fields offered a solution to these problems. The population could be accommodated within the settlement centre, while the surrounding countryside could be freed up both for more intensive and extensive agricultural use. By dividing the arable into a small number of large blocks, within which the whole community had a stake, cooperative action permitted fields to be left fallow in rotation, significantly increasing the area available for grazing at any one time, while an intricate web of access ways along the balks and headlands of the fields offered greater ease of movement. Individual settlements faced this moment of crisis at different times, helping to explain why the phenomenon of nucleation appears to have taken place not during a single phase of reorganisation but over a prolonged period of time. For some communities this critical moment was never reached, allowing the perpetuation or further development of non-nuclear settlement patterns. For others, however, the perceived benefits of nucleation observed elsewhere may have encouraged the adoption of this form of settlement. The advantages of nucleation seem to have been short-lived, and by the thirteenth century the 'village moment' had passed. In the village zones of lowland England there was little land available on which a new village and its territory might develop, while in regions of hamlets and farmsteads, such as the north and west, nucleation offered few solutions to the social and economic needs of these more pastoral communities.[19]

The most recent contribution to the debate, on the other hand, argues that 'the principal factors moulding this landscape of peasant farmers were, not surprisingly, agricultural and environmental'.[20] While accepting the middle Saxon chronology of village formation, Williamson sets out the case for the overriding influence of soils, topography and climate on their development, as we have already described (see above, pages 12–13). Although emphasising the importance of environmental factors, Williamson acknowledges that differences in social, economic and tenurial structure may also have influenced the pattern of settlement. In the context of the heavy midland clays, he notes that while the need to respond quickly to environmental conditions '*might* have been enough on their own to prevent the spread of settlement away from old sites ... these things could just as easily have led to the development of small hamlets – each containing enough farms (three or four, perhaps) to make a viable team – strung out along the margins of the great Midland meadows. That this did not happen was doubtless the consequence of decisions taken by demesne managers'.[21] Individuals, therefore, can be seen to have influenced how the landscape was settled and exploited, but ultimately it was the environment which dictated which choices these farming societies could or could not make.

The Whittlewood evidence

With these three models in mind, we may turn to the evidence from the Whittlewood area. This section traces settlement development from the end of the Roman era to the Norman Conquest, demonstrating that village formation resulted from different processes to those outlined above.

FIGURE 30.
Dispersed settlements and pre-village nuclei in the Whittlewood area before AD 850.

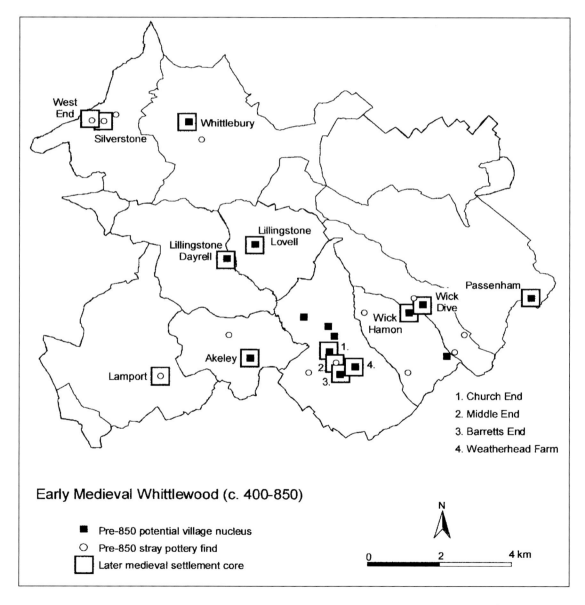

Early Medieval Whittlewood (c. 400–850)

■ Pre-850 potential village nucleus
○ Pre-850 stray pottery find
□ Later medieval settlement core

1. Church End
2. Middle End
3. Barretts End
4. Weatherhead Farm

N

0   2   4 km

Dispersed settlement AD 400–850

In most of the parishes that have been investigated, evidence for a dispersed settlement pattern of early medieval farmsteads has not been found (Figure 30). At Akeley a single significant pocket of sand and gravel is occupied by the present village. On the boulder clays beyond the village, which predominate in the whole parish, no concentrations of pottery have been found to mark the sites of outlying farmsteads of the period AD 400–850, even though there is plentiful evidence for Roman settlement and farming (Figure 20). The failure of the Romano-British farmsteads and their fields to survive beyond the first quarter of the fifth century suggests some retreat from the claylands. Likewise, in the neighbouring parish of Lillingstone Dayrell, a similar pattern of development can be detected. Glacial boulder clay again dominates the local geology, and no early medieval farmstead sites can be detected in the ceramic record in areas later occupied by open fields and assarts. But the difficulties of working the heavy clays seem to have posed no barrier for Romano-British farmers, since extensive manuring scatters are encountered across the parish. One settlement site of the Roman period covering several hectares has been found 750 m (820 yards) north-west of the medieval village, and there are indications of a smaller settlement lying on its south-western fringe. Like Akeley, however, no continuity of field systems or settlement sites can be demonstrated between the Roman and early medieval periods at Lillingstone Dayrell.

By contrast, in the parish of Leckhampstead, a number of concentrations of pottery taken to represent farmstead sites of the period AD 400–850 have been found (Figure 31). At least four of these, none covering more than 2 ha (5 acres), lay below the later village's fields. Two shared their sites with earlier and more substantial Roman complexes, these lying respectively 400 m (440 yards) north of Church End and 600 m (660 yards) south of Barretts End, while the other two appeared to occupy virgin sites. All four lay on boulder clay. Although many such farmsteads have been observed elsewhere, it is relatively unusual to find them located on the clay. In Northamptonshire, the evidence indicates a major retreat to the better-draining, more fertile, and more easily worked soils of the river valleys.[22] At Yarnton (Oxon.), too, even though the density of middle Saxon settlement foci does not fall far short of the Roman numbers, in both periods these sites occupied gravel terraces and avoided the Oxford and Kimmeridge clays.[23] In Whittlewood, a strong case can be made for a move away from the claylands at the end of the Roman period – for instance, in Akeley and Lillingstone Dayrell – but at Leckhampstead pockets of settlement persisted through to around AD 850. Abandonment was thus not total,

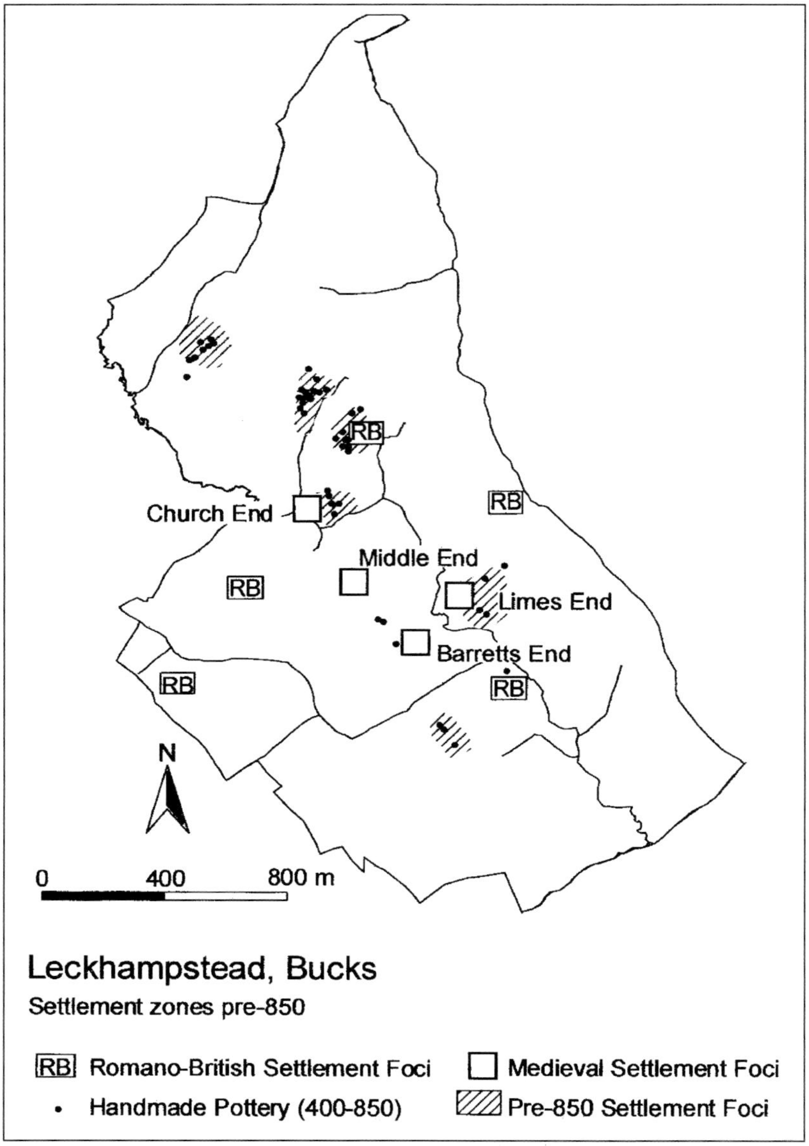

FIGURE 31.
Dispersed settlement in
Leckhampstead parish
before AD 850.

and while the pollen record indicates an expansion of woodland from
Roman levels and more extensive grassland, thin scatters of pottery
in the immediate vicinity of the early medieval farmsteads, presumably resulting from the spreading of domestic rubbish with manure,
demonstrate that some of the land was worked as arable fields.[24] This
indicates permanent occupancy of Whittlewood, the concentrations
of pottery representing farmsteads and not seasonal shielings associated with pastoral transhumance organised from communities based

in the river valleys beyond the study area. What emerges, then, is a more complex picture of settlement and exploitation of the claylands between the fifth and ninth centuries than current models would allow.

Pre-village nuclei

The abandonment of these dispersed settlements has been seen as a critical event, marking the moment of nucleation. Recent investigations at Yarnton have dated the desertion of some of the outlying sites to the end of the eighth century, and identified the reorganisation of what would become the nucleated village in the same period.[25] Elsewhere, the evidence is more equivocal because the handmade pottery wares which mark the sites of these farmsteads can rarely be given a more precise date range than AD 400–850. Nevertheless, the absence of later fabrics which carry more secure dating has been taken to imply that these sites were abandoned by the mid ninth century, and perhaps a century or two earlier.[26] In the Whittlewood area there is a general trend for those sites interpreted as outlying farmsteads to produce no ceramic evidence dated later than AD 850. This is a crux date since it marks the introduction into the area of non-locally produced fabrics, such as St Neots ware, manufactured on the border between Bedfordshire and Cambridgeshire. Thus, the four Leckhampstead sites appear to have had no active life after AD 850, although it is far from clear whether they were deserted close to this date, or had been abandoned at a much earlier period. Some were deserted later. In the parish of Wick Dive, in those areas which were brought under arable cultivation in the later Middle Ages, only one early medieval site has been identified. In the extreme south of the parish, on one of the gravel terraces of the Great Ouse, an attractive position perhaps sought out during the post-Roman settlement reshuffle, this farmstead appears to have survived until the end of the first millennium.[27]

In surviving beyond AD 850, this site was not alone. An important group of pre-850 settlement sites in Whittlewood continued to flourish beyond the mid ninth century. These were the sites that would develop into the main villages. From within the cores of the later nucleated villages of Akeley and Lillingstone Dayrell, for example, there is evidence for occupation before the mid ninth century. Likewise, lying below the later settlement areas of Leckhampstead, our most dispersed village, a further three spreads of pre-850 pottery have been identified by test-pitting, in addition to those found during fieldwalking. All five sites also produce the Saxo-Norman wares indicative of continued occupation through to the first documentary mention of these villages in Domesday Book. In each instance, the area covered by the tell-tale pottery was minuscule and can have accommodated no more than one or two households. At Akeley, the evidence is restricted to a few sherds found 250 m (820 feet) south of the church; at Lillingstone Dayrell the pottery assemblage is larger, but remains concentrated in a small zone 100 m (330 feet) west of the church (Figure 23); while at Church End, Limes End and Barretts End, all in Leckhampstead, each distribution of pottery covers no more than a couple of hectares, and in one case a much smaller area.

There is little to suggest, therefore, that nucleation was in progress in Whittlewood in the mid ninth century. If this had been the case, we would expect that the areas producing pottery beneath later nucleations to far exceed in size those found on the recently abandoned individual farmsteads. They do not, and consequently it is impossible to equate the middle Saxon experience of the Whittlewood villages with places such as Brixworth, Higham Ferrers, Irthlingborough and Raunds (Northants.), where large pottery spreads appear to indicate some concentration of population associated with the abandonment of smaller surrounding sites, or with other contemporary agglomerated settlements like Pennyland (Bucks.) and Yarnton (Oxon.) locally, or more distant sites such as Cowdery's Down (Hants.), Catholme (Staffs.), West Heslerton (Yorks.) and Riby Crossroads (Lincs.), which were large enough to accommodate many households.[28] In fact, in terms of size, those sites found under the late medieval villages of Whittlewood cannot be differentiated from other contemporary settlements interpreted as single farmsteads. The only difference was that they would develop while the others would fail. For this reason we have termed them 'pre-village nuclei'.

From the earliest stages of village development, therefore, the evidence from Whittlewood fails to adhere to current nucleation models in four important respects. First, while there was clearly a retreat of population from the heavy clays, presumably towards the lighter soils of the valley floor, abandonment was not total. Just as later nucleations have been seen to grow from a dispersed pattern of settlement in these favoured locations, this also appears to be the base from which nucleations would spring on the less desirable interfluves. Secondly, the pattern of dispersed farmstead desertion was patchy and not universal. Some sites clearly did not survive beyond AD 850, others remained active until around 1000, while a large proportion, almost half in the case of Whittlewood, remained permanently occupied through to the post-Conquest period and beyond. Thirdly, before AD 850 there is little evidence for a radical reorganisation of population which saw the rejection of dispersed settlement in favour of village nucleation. Settlement in mid ninth-century Whittlewood remained scattered, with nucleations, or proto-nucleations, non-existent. Finally, even when outlying farmsteads were abandoned, it is impossible to detect any associated growth before AD 850 at other settlement nodes which might indicate that a displaced population was congregating at these places.

Village beginnings AD 850–1000

From the second half of the ninth century, there are indications of significant changes in some of the Whittlewood villages. Notably, growth and an expansion in the settled area can be charted. At Church End, Leckhampstead, the pre-village nucleus, previously restricted to

FIGURE 32.
Church End,
Leckhampstead: village
growth, AD 850–1000.
© Crown copyright. All
rights reserved. Licence
number 100046321

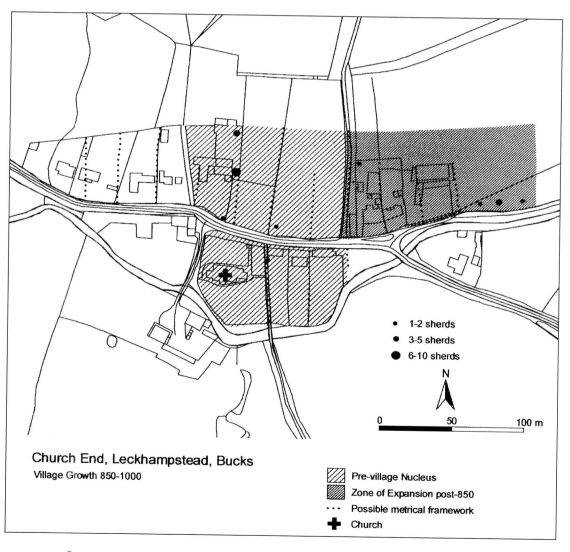

Church End, Leckhampstead, Bucks
Village Growth 850-1000

- 1-2 sherds
- 3-5 sherds
- 6-10 sherds

N

0   50   100 m

/// Pre-village Nucleus
/// Zone of Expansion post-850
··· Possible metrical framework
✚   Church

an area spreading no more than 100 m (330 feet) from the church, was extended over an additional 200–300 m (655–985 feet) to the east along what still remains the main village street (Figure 32). On the basis of the pottery, this expansion took place between AD 850 and 1000. Tracing this expansion by test-pitting rather than open area excavation means that nothing is known about the morphology of this new row: whether, for instance, the plots were of similar size or whether their frontages adhered to some metrical norm, but this possibility cannot be dismissed. Similar expansion occurred at Lillingstone Dayrell, along the road leading to the church. At Wick Dive, finds of St Neots ware together with imported Stamford ware (AD 900–1200) locate the original core of the village adjacent to the church. This material appears to be spread evenly over a strip 200 m (655 feet) long, north of the main village street (Figure 33). At Akeley and Whittlebury, there is evidence of a shift of settlement prior to expansion. Occupation at Akeley after AD 850 moved north to the area around the church, while at Whittlebury spreads of St Neots ware in the northern part of the modern village in the lee

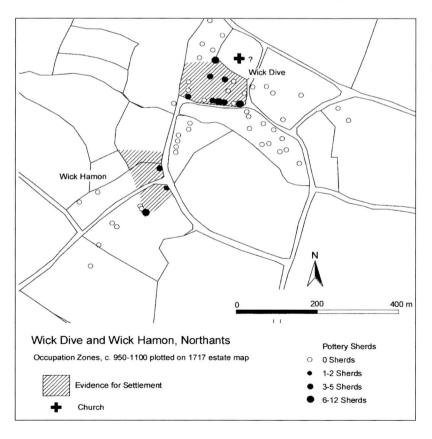

Wick Dive and Wick Hamon, Northants

Occupation Zones, c. 950–1100 plotted on 1717 estate map

Evidence for Settlement

✚ Church

Pottery Sherds

○ 0 Sherds

• 1-2 Sherds

● 3-5 Sherds

⬤ 6-12 Sherds

of the Iron Age hillfort mark the development of a new settlement area, associated with the probable abandonment of two earlier foci immediately to the south and west. In all five cases we might suggest that these pottery spreads record the process of nucleation. Elsewhere, the evidence for village origins is somewhat later. For example, at Lillingstone Lovell, no activity can be detected before the late tenth century, when Cotswold-type Oolitic ware (AD 975–1100) makes its appearance close to the church, while at Silverstone, a small and irregular grouping of farmsteads experienced growth and coalescence at about the same time.

Thus, it appears that while settlements in other parts of the midlands experienced a secondary reordering between AD 850 and 1000, most of the Whittlewood villages still remained at this date in a primary phase of formation. It was only in villages such as Leckhampstead, which had been firmly established by AD 850, that there is any trace of replanning. Even here, due to the nature in which the evidence has been gathered, this remains impossible to prove definitively. Elsewhere, the situation is clearer. Villages, like multi-celled organisms, were still forming biologically and organically from the primordial soup of single-celled settlement. For them, replanning, often on a massive scale, would only take place in the post-Conquest period. In this context it is interesting to note the apparent relationship between the size of population recorded in Domesday Book and the archaeological evidence of village formation. Leckhampstead, our oldest settlement, had a population of over thirty (each recorded person presumably representing a household) in 1086. By contrast, the population in a late arrival such as Akeley, whose territory was almost certainly carved out of an earlier and larger Leckhampstead, was considerably smaller, at just eight people (see below, pages 165–70).

The archaeological evidence from Whittlewood thus identifies a process of village formation that runs counter to accepted models. Rather than seeing the inward movement of people forming a new central place, we see outward growth from existing pre-village nuclei. Consequently, the number and location of pre-village nuclei in each parish in part dictated how the village plan developed. In places such as Akeley, Lillingstone Dayrell, and Lillingstone Lovell, a single pre-village nucleus developed into the later nucleated village. In parishes such as Leckhampstead and Wicken, where many pre-village nuclei survived into, or were established during, the late ninth and early tenth centuries, multiple village and hamlet clusters developed around them. The common experiences of our villages, first the stability in the location of their settlement foci, and secondly their outward growth, thus begins to explains why both nucleated and dispersed plans should emerge together during the period of village formation.

Open-field origins 850–1000

Related changes were taking place in the organisation of the village fields. Evidence gathered from the Whittlewood area offers the possibility of detecting the moment of open-field formation in our twelve parishes. Reconstruction of the extent of the medieval arable zone relies upon a combination of evidence from maps, the identification of ridge and furrow and the linear build-ups of soil at the edges of each furlong called headlands, and fieldwalking material. The map and earthwork data is important but fails to provide the critical dating evidence necessary to pinpoint when the fields and their constituent furlongs were laid out. However, since it was a universal practice to manure ploughlands with an admixture of animal dung and domestic refuse collected at the homestead, containing within it pottery sherds from broken vessels, the recovery of these ceramics through field-walking can be used to locate earlier arable fields and to date when these were being worked. The Whittlewood assemblage contains a number of pottery fabrics. Analysis of these, set against the evidence from the village cores recovered through test-pitting, demonstrates remarkable consistency. In villages in the west of the study area, for example, where sandy wares (1100–1400) appear to have been favoured over the contemporary and competing shelly wares, the fields also contain the same pottery bias. To the east, where shelly wares dominate village assemblages, the manure scatters again show the same proportion. Such results should not surprise. After all, if the principal manure source was the homestead, then the fields would have received the very ceramic material that was being used there. The relationship between what pottery was used in the home and what arrived with manure loads in the fields can, in fact, be demonstrated at all periods. So during the Roman period, the manure scatters can only be differentiated from settlement sites by their density and levels of abrasion (sherds from undisturbed settlement sites have suffered less than pottery rolled during successive ploughing episodes), and not by the types of pottery that they contain. The same is the case in the early medieval period. Around the farmsteads dated to AD 400–850, identified as concentrations of coarse handmade sherds, small halos of the same pottery can be found marking their limited arable zone.

In fact, there is only one period during which this close relationship between village and field ceramic assemblages is not present, between AD 850 and 1000 (Figure 34). Our exploration of village cores has

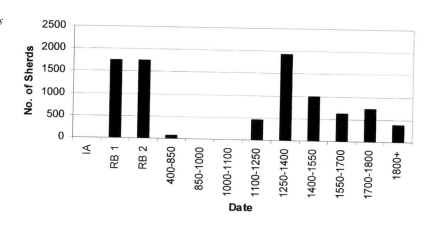

FIGURE 34.
Number of pottery
sherds in manure
scatters recovered during
fieldwalking in the
Whittlewood area.

shown that in all cases St Neots ware type I was being used in the
home. Despite extensive field survey, however, not a single sherd of
this fabric has been recovered in manure scatters. St Neots ware is a
coarse shell-tempered pottery. The shell inclusions are prone to erosion,
but the main body of the pottery is fairly resilient. Certainly St Neots
ware cannot be considered to be more friable, and thus more liable
to collapse, than pottery of the period AD 400–850. Since significant
quantities of earlier handmade wares have been found through fieldwalking, we may conclude that the absence of St Neots ware is real,
and not the consequence of plough attrition leading to its destruction.
Moreover, with field assemblages producing large amounts of Romano-
British wares as well as wares of AD 400–850, the possibility that
alluvial and colluvial activity has masked these deposits can be ruled
out. A traditional explanation of its absence from the record would
suggest that no arable cultivation was taking place, but this seems
highly improbable. We have already suggested that this was a period
of arable expansion, which is indicated too by increased rates of soil
erosion visible in valley deposits (see above, pages 69–70).[29]

The absence of St Neots ware, therefore, must indicate a short
period during which manuring strategies changed, a moment when
household waste was not used to manure the fields. There are grounds
to associate this with the laying-out of the open fields. For the first
time, arable holdings were geographically divorced from the farmstead. It may have become inconvenient, therefore, to cart domestically
sourced detritus to intermixed strips often at some distance from the
village. Furthermore, by laying out open fields over former settlement sites already rich in organic matter, as seems to be the case in
Leckhampstead parish, or over areas of former pasture, the nutrient
pool of which was not depleted by overworking, large parts of the
new system may not have initially required further manuring. If they

did, an adequate return could be had from dung spread on the hoof by those animals allowed to graze the fallows or on the stubble after harvest. We would argue that the return to manuring with household material, a strategic change marked by the arrival of late eleventh- and early twelfth-century sherds in the fields, may have been forced upon farmers in order to counter soil nutrient depletion after a period of repetitive cultivation, and to protect or increase yields to feed a growing population and to generate sufficient income to pay higher rates of rent and tax.[30]

The early arrangement of these open fields is not clear. However, there is nothing to suggest either the initial laying-out of long furlongs or their later subdivision.[31] On the basis of the manure scatter data, for example, it is difficult to see the arable zone extending much beyond 1.5 km (1 mile) from the village centre in the twelfth century. Arable cultivation only reached the peripheries of the parish at this period when the boundary lay within this radius. Elsewhere within each territory there was clearly space to expand, and this growth can again be traced in the ceramic record, with new land being opened up to the plough into the late thirteenth century. So the fieldwalking evidence points to incremental growth of the arable over time, rather than an initial intake of an extensive acreage. Nor does the surviving ridge and furrow show anything other than a short and interlocking furlong arrangement. Strip alignments never appear to have stretched more than 200 m (655 feet), and follow the local microtopography so closely that it seems unlikely that, underlying the furlongs that can be mapped accurately, there was ever an earlier arrangement of long furlongs. Indeed, excavation of headlands in the parishes of Silverstone and Wicken, where pre-medieval ditches have been found running parallel to and under the medieval soil accumulation, seems to point to at least the partial survival of early field systems which influenced the later open fields, a phenomenon that is now being recognised elsewhere in the midlands and beyond (see above, pages 7–9).[32]

If the middle Saxon chronology of open-field formation posited in other parts of the midlands is accepted, then the evidence from Whittlewood suggests that this form of farming arrived relatively late. In fact, it would appear that the open fields of our villages were laid out at a time when elsewhere, in central Northamptonshire for example, an existing system was being replanned. This chronology finds parallels in Whittlewood's settlement histories, which show a similar dislocation; while villages further afield were being internally reorganised, in Whittlewood these were still in the process of initial formation. It is feasible, therefore, that the choice of using short furlongs from the outset in Whittlewood was made because the use of the long furlong was already being rejected in these other places. And our villages, too, may have been able to adopt the now more fashionable regular arrangement of tenements in just the same way. Although the landscape of our medieval parishes was radically altered during the period AD 850–1000, it appears that this represents a stage of development that preceded replanning. The changes that were undertaken, however, were likely to have been informed by the experience of those areas where early arrangements were now found to be inappropriate, the settlements and fields of which required reorganisation. Through emulation, perhaps, Whittlewood avoided some of the problems associated with early unplanned village layout by adopting the most current design ideas. This certainly appears to be the case with regard to its open fields.

Meadow and green

The villages of the Whittlewood area had access to plentiful land for grazing. There was a good deal of meadow, especially within the valley of the Great Ouse, where an unbroken but often narrow swathe running between Buckingham and Stony Stratford has been preserved to this day (Figure 35). Smaller ribbons of meadow also lay along the tributary streams, ensuring that all manors possessed some of this valuable resource. For example, a seventeenth-century terrier of Akeley, a parish without access to the Great Ouse, records seven areas of meadow on the demesne of varying size.[33] But it would seem that meadow, however it was disposed, never became the principal settlement attractor, as Williamson has suggested.[34] Certainly, almost all of the nascent villages were located along watercourses, with presumably easy access to limited meadowland. But even where there were large blocks, only at Passenham – the name refers to the meadow (*hamm*) of Passa – does there appear to be a close association between settlement and this resource. In Leckhampstead and Wicken, for example, early settlement ignored the principal meadows, choosing positions along their respective tributary streams amongst smaller patches of wet grassland. This may have been due to the availability of pasture elsewhere on their estates. All these manors possessed significant quantities of woodland, and their location midway between these two resources may have provided the most efficient model for their exploitation. It might also be noted that by failing to draw settlement to its fringes, so meadowland largely failed to affect settlement form. Certainly, it might be argued that dispersed settlements such as Leckhampstead or Silverstone developed this form to exploit small parcels of meadow, and that the nucleated form of Passenham reflects the large block of meadow near which it was sited. However, elsewhere the correlation

FIGURE 35.
Meadowland on the
river Great Ouse at
Leckhampstead.
RICHARD JONES

is less evident: the polyfocal form of Akeley bears no relation to how its meadow was distributed, and in the nucleated villages of Lamport, Lillingstone Dayrell, Lillingstone Lovell and Wicken, the presence of ribbons of meadow did not encourage dispersed settlement along its edge.

More magnetic may have been small clearings or 'greens'. Names such as Akeley, Cleley, Foxley and Puxley (all incorporating the element *leah*, meaning a clearing or open space in wooded country), and names in *–feld*, such as Luffield and Wakefield (which signify open country near woodland), suggest that at the moment of settlement formation and administrative reorganisation, clearings were a recognisable feature of the landscape, although perhaps they were rare enough to distinguish the territories that took their name. Seventeenth- and eighteenth-century maps also provide evidence for greens, in place-names such as Chapel Green, or in field names such as Elm Green, Sutfeld Green (in north Wicken) and Brownswood Green (a detached part of Cosgrove, now in Potterspury). The origins of these greens

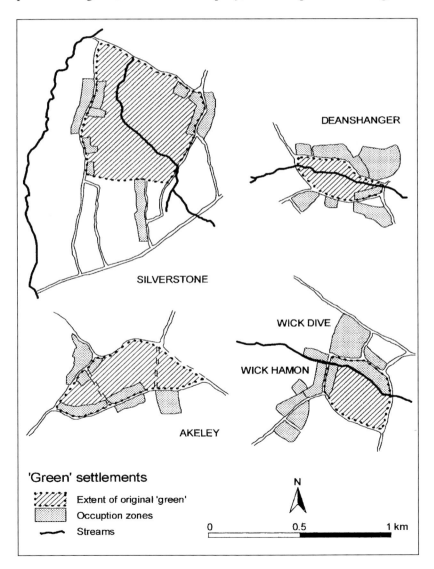

FIGURE 36.
Plan of villages in Whittlewood showing the location of 'greens'.

97

are unknown; however, there are indications that 'green'-like features provided the early focus for some of our villages. This was certainly the case at Deanshanger, where the Forest Map shows the settlement arranged around a small oval green. A similar arrangement at Wicken might explain the curious eye-shaped road pattern that still survives, and there is strong evidence to suggest that Akeley formed around another green. On a larger scale, the central space within the ends at Silverstone may have begun life as a green or an oval clearing (Figure 36). Four features link all these sites. The first is that these settlements contained more than one focus: Wick Dive and Wick Hamon appear to represent two contemporary settlements on the fringes of its green; at Akeley there were again two settlements on the green-edge; at Silverstone possibly three. Secondly, all these settlements appear to have been dependent on another place: Akeley on Leckhampstead, Silverstone on Greens Norton, Deanshanger on Passenham and Wicken on an unknown estate centre. Thirdly, where there is evidence, as at Akeley, Silverstone, Wick Dive and Wick Hamon, all seem to belong to a secondary phase of settlement development dating to the tenth century. Finally, and perhaps most importantly, only small amounts of meadow are recorded in Domesday Book (Figure 37).

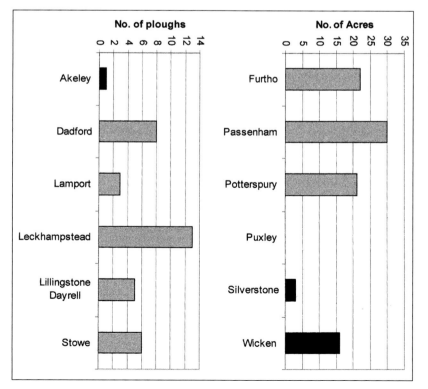

FIGURE 37.
Quantity of meadowland recorded in Domesday Book, expressed in acres for Northamptonshire manors, and numbers of ploughs for Buckinghamshire manors. Villages with 'greens' shown as black bars.

These greens may represent substitutes for meadow. Certainly, many were low-lying and watered by streams, perhaps permitting the long growth of valuable grass. Over time, however, some were encroached upon by expanding settlements, seen in Whittlewood most clearly at West End, Silverstone, at Akeley and Wick Dive, where they were colonised in the twelfth century, and at Wick Hamon in the thirteenth century. Some greens were brought into the open-field system, while others appear to have remained uncultivated and unoccupied, as at Deanshanger. But it is in these features that the influence of the environment upon settlement location and form seems most clear. In a local context, these greens were of equal attraction to the early medieval occupants of Whittlewood as the streams on which their settlements congregated. And they were perhaps more enticing, for in places such as Deanshanger and Wicken, we actually see greenside sites chosen preferentially over both large and small blocks of meadow.

The Norman Conquest

Reference has already been made to the effects of the Norman Conquest on settlement form and social structure in England, notably the replanning of villages by Norman lords and the reduction of sokemen to villeinage (see above, pages 10–11). Likewise, in Whittlewood, it has been suggested that the replanning of settlement took place after the Conquest, in the twelfth century and later, a case argued in detail in Chapter Eight. The question thus arises: to what extent were the villages, fields and inhabitants of the Whittlewood area directly affected by the Norman victory at the Battle of Hastings?

Domesday Book records the wholesale dispossession of English lords in the project area, as it does in most other parts of the country. At Akeley, for example, the manor held by Ælfric, son of Goding, in 1066 was in 1086 in the possession of Walter Giffard and his undertenant, Robert. Similarly, the manor held at Potterspury by Earl Tostig, who was killed at Stamford Bridge in 1066, was held by Henry de Ferrers 20 years later. No Saxon landholder in the study area seems to have survived the general upheaval in landholding, although some may have continued to reside there, perhaps in an official capacity which Domesday Book fails to record, as a bailiff, subtenant or lessee.[35] In the late eleventh and twelfth centuries, most Norman lords leased their lands for a fixed annual rent. The values recorded for each manor in Domesday Book are probably an estimate of the sum for which it could be let.[36] In the Whittlewood area, these values ranged from £10 at Passenham, still in 1086 a royal estate, to as little as 4s for a holding at Puxley and 5s for one of the manors of Silverstone. In general, the recorded figures are modest. Like their Anglo-Saxon predecessors, most of the new Norman lords of Whittlewood held only one or two manors, and formed part of the countrywide group of 6,000–7,000 lesser landholders with estates worth up to £5 a year.[37]

There may have been attempts to increase revenues following the Conquest. For example, the value of Lillingstone Dayrell, which Hugh held of Walter Giffard, increased from £2 'when acquired' and £2 10s 'before 1066' to £3 in 1086. We do not know if this resulted from a replanning of the settlement or a change in social structure. Only at Stowe, which Domesday Book records as 'waste' when acquired, can the possibility be raised of a reorganisation of the settlement and fields by the lord and tenants. An alternative explanation, that the manor was ravaged by the Conqueror, appears less plausible, although we are not able to confirm this archaeologically.[38] Of considerable value to their new owners were the woodland resources of the Whittlewood manors. At Lillingstone Dayrell, for example, there was sufficient woodland to support 1,200 pigs, which must have been brought by the peasantry from outside and for which Hugh, as lord, was able to charge pannage. We do not know the rate at which pannage was levied, but we may suppose that this was one of the means used to raise the value of the manor (see above, page 70; see below, pages 108–10).

There can be little doubt that peasants bore the brunt of the extra demands for revenue which the general rise in Domesday values suggests. Domesday Book divides the population of the Whittlewood area into three main groups: villeins, bordars and slaves. The villeins were the most numerous, making up 48 per cent of the recorded population, while the bordars accounted for 35 per cent. Our current understanding of these two groups is that the villeins held a relatively large holding (in the region of 6–12 ha, or 15–30 acres), while the bordars were smallholders typically with 2 ha (5 acres) or less.[39] Sokemen (privileged peasants) were almost completely absent, but there is no evidence to suggest that their status had been reduced as a result of the Conquest. In the following two centuries, the pattern of tenure in the study area seems to have been relatively stable. At Akeley, for example, the four bordars of 1086 were probably represented by the four cottagers recorded in the Hundred Rolls survey of 1279. Likewise, at Dadford, the Domesday population consisting entirely of bordars was replicated in 1279 by one made up of cottagers.[40] In terms of the social structure of the peasantry, therefore, the Norman Conquest and its aftermath may not have had a profound effect in Whittlewood. Nevertheless, it is likely that lordship became a more potent force in the localities, increasing the burdens of the peasantry under its control, and making it more rather than less likely that lords would engage in the replanning of settlements.[41]

The Whittlewood nucleation and open-field model

Chronology

Villages formed in the Whittlewood area during the 150 years after AD 850. No evidence can be found for large agglomerated settlements before that date. Where spreads of pre-850 pottery have been retrieved from under later villages in Whittlewood, these remain restricted to small areas of no more than 1–2 ha (3–5 acres), suggesting that before the mid ninth century these sites were occupied by only one or two households. In other places, the first signs of occupation, again of small size, can only be dated to the late tenth century. Reorganisation of the landscape accompanied the growth of these nascent villages. Ceramic evidence indicates an important and short-lived change in manuring strategy which must be related to the laying-out of the open fields between AD 850 and 1000.

Process

The villages of Whittlewood grew outwards from existing nuclei. There is little to suggest that this growth resulted from the forced or voluntary abandonment of dispersed farmsteads and the movement of an outside population to a central place. Some evidence survives for the fusion of a number of initially dispersed settlements to form a single polyfocal centre, caused by growth, but the deliberate plan-ning of a village in its earliest phase of development seems not to have occurred. Instead, settlement clusters appear to have developed from those places inhabited in the mid ninth century and from similarly small sites which have their origins in the period AD 850–1000. But there seems to have been little need for a major rearrangement of the existing settlement pattern.

Consequently, in the absence of a break with the past, the initial settlement pattern remained an extremely important influence on the subsequent development of each village. A single pre-village nucleus would spawn a single nucleation, several original foci would produce dispersed villages comprising a number of hamlet clusters. Geography also played its part. If the pre-village nuclei were located some hundreds of metres apart, despite outward growth they would remain separate and develop independently of others. Two or more nuclei set close together might coalesce to form a single polyfocal settlement. Lacking control, from the outset villages might adopt very different plans.

Stimuli

Settlement form in Whittlewood in the period before the Conquest remained conservative, building upon earlier structures rather than replacing those with alternative models. Initial forms were retained because they faced no moment of crisis. The area was rich in natural resources and underpopulated on the eve of village formation and remained so throughout the period of village and hamlet development. There remained considerable opportunity for settlement expansion, and it is difficult to envisage internal boundary disputes, impeded movement or problematic access to resources in such a sparsely populated region. There was sufficient grazing and meadowland to provide winter fodder for livestock, and ample scope to extend the arable without detrimentally affecting the critical balance between cereal production and animal husbandry. No correlation can be drawn between soil conditions or the disposition of meadow and the various nucleated and dispersed settlement forms that developed, although 'green'-like clearings and access to water certainly played an important part in determining where these early villages began to take root. Nor was there anything particular in the social structure, when first defined in the late eleventh century, that was likely to have profoundly influenced the settlement plans.

Lacking positive or negative stimuli for change, therefore, early village forms came to be perpetuated, whether they were nucleated or dispersed. Under these circumstances, the disincentives to nucleate seem clear. The upheaval that nucleation required must have acted as a strong deterrent to change, particularly in the absence of social or economic necessity. More difficult to explain, however, is the failure within the territories of the more nucleated settlements of communities to exploit the opportunities available to develop additional settlement foci. Perhaps low rates of population rise did not warrant the breaking of new ground. But it may have had more cultural origins. It might be wondered whether the nucleated settlements of the surrounding champion lands, which had developed under conditions of stress, had come to be perceived as useful and efficient adaptations to the problem of living together off the land, models to be followed and their success to be shared at the later moment of village growth in Whittlewood. Certainly, the open-field system which characterised the champion areas appears to have been embraced by the communities in Whittlewood, although it was adopted only after it had proven successful elsewhere. But even with their introduction, with space never at a premium, fields could also be laid out without radically altering the existing settlement pattern.

Despite this, the settlements of Whittlewood did not remain immune to the prevailing fashion to move towards more clustered forms seen across the Central Province. The idea of individual farmsteads spread across the landscape was abandoned in favour of larger communal groupings centred on one or more preferred sites. Even Whittlewood's dispersed settlements were made up of small nucleations rather than single isolated properties. The concept of nucleation must therefore have underlain the development of every element of its settlement pattern, even if it did not drive it to the extremes seen elsewhere. And it is possible to recognise in the archaeological data when this moment arrived. If locally in the period after AD 850 centripetal forces were not at play, drawing a scattered population to a central place, this was certainly the point at which further proliferation of settlement ended, with growth confined for the next 250 years to areas around those places that already existed.

Implications for other village models

The Whittlewood evidence offers both a new chronology and an alternative process to village formation. It does not stand in opposition to the models already proposed, indeed to a large extent it supposes that these were followed elsewhere. It might be doubted, for example, if the clustered settlements of Whittlewood would have formed at all had villages not been established at an earlier date in other parts of the midlands, providing a template that our communities could imitate in the absence of any other local stimuli to develop along similar lines. In the timing of these events, Whittlewood reinforces the notion of regional variation: villages formed in different parts of the country at different times. The settlements of Whittlewood, for example, may have begun to grow later than the middle Saxon date proposed for the settlements of central Northamptonshire, but they may already have been in existence before villages began to form in Nottinghamshire, where there is no evidence of nucleation before 1000.[42]

Furthermore, the Whittlewood data may have identified early settlement status as a significant influence upon the timing of nucleation in particular places. Those sites with the best evidence for early nucleation, that is, before AD 850, such as Brixworth, Higham Ferrers, Irthlingborough and Raunds (Northants.), were all major estate centres. Contemporary agglomerations known at Cowdery's Down (Hants.) and Brandon (Suffolk) have also been shown to be of high status.[43] By contrast, early nucleation on lower-status sites is less often encountered, Yarnton (Oxon.) being a rare example.[44] The question then emerges: has a nucleation model developed on evidence obtained from a particular class of settlement been too widely applied? Did villages which developed from non-estate centres, of which the eight villages in Whittlewood are examples, in fact follow a later nucleation chronology in line with our evidence? This seems to find considerable support. Excavations at Great Linford (Bucks.) identify

village expansion in the mid tenth century.[45] Recent investigation at
Great Easton and assessment of the evidence from Leicestershire as
a whole has convinced some of a nucleation date contemporary with
the introduction of Stamford wares (AD 900+), and thus in step with
developments in Whittlewood. Small concentrations of handmade
wares under Leicestershire villages also point to nucleations around
existing sites, evidence for pre-village nuclei even if they have not
previously been so named.[46]

The identification of a process of outward growth underpinning
nucleation, and leading to the perpetuation of elements of an earlier
settlement pattern, in opposition to the traditional model of inward
movement of people involving the abandonment of outlying farmsteads, enables the rereading of data which has previously only been
interpreted against the earlier hypothesis. In Buckinghamshire and
Leicestershire, the great majority of all Saxo-Norman pottery from
these counties (80 and 90 per cent respectively) has been recovered from
within or immediately outside later village cores.[47] In the absence of
this material from middle Saxon farmstead sites, this has been posited
as evidence for completed nucleation before the middle of the ninth
century. But this is the very pattern observed in Whittlewood, where
it can be shown that this material charts the increase in settlement as
nucleation took place between AD 850 and 1000.

The Whittlewood model may find applications beyond the twelve
parishes on which it has been based. Across the midlands, middle
Saxon nucleation did occur on a small number of sites, often those
already of high status. But over the same area, and perhaps further
afield, a more common experience was village formation in the period
after AD 850. This was accompanied by the laying-out of open fields,
and occurred at the same time as early villages were being radically
reordered. Below many were pre-village nuclei from which they grew.
This is a developmental trajectory that can be proven. What cannot
be substantiated anywhere but in a few special cases, either because
the evidence remains too vague or because it simply did not happen,
is a link between nucleation and the abandonment of outlying farmsteads, the freeing-up of the countryside, and the laying-out of the
open fields. In different parts of the country, evidence for deliberately
planned villages can be found, although these are invariably of a late
date, and evidence can be found for the coalescence of more than
one centre forming a single nucleation. But outward growth from
pre-village nuclei probably lies behind the majority of village developments, particularly since this was the root not only of nucleated
settlements but more dispersed villages too.[48]

CHAPTER SIX

The Forest

The woods and forests of late medieval England possess a paradoxical image. On the one hand, they have been characterised as landscapes of 'oppression, avarice, and selfish indulgence', where kings and nobles engaged in their passion for hunting, and the local inhabitants were harassed by the restrictions and rapaciousness of forest law.[1] In the words of Robert Bartlett, 'the wild woods were, in some ways, the least free places in England'.[2] On the other hand, those same woods and forests could also offer a life of independence and opportunity. The ballads of Robin Hood, for example, depict 'the cheerful side of the life of the forest, where merry and carefree men consorted in defiance of the law'.[3] More prosaic records, too, suggest that woodland inhabitants enjoyed a more varied and less constrained existence than many of those who lived in champion countrysides. As Christopher Dyer has commented, 'their mentality tended to individualism and nonconformity: they turned more readily than the stolid champion peasants to rebellion and crime'.[4] These contrasting images point to the richness and complexity of woodland society, and reveal some of the challenges and rewards of living in the forest.

The forest has also presented historians with a further dichotomy. On the one hand, it is argued, forests were essentially an economic resource, possessing a largely functional value as a source of timber, grazing, venison and raw materials. The imposition of forest law allowed the king to retain rights over land that did not form part of the royal demesne and gave him the opportunity to raise large sums of money in fines from the inhabitants. According to this interpretation, forests were there for profit.[5] On the other hand, it may be suggested that the creation of the forest was a political decision, taken by William the Conqueror to enhance his regality. The exclusive right to hunt in designated areas of countryside was one of the royal powers which the Norman dukes appropriated from the Carolingian kings in the tenth century. The extension of this right to his newly conquered kingdom, and on an appropriately large scale, was a powerful symbol of William's mastery over his English subjects. Furthermore, hunting was an essential part of royal and aristocratic culture: it allowed king and magnates to bond together in an enjoyable leisure pursuit that was an ideal preparation for war. An invitation to hunt in the royal forest was thus a useful form of political patronage, and provided the king with an opportunity to display his authority and largesse. It is no accident that so many royal residences lay in or close to areas of forest.[6] Of course, medieval kings may not have recognised the distinction between the economic and political functions of the forest, and in many ways they were intertwined. But we will consider the merits of these differing interpretations in our study of Whittlewood Forest.

In this chapter we examine the creation of the forest by the Norman kings, and the imposition of forest law on the inhabitants of the Whittlewood area. The woods, parks and lawns of Whittlewood in the Middle Ages are described, and the struggle for disafforestation is discussed. In addition, the impact of the forest on settlement, society and landscape is considered in discussions of issues such as assarting, poaching and rural industry. But we begin by examining the regeneration of woodland in the study area in the centuries following the Roman withdrawal.

Woodland regeneration

For much of the Roman era, Whittlewood was largely an open landscape of arable and pasture, with restricted and probably closely managed areas of woodland. Following the end of the Roman period, however, the study area experienced a significant retreat of settlement (see above, pages 59–61).[7] The decline in the density of settlement almost certainly led to the abandonment of arable and pasture fields, and the creation of suitable conditions for the regrowth of woodland. Analysis of pollen samples taken from the Whittlewood area reveals woodland regeneration in the period AD 400–600. Scots pine was especially prominent, suggesting a change in land use and possibly woodland management. The woodland appears not to have been dense; the presence of grass pollen indicates areas of wood pasture, while thistles revealed that some land had been abandoned.[8] The spread of woodland across former agricultural land is demonstrated too by the ceramic evidence: much of the medieval and post-medieval woodland of the Whittlewood area lay across fields which have yielded significant quantities of Romano-British pottery, indicative either of farming or settlement (Figure 38).

The regeneration of woodland should probably not be thought of as a linear development. The formation of woodland and wood pasture in the early Middle Ages, either through neglect or because of

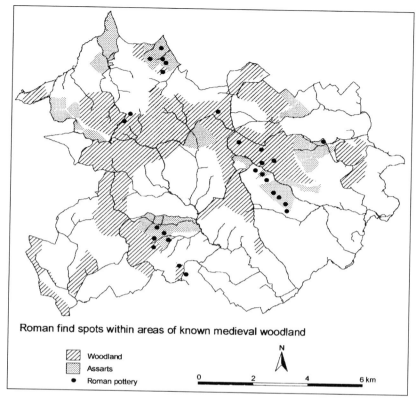

Roman find spots within areas of known medieval woodland

FIGURE 38.
Roman findspots within
areas of known medieval
woodland.

	Woodland
	Assarts
•	Roman pottery

N

0   2   4   6 km

deliberate policy, may have occurred alongside the clearance of trees, and the conversion of land to settlement and farming. Place-names can sometimes be used to suggest the type of environment in which a settlement formed. For example, the element *leah*, as in Akeley, Cleley and Puxley, indicates a place located close to woodland, in a glade or clearing, most such names probably being coined in the period AD 750–950.[9] The element *hangra*, at Deanshanger, also signifies woodland, meaning 'sloping wood'.[10] Other woodland names in the project area include Stockholt ('stump-wood'), a late creation, and Whittlewood ('wood of Witela').[11] Place-names thus demonstrate both the existence and clearance of woodland in the Whittlewood area before the Norman Conquest.

The high density of Roman settlement and field systems indicated by the ceramic evidence does not suggest that Whittlewood lay on soils which were unsuitable for farming. Likewise, the clearance of woodland for settlement implied by early medieval place-names reveals that the area could support a population which made its living, at least in part, from agriculture. Thus Whittlewood was not chosen to become a forest after the Conquest simply because no other use could be found for the land. Although the large amounts of wood-land in the study area at the time of Domesday Book suggests that there were practical reasons for creating a forest there (see below), we have to consider the possibility that those woods had been delib-erately encouraged, managed and maintained. As we discussed in Chapter Four, Whittlewood may have served as a hunting ground for Saxon kings. Royal estates had for many centuries held rights in the Whittlewood area. As the multiple estates fragmented, attempts were made to preserve royal control over designated areas of woodland; for example, in Silverstone, Whittlebury and Wakefield, limiting the opportunities for settlement and clearance (see above, pages 68–9). The Norman kings thus inherited a landscape that was culturally as well as physically determined. The creation of Whittlewood Forest was not simply a mechanical response to post-Roman woodland regeneration.

Domesday woodland

The Whittlewood area was clearly well wooded at the time of the Domesday survey in 1086 (Figure 39). The important royal manor of Greens Norton, for example, contained woodland measuring four leagues long and three leagues wide, one of the largest concentra-tions of woodland in eleventh-century Northamptonshire.[12] This was equivalent to about 4,895 ha (12,096 acres), according to Oliver Rackham's method of calculation, and almost certainly extended into the heavily wooded parishes of Silverstone and Whittlebury, both of which were chapelries dependent upon Greens Norton.[13] Thus there was still a Norton wood in Whittlebury in the thirteenth century, much of which was cleared to create a monastic grange.[14] Although the king held substantial tracts of woodland in the study area in 1086, in Passenham, Greens Norton (at Whittlebury) and probably in Silverstone, most Domesday woods were in private hands, and they contributed to a lord's manorial income. At Greens Norton, for example, Domesday Book records that 4s was raised from the collec-tion of honey. Another source of profit was pannage, the seasonal practice of taking domesticated pigs into the woods in autumn to fatten on acorns (or beech mast, if any) before being slaughtered and salted down. In Buckinghamshire, woodland was measured in terms of the number of swine it could support: 600 at Leckhampstead, 540 at Stowe, and so on. According to Rackham, 'the acorn crop is (and was) very erratic … we cannot hope to get an objective equation between pigs and acres: we can rarely tell whether a wood for few swine was a *small* wood, a *hornbeam* wood (not yielding acorns), a

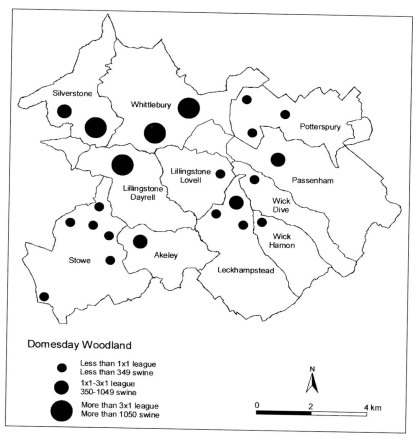

FIGURE 39.
Domesday woodland.

coppice wood (without big enough oaks), or a wood owned by a pessi-mist'.[15] Nevertheless, in attempting to reconstruct the landscape in parts of the study area at the time of Domesday Book, a correspond-ence has been detected between the number of pigs recorded and the likely area of woodland.

At Akeley, extensive archaeological fieldwork has demonstrated that more than 50 per cent of the parish lay outside the settled and cultivated area, in zones from which little or no eleventh-century pottery indicative of settlement or farming has been recovered. Some of this land was almost certainly meadow but most, about 280 ha (700 acres), was probably woodland or wood pasture (Figure 40). It has been suggested that a pig corresponds to 1–1.5 acres of Domesday woodland.[16] However, at Akeley the number of swine recorded (806) was larger than the estimated size of the woodland, giving a ratio of pigs to acres of 1:0.87. Perhaps the acorn crop was unusually abundant at Akeley, a product of the many oak trees in Whittlewood Forest of which later records give notice.[17] In Lillingstone Dayrell, too, the

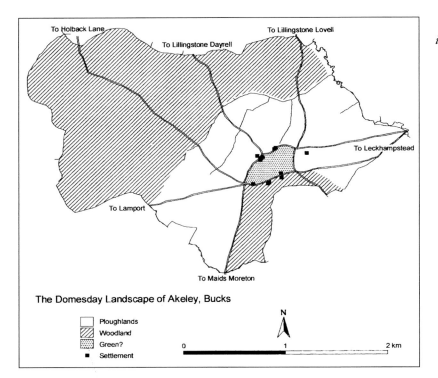

The Domesday Landscape of Akeley, Bucks

Ploughlands
Woodland
Green?
Settlement

N

0   1   2 km

FIGURE 40.
A conjectural
reconstruction of the
Domesday landscape of
Akeley, based on textual,
archaeological and
topographical evidence.

number of swine recorded in Domesday Book (1,200) was larger than
the estimated area of eleventh-century woodland, about 425 ha (1,060
acres) including Heybarne. This gives a similar ratio of pigs to acres
of 1:0.88. However, this pattern may not be universal. In the parishes
of Leckhampstead and Stowe, the extent of woodland in the eleventh century was probably larger than the number of swine recorded,
within the range of 1–1.5 acres per pig.[18] But the Domesday landscape
of these parishes cannot be reconstructed with the same degree of
confidence as at Akeley and Lillingstone Dayrell.

Creation of the forest

Although Anglo-Saxon kings engaged in the pleasures of the hunt,
it seems that the idea of a royal forest was a Norman innovation,
imposed by the Conqueror and extended by his sons, especially
Henry I (1100–35), during whose reign the first record of Whittlewood
Forest occurs.[19] Forest law encompassed not only areas of woodland,
in which the king's deer were free to roam, but also villages and
towns, together with their fields of arable and pasture, the inhabitants of which were restricted in the exploitation of their own lands.
The law's primary purpose was to protect the king's hunting, but the

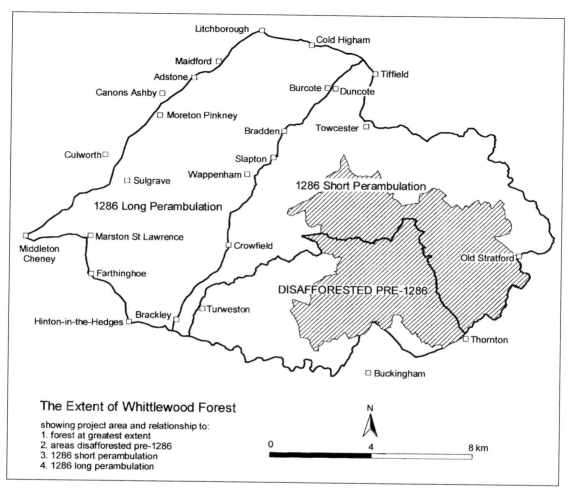

Litchborough
Cold Higham
Maidford
Adstone
Tiffield
Canons Ashby
Burcote
Duncote
Moreton Pinkney
Bradden
Towcester
Culworth
Slapton
Wappenham
1286 Short Perambulation
Sulgrave
1286 Long Perambulation
Marston St Lawrence
Crowfield
Middleton
Cheney
Old Stratford
Farthinghoe
DISAFFORESTED PRE-1286
Brackley
Turweston
Hinton-in-the-Hedges
Thornton
Buckingham

The Extent of Whittlewood Forest

showing project area and relationship to:
1. forest at greatest extent
2. areas disafforested pre-1286
3. 1286 short perambulation
4. 1286 long perambulation

N

0   4   8 km

FIGURE 41.
The changing extent
of Whittlewood forest
during the thirteenth
century, based on surviving
perambulations.

forest also became a significant source of royal income. Fines for such offences as killing deer, clearing woodland or keeping hounds in the forest were high.[20]

All the parishes of the study area lay within Whittlewood Forest in the late twelfth and thirteenth centuries (Figure 41). The restrictions and cost of living in the forest were undoubtedly resented, especially among landowners, whose freedom of action was curtailed by the officials who imposed forest law. The trouble and expense involved in ploughing up even small pieces of land in the forest were considerable, and contributed to the growing clamour for disafforestation heard during the reign of Edward I (1272–1307).[21] Nevertheless, despite the protests, some sort of accommodation must have been reached between the king's forest officials and the local inhabitants, whereby a considerable tract of woodland around Wakefield Lawn and extending

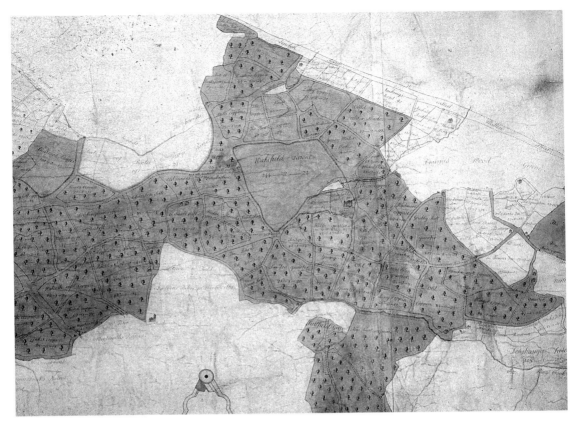

across Whittlebury and Silverstone was preserved for the royal hunt, but more peripheral areas were permitted to be farmed or enclosed for use by landowners and their tenants (Figure 42). No evidence of these negotiations survives; however, despite the high demand for land in the thirteenth century, decisions relating to the extension of farmland and settlement were clearly made not only on the basis of utility and profit but also with careful consideration for the maintenance of royal prestige and prerogative.

There can be little doubt that the Norman and Angevin kings hunted in Whittlewood Forest. Henry I stayed at Silverstone at least once during his reign, in the 1120s.[22] Hunting lodges were built at Silverstone and Wakefield in the twelfth century, both of which were maintained by Henry II.[23] Indeed, between 1178 and 1183 the king spent large sums of money on the domestic buildings at Silverstone, work supervised by two of his foresters.[24] Silverstone continued to serve as a royal residence throughout the thirteenth century, both Henry III and Edward I funding extensive campaigns of repair work and rebuilding. Royal interest in the lodge faded, however, during the

FIGURE 42.
Detail of the *c.* 1608 map of Whittlewood Forest, showing Wakefield Lawn and the surrounding coppices.

NORTHAMPTONSHIRE RECORD OFFICE AND HIS GRACE, THE DUKE OF GRAFTON reign of Edward II, and in the mid fourteenth century Edward III acquired a new base, the castle of Moor End, close to the forest.[25]

The principal hunting grounds in Whittlewood Forest were the parks and lawns. Medieval parks were fenced enclosures, containing a mixture of woodland and grassland, which provided cover and fodder for the deer, but from which the animals were unable to escape.[26] The royal park at Handley, for example, which lay to the north of Silverstone, occupied about 365 ha (900 acres) and comprised ten coppices and a lawn when it was disparked and converted to arable in the seventeenth century; this transformation saw the substitution of a purely functional landscape for one that had been more mixed in character.[27] In the Middle Ages Handley was frequently used as a source of timber and deer, both to meet the king's own needs and to provide favours for individuals and religious houses; for example, the prior of Luffield was given two oaks to repair his church in 1253.[28] Occasionally, however, orders were issued to prevent further despoliation, to give both vert and venison time to recover.[29] Rights of common grazing often existed in medieval parks, such as agistment – the right to pasture cattle – for which a payment was usually made.[30] Thus, at Handley 13s 4d was collected in 1344.[31] Earlier this practice had been prohibited by the king, presumably in order to protect the deer's fodder.[32] Probably for the same reason, the keeper of Handley enjoyed fewer rights of pannage and other liberties in the park than elsewhere in the bailiwick of Wakefield: a delicate balance between conservation and exploitation needed to be preserved.[33] Forest law was applied in parks just as in the neighbouring woods. In 1279–80 eight swanimote courts were held in the park of Handley, from which 6s 6d was paid to the king in fines.[34] Parks were maintained for a variety of reasons – profit, prestige, pleasure and patronage; their preservation depended on striking a balance between these uses.

Like parks, lawns provided grazing for deer, as well as domestic animals, such as cattle, sheep and pigs. Two lawns are depicted on the Forest Map, at Wakefield and Shrob.[35] The earliest record of Wakefield Lawn occurs in about 1220, by which time the royal residence at Wakefield had probably been abandoned in favour of Silverstone.[36] The likelihood is that the lawn was fenced, as it was in the seventeenth century (Figure 42). Thus, in 1253 an inquisition *ad quod damnum* recommended that Wakefield Lawn be opened to the inhabitants of the forest villages for common of pasture, a right they had enjoyed before it was enclosed.[37] The lawn at Shrob may have been the creation of Henry VIII.[38] Nevertheless, there was probably an area of open ground there from an early date. The name derives from a word related to 'shrub' and 'scrub', which suggests the absence of heavy tree-cover.[39] Moreover, Shrob appears to have been carefully protected: it was apparently the only part of Whittlewood Forest in which the local inhabitants enjoyed no rights of common.[40]

The king's deer were not only preserved in enclosed parks and lawns. They also roamed the woods and ridings of the forest. It was probably these deer that the king sent his huntsmen to capture and salt in 1237 when he ordered bucks to be taken in Whittlewood outside the royal demesne, presumably in the private woods of local lords.[41] Similarly, a deer pursued through Wakefield bailiwick in 1369 was caught along a riding called *Appeltrowrode*.[42] Deer chased through the woods might also pass through surrounding fields of grain, the ditches and hedges of which had to be insubstantial enough to allow them and their pursuers freedom of access.[43] On the other hand, they might enter through deer-leaps into the private parks of neighbouring landowners. This was the intention behind the construction of a deer-leap in Potterspury park by William de Ferrers, Earl of Derby, in 1230, which he was allowed to move to a more favourable position in 1234.[44]

The king's deer did not, however, enjoy complete freedom of movement within Whittlewood Forest. The woods of the forest are shown on the Forest Map divided into coppices, which were separated by broad ridings. This arrangement is almost certainly medieval in origin. For instance, a number of the coppice names recorded on the Forest Map can be found in documents of the thirteenth and fourteenth centuries.[45] The coppice system was established in order to manage woodland which was used for both hunting and the production of timber. Coppices were cut in rotation, the timber and wood felled in such a way that natural regrowth was ensured and encouraged. Grazing animals, including deer, were excluded by banks, ditches and hedges, at least for the first few years of regrowth, so that the new shoots were not eaten.[46] An order for the enclosure of a coppice 'by as many labourers as shall be necessary' was issued by the king in 1356.[47] It is possible that these newly felled coppices were the preserves (*defensis*) in which no one was allowed to common, according to a grant of 1255.[48] Many of the coppice banks within Whittlewood still survive, up to 4 m (13 feet) across and 0.5 m (1.5 feet) high (Figure 43).[49]

What was the character of this woodland in the Middle Ages? There is likely to have been a range of both dense and more open woodland, suitable both for coppicing and for grazing livestock. In 1248, for example, an inquest was held at *Hynewode* near Luffield Priory, which reported that the prior would cause no damage to the king or the forest if he ploughed up an area of undergrowth (*rifletum*) which lay between the priory's arable land and the dense woodland (*magnum*

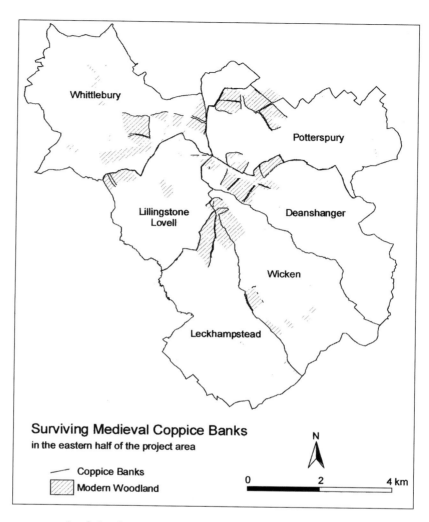

Surviving Medieval Coppice Banks

in the eastern half of the project area

Coppice Banks

Modern Woodland

Whittlebury

Potterspury

Lillingstone Lovell

Deanshanger

Wicken

Leckhampstead

N

0   2   4 km

FIGURE 43.
Medieval coppice banks identified by fieldwork.

coopertum) of the forest.[50] The 'great cover' must refer to the coppices of Hazelborough, still an area of thick woodland today. By contrast, at the forest eyre of 1348, it was heard that the lords of Silverstone had cleared more than 100 acres (40 ha) of woodland and felled 500 trees.[51] If an accurate record – five trees per acre – this suggests an area of wood pasture, with wide spaces of grassland between the oaks. The king, too, might order areas of woodland to be cleared. Such clearings, known as trenches, were sometimes made in the forest, usually along paths or roads in an attempt to discourage robbers. The timber and wood felled on one such occasion in 1279 was ordered to be sold for the king's benefit.[52]

Disafforestation

Whittlewood Forest encompassed the lands and woods of many lords who chafed under the restrictions imposed by forest law and the extortions of forest officials.[53] Political expediency ensured that such restrictions were sometimes lifted. For example, landowners might be granted the right to create private parks within the forest. Thus, William de Ferrers was given licence to impark his wood at Potterspury in 1229. Likewise, a private park was held by the lord of Wick Hamon in Wicken.[54] Nevertheless, such parks fell within the jurisdiction of the king's forest officials. Even after disafforestation, in 1368, it was reported that two deer-leaps had been constructed in the earl of Warwick's park at Potterspury 'to the detriment of the king's forest', although by this time it may be doubted whether any action could be taken.[55] Other restrictions included the sale of timber in the forest, and the clearance of land for farming, so that landowners were required to seek permission before they could exploit the resources of their estates.[56] In many cases permission was granted, either beforehand or retrospectively, as was the case with the lords of Silverstone, to whom the royal manor passed in the fourteenth century, whose clearance of 500 trees apparently went unpunished at the forest eyre of 1348.[57] But, in the thirteenth century, landowners displayed increasing impatience at the imposition of forest law and demanded its curtailment.

The clamour for disafforestation was heard by King John, who promised to limit the extent of the royal forest and investigate the 'evil customs' of the foresters in Magna Carta.[58] However, it was not until the reign of Edward I that the boundaries of Whittlewood Forest began to contract. The part of the forest lying in Buckinghamshire was probably the first to be removed, in the period following the eyre of 1255 and before the perambulation of 1300 (Figure 41).[59] Two perambulations of the Northamptonshire portion of the forest were made in 1286, to little apparent effect.[60] However, following the crisis of 1297–98, Edward I was compelled to act, and a third perambulation of Whittlewood in Northamptonshire was made in 1299. This further reduced the size of the forest, compared with the shorter of the two perambulations of 1286, and became the definitive version of the boundaries of Whittlewood for the remainder of the Middle Ages. Wicken was disafforested, but the other Northamptonshire parishes of the study area remained within the forest bounds. The only part of Whittlewood outside Northamptonshire was Heybarne.[61] Thus, with a few exceptions, Whittlewood was effectively confined to areas of royal demesne. With the size of the forest reduced throughout

England, complaints against forest law faded from the political agenda.[62]

The impact of the forest

In seeking to explain the development of landscape and settlement in the study area, the creation of the forest as an institution following the Norman Conquest has to be considered a factor of some importance. In this section we examine the effects of the forest on the people of Whittlewood and the influence it had on their lives.

Settlement
The initial growth of most of the villages of the project area occurred before the Norman Conquest. Their inception and early development, therefore, were probably not affected by the establishment of the forest. Indeed, even following the imposition of forest law, it is difficult to demonstrate any discernible impact upon the size or layout of most of the villages within the forest bounds. Continuity rather than change seems to be the overwhelming theme. In a few cases, however, the institution of the forest may have had a direct effect. For example, the Domesday manor of Wakefield seems to have disappeared in the early twelfth century, probably because it was appropriated by the crown and a royal residence established there. Any incipient settlement (there were three villeins and a bordar in 1086) was evidently extinguished and the area was given over to the king's hunting lawn and woods (see below, pages 211–12). In the reign of Henry II, the forester of Wakefield (and Whittlewood) was established at Puxley, the expansion of which settlement until the mid fourteenth century may have owed much to its association with the keepership of the forest. Equally, it might be suggested (again without detailed evidence) that the decline of Puxley after the Black Death resulted as much from the fading importance of the forest as from any effects of plague.[63]

More positive assertions can be made in the case of Silverstone, the development of which was almost certainly affected by the foundation in the twelfth century of a royal hunting lodge. Probably located at a crossroads close to the present church, the lodge occupied a central position and may have been a focus for the growth of the village until its abandonment in the early fourteenth century. The recorded population of Silverstone increased more than fivefold, from seven in 1086 to thirty-seven in 1301, at a time when the national population may have only doubled or, at most, trebled. Extensive fishponds were constructed to the north of the lodge, preventing the expansion of settlement in this direction and perhaps encouraging the growth of the village's distinctive 'ends'. At West End a pottery kiln flourished in the period *c.* 1180–1250, which may have been intended to supply the king's house, a suggestion given credence by the peculiar distribution of its recovered wares.[64] Royal servants were granted land in the parish, possibly as *locatores* (men who deliberately encouraged colonisers to settle), thereby providing further impetus for growth. For example, when William de Braundeston died in 1273, he was reported to have held a messuage, a croft, three virgates and six cottages of the king-in-chief, by serjeanty of keeping the king's wine at Silverstone.[65] Several generations of a family named Engineer (a maker of siege engines) can be found at Silverstone from the late twelfth century; perhaps Roger (died *c.* 1200) accompanied Richard I on crusade and was rewarded with land on his return.[66] The extensive improvements to the lodge in the twelfth and thirteenth centuries may also have encouraged building workers to settle in the village.

Thus, at Wakefield, Puxley and Silverstone, the establishment of the forest probably had a direct and lasting impact upon the development of settlement. The infrastructure of the forest, in terms of residences and keeperships, became part of the fabric of these places, influencing the extent and shape of further settlement growth. In other villages, such features cannot be so easily recognised. Was the forest therefore irrelevant to changes in village layout during the Middle Ages? No certain answer is possible, although the suggestion might be advanced that the radical reordering of village plans, for example at Lillingstone Lovell and Wick Hamon in the thirteenth century – discussed more fully in Chapter Eight – was the outcome of a deliberate attempt by lords to express their power and authority within the village in ways that were inhibited by forest law in woods and fields. The village was the stage, perhaps, on which lords in the forest displayed their command (see below, pages 160–4, 183). The regulation of the forest may also have influenced changes in the landscape surrounding the villages, which included the appearance of dispersed settlement elements away from village cores. In the Whittlewood area, woodland clearance for the purposes of extending arable, pasture and settlement continued until the very eve of the Black Death.

Assarting

Although the clearance of woodland in Whittlewood Forest began before the Norman Conquest and continued in the twelfth century, as revealed by terse references in the Exchequer pipe rolls, it is not until the thirteenth century that adequate records survive to describe the process in detail. In the 150 years or so before the Black Death, the king's forest officials recorded the clearance of hundreds of acres of wood pasture and their conversion to other uses. These were called assarts or, in the case of buildings and enclosures in the forest, purprestures, and both were regulated by the crown.[67] The size of assarts varied enormously, ranging from tiny fractions of an acre to swathes of land of 40 ha (100 acres) or more. They were carved from the forest both by lords and peasants, and might be held either in common or by individuals. Forest officials could not prevent, but were probably able to influence, the geography of assarting in Whittlewood Forest – for example, preserving the king's woods around Wakefield Lawn – even if the extent of clearance was determined more by demographic, economic and social factors. Thus, the political and cultural significance of the forest hindered the agricultural and economic exploitation of the area.

Until the Black Death of 1348–49 land was a relatively scarce resource, and demand for arable, necessary to feed a population which may have peaked at 5 million or more *c.*1300, was high. Much of the land assarted in Whittlewood Forest was cultivated and, like the open fields, sown with wheat and oats.[68] Some assarts were cleared and held in common. For example, the vill of Silverstone assarted 10 acres (4 ha) in a place called *Blodhanger* and a further 2 acres (0.8 ha) in *Baggenho*, names which reappear as Bloodhanger and Bagnalls in Black Pit Field on the enclosure map of 1826 (Figure 44).[69] The northernmost of Silverstone's open fields also originated as newly assarted land called *Swynhey* which was evidently incorporated into the arable in about 1278. At the same time, other land belonging to the manor of Greens Norton was said to have been 'broken by ignorance of the king's tenants of Silverstone because they believed that it belonged to the manor of Silverstone'.[70] In the rush to clear additional ploughlands, manorial (and parish) boundaries were either forgotten or ignored.

In other parishes, too, assarted land was incorporated into the open fields. At Deanshanger, for instance, furlong names such as 'stocking' and 'overbreach' are indicative of woodland clearance.[71] Other land, however, was cleared and farmed separately. Examples include the farmsteads at Stockholt, in Akeley; Heybarne, in Lillingstone Dayrell; and Monksbarn, in Whittlebury, the latter made up of a number of individual assarts granted to Luffield Priory.[72] Although the arable in these enclosures lay outside the open fields, rights of common pasture might persist; for example, at Monksbarn the 'whole countryside' was able to pasture 'after the grain and hay have been carried from the fields'.[73] In this way the mixed farming practices of the Whittlewood area were preserved and the extension of the arable at the expense of wood pasture did not necessarily lead to a diminution in the size

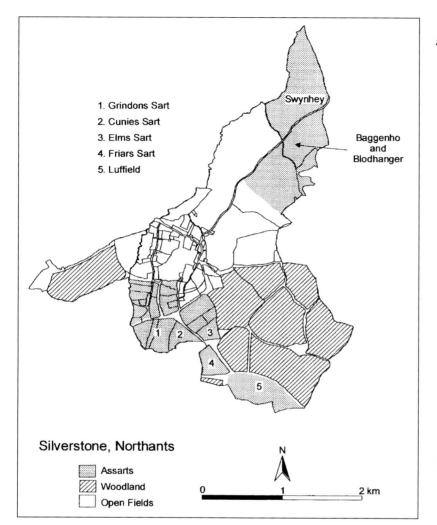

1. Grindons Sart
2. Cunies Sart
3. Elms Sart
4. Friars Sart
5. Luffield

Swynhey

Baggenho
and
Blodhanger

Silverstone, Northants

N

Assarts
Woodland
Open Fields

0   1   2 km

FIGURE 44.
In northern Silverstone
land was cleared of trees
and incorporated into the
village's open fields during
the thirteenth century. To
the south of the village
assarts were enclosed and
held in severalty.

of herds and flocks. Nevertheless, the potential reduction of common pasture may have led to tension within the community (see below, pages 142, 146).

Assarting not only increased the extent of the arable, it also introduced dispersed settlement elements into many of the parishes of the study area. As well as the isolated farmsteads of Stockholt, Heybarne and Monksbarn, a considerable number of cottages were built, often on tiny plots of land carved from the waste. In Puxley, Hugh de Stratford cleared just a quarter of a rood (250 sq m) on which he built seven cottages, two of which he held himself, and the other five he leased.[74] The expansion of Puxley in the thirteenth and early fourteenth centuries owed much to the energies of those willing to clear such smallholdings, often described as lying in Puxley Green, as well as larger holdings such as that held by Henry Gobion at Grubby Hill, and which later developed into the enclosures depicted on the Forest Map (Figure 42).[75] At Silverstone, the hamlet of Cattle End was founded as an assart settlement in the early thirteenth century, and must have comprised many of the small enclosures described in the regard rolls; for example, the house and rood of oats held by William Smith (*Faber*) in the reign of King John.[76] Other dispersed settlements created by assarting included the chapel and associated dwellings dedicated to Thomas Becket in Lillingstone Dayrell, the hamlet of Elm Green in Wicken, and the forest lodges built to accommodate the variety of officials who implemented forest law.[77]

FIGURE 45.
Detail of the *c.* 1608 map of Whittlewood Forest, showing the village of Whittlebury and the enclosures at Monksbarn (top right) and Nether End (left).

The imposition of forest law almost certainly limited the amount of assarting allowed in Whittlewood Forest. This may have restricted the growth of some settlements (or their fields); for example, Puxley lay close to the woods surrounding Wakefield Lawn. In Potterspury, with the exception of a rectangular strip of land in the north-west of the parish and a moated site in the south-east, no assarting or settlement is apparent to the south of Watling Street (Figure 42). Although Brownswood Green was a detached portion of Cosgrove, it might still be asked whether the villagers would have made further encroachments into the woods north of Wakefield Lawn had it not been for the vigilance of the king's forest officials. Similar hypothetical questions might be raised in relation to the extension of Whittlebury in the mid thirteenth century. The houses marked on the Forest Map extend to the edge of the woodland and no further, perhaps because of limitations imposed by the king (Figure 45).

Poaching
All classes of medieval society engaged in hunting. The aristocracy sought to emulate the king's rights over the forest by creating private parks. Like the forest, parks had an economic value and were a source of profit; but they were also a cultural expression of status and prestige and, relatively speaking, a wasteful use of resources. Four private parks existed in the study area at various times in the Middle Ages, at Potterspury, Stockholt, Stowe and Wicken. The king also permitted favoured individuals to hunt in the royal forest itself. A number of writs allowing deer to be taken in Whittlewood Forest survive; for example, that granted to William Beauchamp, Earl of Warwick, who killed a stag and three bucks in 1292.[78] Others were pardoned retrospectively, such as the abbot of Stanley, in Wiltshire, who took a hind in Whittlewood in 1304, and zealous forest officials sometimes needed to be restrained from molesting those with permission to hunt, such as Edmund, Earl of Cornwall, in 1283 and 1286.[79] A few high-born poachers, however, were presented at the forest eyres, including Robert Kilwardby, Archbishop of Canterbury, whose followers were accused of killing fourteen deer over three days when they stayed at Luffield in 1277.[80]

Local lords also engaged in poaching, either for sport or for more mundane reasons of consumption and sale. For example, Simon de Patishulle was fined 2 marks (£1 6s 8d) because his dogs were found after dark in his wood at Heybarne devouring a young stag wounded in the right haunch by an arrow in November 1250.[81] Simon was probably responsible for the building of a farmstead at Heybarne, from which pottery dated c. 1250–1400 has been recovered. In 1279 he held a carucate of ancient assart there of the lord of Lillingstone Dayrell, which land was later ploughed until its abandonment towards the end of the fourteenth century (see below, pages 178–80, 212–13).[82] Although Heybarne was probably established with its potential for farming chiefly in mind, its remote location surrounded by woodland made it a good base from which to lead illegal hunting parties. Likewise, the farmstead at Stockholt may have been used for a similar purpose. In 1249 four men set off with bows and arrows from the house of Roger de Wauton, the holder of Stockholt, but were apprehended in Stockholt wood before they had fired a shot.[83]

Most of those prosecuted for poaching at the forest eyres, as in other forests, were peasants.[84] For these people, the dangers involved and the harsh penalties if caught were outweighed by the urge to supplement their meagre diet with fresh game or their income with the proceeds from the sale of meat and skins. A buck taken from Wicken wood in 1250, for example, and received at the house of Hamo Hasting of Wolverton, a local landowner and donor to Luffield Priory, may well have been killed to order.[85] Eyres were held in Whittlewood in 1209, 1255, 1272, 1286 and 1348, with the number of venison cases ranging from about two dozen in 1255 and 1286 to no more than six in 1272 and 1348.[86] These cases represent only the tip of a much larger iceberg of poaching in the royal forest. There can be little doubt that many poachers escaped detection or failed to attend the infrequently held eyres. Even those who did appear before the forest justices may have committed many more offences than the few with which they were charged. William de Lynford of Silverstone, for example, was described as a 'customary poacher of venison' in 1286.[87]

Most of the venison cases presented at the eyres were concerned with offences in and around the king's demesne woods and parks. Unlike cases involving the vert, which encompassed a much wider area, there seems to have been a conscious effort to prosecute those who poached deer in places where the king himself may have hunted. In an attempt to ensure a plentiful supply of deer for the royal chase, foresters may have been particularly vigilant in the woods close to Handley, Silverstone and Wakefield – these were, after all, the places where the foresters themselves lived. We ought not to be surprised, therefore, to find so many prosecutions involving residents of Silverstone and Wicken, the two villages named most often, or more occasional references to poachers from Deanshanger, Lillingstone Dayrell, Lillingstone Lovell, Passenham, Potterspury and Puxley. These places were not necessarily more frequently involved in poaching than other villages nearby, such as Syresham or Stowe. Instead, they may have been targeted by the foresters because of their proximity to the king's woods and parks. Such an hypothesis may help to explain why certain villages in other forests also seem to have produced more than their fair share of poachers.[88]

The inhabitants of the study area may thus have suffered from the attentions of the king's forest officials to a much greater extent than those who lived in more peripheral parts of Whittlewood. On the other hand, the king's woods and parks may have been better stocked with deer, providing more frequent opportunities for the chance taking of game, such as the buck which strayed into the fields of Silverstone in 1245 and was killed by two hounds.[89] The records of the eyre suggest that for the peasantry the effects of forest law could be severe. Not only were individual poachers heavily fined or even hanged, but whole villages were also frequently amerced. Inquests involving the four nearest townships were held whenever a dead deer was found, with the result that places such as Silverstone and its neighbours were repeatedly called to appear and invariably amerced.[90] The undoubted burden of the eyres, however, needs to be balanced against their infrequent sessions and the relatively small number of venison cases heard. Most poachers must have had a reasonable chance of escaping detection or, if caught, of their case failing to be among those presented at the eyre. The benefits of poaching, either for consumption or for sale, were probably considerable in an era when many peasants struggled to make a living.

Rural industry

The king's forest officials were not only charged with protecting the king's deer. They were also responsible for ensuring the survival of the vert, the deer's habitat or cover. For the inhabitants of woodland societies, the exploitation of wood, timber and wood pasture was more widespread and more important for their survival than the illegal hunting of game (see below, page 128). Wood was used for building, fencing and fuel. The right of villagers to collect wood for their immediate needs was enshrined in custom and only occasionally recorded in writing. At Deanshanger, the villagers were entitled to take wood to repair hedges and houses (called haybote and housebote), fencing for their grain and dead wood for their fuel, in return for rendering wheat, geese and hens to the forester of Wakefield. A similar agreement was reached with the inhabitants of Potterspury, and it is possible that other villages also entered into reciprocal arrangements with the king's forest officials.[91] On the king's manor of Silverstone in 1288, the virgate holders were entitled to take haybote, housebote and half an oak before Christmas for their fuel. Half-virgaters were allowed a quarter of an oak.[92]

For some villagers, wood was taken for small-scale commercial and industrial purposes. Whittlewood was not, however, endowed with extensive mineral resources, so that there appears to have been little or no iron-working or coal-mining, as in other forests, such as Rockingham, Cannock and Dean.[93] Whittlewood was characterised chiefly by agriculture rather than industry. Nevertheless, surname evidence reveals the presence of carpenters, charcoal burners, potters, sawyers and smiths in Whittlewood at the time of the lay subsidy of 1301 and the Silverstone custumal of 1288.[94] Such people would have needed considerable quantities of wood to pursue their craft and undoubtedly drew the attention of the king's forest officials. For example, in 1345 William Drury of Foscote (near Silverstone) was found to have felled three oaks in Handley worth 5s each 'to the damage of the king', which he used to make charcoal at his hearth (*astrum*).[95] Other trees felled at about the same time may have been used for a similar purpose. Certainly the demand for charcoal was high. In 1306 a writ was issued ordering 100 pollards to be lopped in Whittlewood to make charcoal for the king's children staying in Northampton castle.[96] The likelihood is that the charcoal was made locally; charcoal pits have been identified within coppices near Deanshanger, Silverstone, and Whittlebury (Figure 46). However, we do not know how many of the trees felled in the forest were intended to supply this particular industry.

Wood was also needed to fuel the pottery kilns of the area, the most active of which were located in Potterspury. At least half a dozen kilns were operating in Potterspury between the middle of the thirteenth century and the end of the fifteenth, the wares from which have been recovered from almost every late medieval site in the study area, as well as from large parts of the east midlands.[97] References to potters in the fifteenth and sixteenth centuries have been found, but they tell us little about the size of the industry or whether those engaged in pottery-making were employed full-time or made part of their living from other activities.[98] Certainly, in the sixteenth century, a number of Potterspury's inhabitants were described as craftsmen or artificers: not only the potters John Ingram and William Smith, but also butchers, carpenters, millers, tailors, tanners and wheelwrights, suggesting that by this time there was some occupational specialisation.[99] Although pottery-making was centred on Potterspury in the Middle Ages, other kilns also operated in the study area, as at Silverstone *c.* 1200.[100]

Domesday Book shows that smiths were active in the woods of Greens Norton before the Norman Conquest, paying £7 to the king, presumably in order to take wood to fuel their hearths.[101] At Stowe

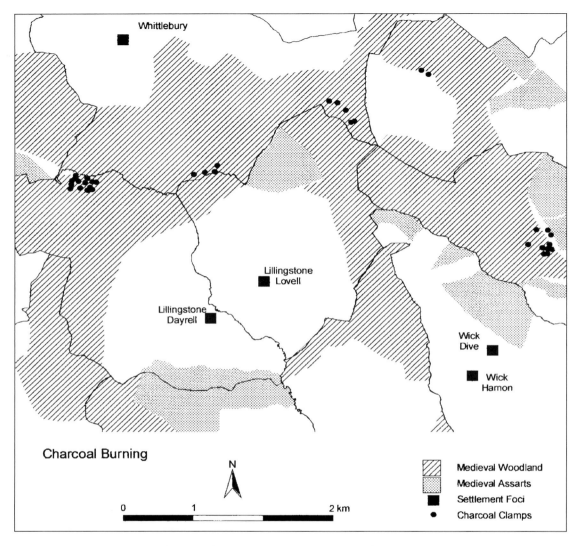

Whittlebury

Lillingstone
Lovell

Lillingstone
Dayrell

Wick
Dive

Wick
Hamon

Charcoal Burning

N

0   1   2 km

Medieval Woodland
Medieval Assarts
Settlement Foci
Charcoal Clamps

there was a smithy in the thirteenth century, at which two half-virgate holders in the village in 1279 called Smith (*Faber*) may have worked during slack times in the agricultural year.[102] An 'old smithy in the middle of the vill' of Lillingstone Dayrell was recorded in 1288–89, and there was a smithy 'at the end of the vill' in Potterspury, the rent for which was halved to *6d* in 1416–17.[103] The demand for ironwork was probably sufficient to sustain a smithy in most of the villages of the study area, which must have consumed large quantities of wood. Manorial reeves regularly bought iron and steel for the repair of ploughs, carts and buildings, much of it no doubt sourced locally. For example, at Passenham in 1383–84, an agreement was

FIGURE 46.
Charcoal was much in demand in the Middle Ages and charcoal burning was likely to have been a common by-employment among the forest villagers.

reached with William Smyth, smith, to maintain the ironwork of the manor's ploughs and ensure the horses were properly shod.[104] Supplies of wood would also have been required to fuel the malt-kiln recorded at Lillingstone Lovell in 1374, and for making the bricks and tiles recorded there in 1551–52.[105] Likewise, the various carpenters and other woodworkers of whom there is occasional notice needed timber of different shapes and sizes, which they must have either purchased or stolen from the forest. A plough bought by the reeve of Passenham in 1380–81 for 1s 2d was made by one William Carpenter, who was also hired to trim the sheath and share-beam.[106] Finally, oak bark was needed to tan hides for making into leather; tanners were recorded at Potterspury and Abthorpe (near Silverstone) in the sixteenth century, one of whom rented a close of pasture at Heybarne, presumably to graze cattle.[107] Earlier evidence of leather-working is limited to the discovery of a skeleton of a young dog – possibly a hunting dog – dating to the late thirteenth century at Leckhampstead (Figure 47).

FIGURE 47.
Skeleton of a medieval dog found in a test-pit in Leckhampstead.
RICHARD JONES

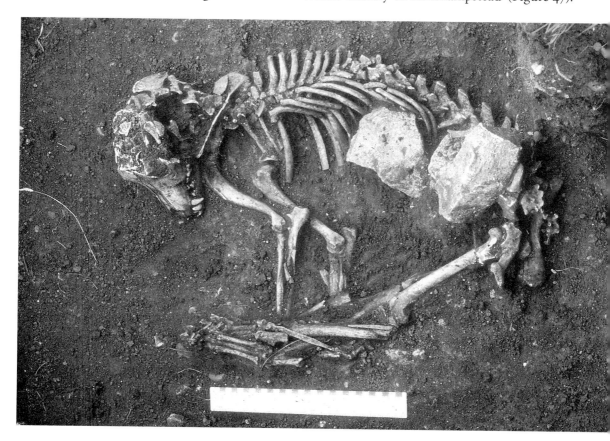

Cut marks reveal that the carcass had been skinned. Skins from smaller animals such as dogs were often used to make leather for gloves, pouches and shoe uppers.[108]

The inhabitants of the medieval English forest almost certainly engaged in a wider range of non-agricultural occupations than those who lived in champion countryside.[109] The small size of many holdings, especially among the assarts, meant that a large number of people depended for their livelihood on the resources of the woodland, from which they also needed to raise the often heavy fines levied by the king's forest officials.[110] Records surviving from the Middle Ages reveal something about their occupations, as charcoal burners, potters, smiths and carpenters, but we can rarely tell whether such work was full- or part-time. Such people, however, were not necessarily the poorest in society. If John le Collier of Whittlebury really was a charcoal burner in 1301, he was among the wealthiest third of villagers who contributed to the lay subsidy of that year.[111] In later centuries, more detailed records reveal the importance of woodland occupations to the economy of the Whittlewood area.[112] Following disafforestation, moreover, in 1853, there was a lament for the loss of those pursuits which depended on the survival of the woodland: 'with its tree-fellers and hewers, its sawyers and hurdlers, its spoke-choppers and faggoters, its lath-renders, rake- and ladder-makers, and what not, the Forest found food for hundreds of families, where the cleared land now scarcely furnishes employment for thirty or forty people'.[113] Here we have a clue to how some of the medieval smallholders of Whittlewood may have made their living.

Conclusion

For king and peasants alike, Whittlewood Forest possessed an economic value as a source of timber, grazing, venison and raw materials; in short, of profit. But Whittlewood was also a political and cultural institution, maintained in the face of protests by the king as a place of prestige, pleasure and patronage. The location of the demesne woods of the forest was not physically determined: much of the land was ploughed at other periods in its history. Instead it was deliberately chosen, managed and preserved, first by the Saxon kings who held many rights there, and subsequently by the Norman kings and their successors. The forest was a symbol of majesty and prerogative, the core of which was successfully defended throughout the Middle Ages, even as more peripheral parts were imparked, enclosed and cleared for agriculture and settlement by lords and peasants. The preservation of woodland in the period 1200–1350 played an important role in shaping the pattern of landscape and settlement, and may have prevented the inhabitants of villages such as Potterspury and Whittlebury from expanding their farmland or constructing houses in areas close to the king's woods, some of which were preserved around Wakefield Lawn. Would the landscape have been different had the forest not existed? We cannot be certain, but the perception of the forest shared by many contemporaries was evidently one of restriction.

CHAPTER SEVEN

Farming the Forest

Medieval Whittlewood not only provided kings and lords with a well-managed and closely supervised hunting landscape; it also offered an extensive and diverse farming landscape to the inhabitants of the forest villages. The open fields, which ceramic evidence suggests were laid out during the tenth century, were farmed throughout the Middle Ages and beyond, in some cases surviving until the era of parliamentary enclosure. In the period before the Black Death, when the population reached its medieval peak, additional areas of arable were cleared from the surrounding woods and either added to the open fields or held as enclosed assarts. Cattle, horses and other animals, used as traction for ploughs and carts, and for dairying, meat and other products, were grazed on the stubble after harvest, in the fallow fields, in areas of permanent pasture and in assarts and woods. After the Black Death, when population fell, arable farming declined and a greater emphasis was placed upon pastoral production, especially sheep, which were introduced in large numbers and were valued for their wool. These changes in farming practices can be shown to have had a considerable impact upon the people of Whittlewood, their settlements and the landscape.

The principal land uses in the project area in the later Middle Ages were arable, pasture, meadow and woodland (Figure 48). A small amount of moor – low-lying rough grazing ground – was recorded at Potterspury in 1315, probably located in the area known as Moor End, but no mention has been found of other land uses, such as heath, marsh and waste.[1] Late medieval Whittlewood seems to have been a carefully managed landscape – the woodland, for example, was divided into coppices – with little land left unimproved for rough grazing. In the eleventh century, Domesday Book suggests that the study area was lightly populated compared to other parts of the midland region; the large amounts of woodland recorded were ideal for livestock husbandry (especially pig farming), with limited arable cultivation.[2] This was a legacy of the area's post-Roman woodland regeneration and subsequent use as a hunting landscape. However, by the end of the thirteenth century, documentary and archaeological evidence both

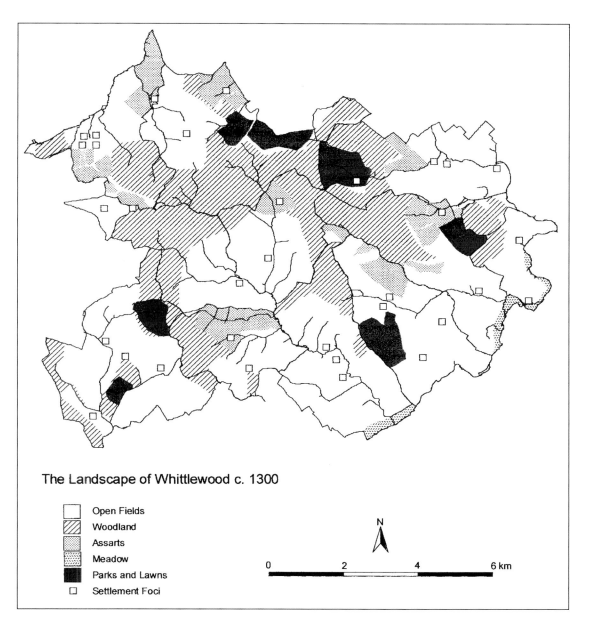

The Landscape of Whittlewood c. 1300

Open Fields
Woodland
Assarts
Meadow
Parks and Lawns
□ Settlement Foci

N

0   2   4   6 km

FIGURE 48.
Reconstruction of the
landscape of Whittlewood
based on historical and
archaeological evidence.

show a significant expansion of population, settlement and arable
production. At Lillingstone Dayrell, for example, the recorded population rose threefold from eleven in 1086 to thirty-three in 1279, and
there was a corresponding increase in the size of the village, revealed
by its physical remains. New settlements were created, such as Cattle
End, Elm Green and Heybarne, and more land was cultivated for
crops, demonstrated both by the extension of manuring, as revealed

by pottery scatters, and the proliferation of references to assarting (see below, pages 136–8, 159–60).[3] Rising demand for basic food-stuffs, especially bread, ale and pottage, increased the profitability of grain-growing, and both lords and peasants responded by seeking to enhance the supply of crops. Arable farming thus developed, in spite of the restrictions imposed by forest law. The emphasis changed after the Black Death of 1349.

How did the lords and peasants of Whittlewood react to the fluctuating demands for agricultural produce? To what extent did they engage with the market in an increasingly commercialised and sophisticated economy? What were the implications for the development of the landscape? Part of the answer to these questions can be found in a range of documentation which itself was a response to the changing economic and social conditions of the period. At the beginning of the thirteenth century, many lords in England switched from a policy of leasing their demesnes to managing them directly, in order to take advantage of the growing profitability of farming. They employed stewards, bailiffs and reeves to account in detail for their rents and produce; as a result, the evidence for farming practices becomes more plentiful, in the form of manorial account rolls, court rolls, extents and surveys.[4] This chapter employs the surviving manorial records of the Whittlewood area, together with evidence from archaeological fieldwork, to examine the changing patterns of agriculture between *c.* 1250 and *c.* 1400, first in the demesne sector and then among the peasantry. The links between the forest villages and nearby market towns are also considered.

Demesne agriculture

In the Middle Ages less than half of the cultivated land of the project area was managed directly by lords. Most was in the hands of free and customary tenants. Thus, in 1086 about 44 per cent of the plough-teams recorded in Domesday Book were held in demesne. In our Buckinghamshire parishes (not including Boycott and Lillingstone Lovell) the Hundred Rolls inquiry of 1279 reveals that about 40 per cent of the arable was under seigneurial control, a surprisingly high proportion. In Stodfold Hundred as a whole, Kosminsky found only 32 per cent of arable in demesne, and a similar figure was calculated for the whole of the midland region covered by the Hundred Rolls survey.[5] Despite the dominance of non-seigneurial producers, therefore, the demesne sector was of considerable importance in the parishes of the study area. This was reflected in the widespread involvement by lords in all aspects of the area's farming.

Some manors in the project area formed part of federated estates whose lords held lands in a number of counties. In the fourteenth century, for example, Passenham was part of the earldom, later the duchy, of Lancaster, and Potterspury was held by the earls of Warwick. The various manors of Stowe parish were mostly in the possession of the abbeys of Oseney (Oxon.) and Biddlesden (Bucks.), and Akeley was held by the priory of Longueville in Normandy. On these manors farming practices may have been influenced by decisions taken as part of a wider estate policy. By contrast, on manors with resident lords whose estates were much smaller, such as the Chastiluns at Leckhampstead, the Dayrells at Lillingstone Dayrell, and the Dive family at Wicken, demesne agriculture was organised to supply the family's immediate needs, both for consumption in the household and for sale on the market.

Lords held a variety of demesne assets: not only arable, pasture, meadow and woodland, but also deer parks, dovecotes, fishponds, horse-mills, sheepcotes, smithies, watermills and windmills. Of these, dovecotes, fishponds and mills were particularly widespread, suggesting considerable levels of seigneurial investment. The creation of a manorial complex at Lillingstone Lovell, for example, probably in the late thirteenth century, necessitated the diversion of the main road through the village and the development of a sophisticated system of water management to supply a series of five interlinked fishponds.[6] At Wick Hamon, the excavation of the manorial site, dateable to the thirteenth century, has revealed evidence of an elaborate dovecote together with a bakehouse and/or brewhouse.[7] At Furtho a fifteenth-century dovecote still survives, with room for about 330 nests (Figure 49).[8] In total at least a dozen dovecotes were built by lords in the project area. Watermills were recorded on three manors at the time of Domesday Book; 250 years later their number had trebled, a remarkably steep increase compared to other parts of the country, to which may be added three or more windmills. The windmill at Potterspury was built in the early fourteenth century, and in 1315 was said to be worth 6s 8d a year. In 1416–17, however, it was described as 'fallen down and all in decay', a victim to the decline in demand for grain milling which was evident across the country after the Black Death.[9]

The decision to build dovecotes, fishponds, mills and other assets may have been taken for a number of reasons: to provide fresh produce for consumption in the household; to enhance a lord's status in the eyes of his neighbours; to provide a service for the tenants of the estate; and to make a profit, for example by leasing a mill or by selling produce on the market. Pigeons from the dovecote at Silverstone, for instance, were sold for 4s 6d in 1279–80.[10] Fish from the same

FIGURE 49.
The dovecote at Furtho.
FRAN HALSALL

manor were regularly consumed at the king's table, at Westminster, Woodstock and elsewhere.[11] In the years around 1300, however, most profit was to be made by selling grain, and in the Whittlewood area many lords seem to have made the production of crops the principal focus of their farming enterprises.

Arable farming
Around 1300, lords in Whittlewood engaged in arable farming on a large scale. At Wick Dive, for example, 232 acres (94 ha) of sown arable were in demesne in 1281. At Leckhampstead and Potterspury, in excess of 300 acres (120 ha) of arable were recorded at about the same time.[12] According to Campbell, 'any demesne which regularly cropped 250 acres or more ... ranked as a very major enterprise'.[13] On smaller demesnes, too, arable farming was extensive: 110 acres (45 ha) were held by John de Montalt, lord of one of three manors in Lillingstone Lovell at the end of the thirteenth century, which in 1279 was assessed at just 1.25 hides.[14] On this manor and others, extents reveal that relatively little land was devoted to other uses, such as

meadow and pasture. The grazing necessary to support the animals on which arable farming depended (for traction and manure) was often found in the common pastures of the forest rather than private closes. Others may have pastured their animals in private deer parks and woods. At a time of high demand for grain the resources of the forest enabled lords to extend the acreage devoted to crops without loss of adequate pasture.

On most manors the demesne probably lay scattered across the open fields, intermixed with the land of the tenants. At Lamport, for example, the description of a tenant holding in a charter of 1439 makes clear that some of the strips lay alongside those belonging to the lords of Lamport and Stowe.[15] Likewise, at Deanshanger, for which there survives a detailed field book of 1566, the farmer of the demesne, Robert Fowkes, held 198 acres (80 ha) divided into strips, usually of half an acre each, which were listed by field and furlong, lying among those of the tenants, not consolidated into blocks.[16] Large arable enterprises demanded considerable amounts of labour, which in the Middle Ages was mostly supplied by the inhabitants of the forest villages. Labour services were owed on a number of Whittlewood manors, although their extent varied considerably. They were heaviest at Potterspury, where twenty villeins were obliged to work on the demesne for three days a week throughout the year at the end of thirteenth century.[17] Elsewhere they were less onerous; for instance, at Passenham and Silverstone, tenants were required to work at specific tasks, such as ploughing, harrowing, haymaking and reaping, but only for a few days in the year.[18] For the most part, therefore, the lords of the Whittlewood area depended upon hired labour.

Arable farming was profitable around 1300 because the demand for grain was buoyant, ensuring high prices, and labour costs were low. The lords of the Whittlewood area sold a substantial proportion on the market. On the royal manor of Silverstone, for example, the principal cash crop was wheat: in 1277–78 and 1279–80 about two-thirds of the harvested grain (net of tithe) was sold.[19] Of all the grains, wheat, the main bread grain, was the most highly valued in the Middle Ages. In 1279–80 wheat accounted for nearly 70 per cent by value of all the grain sold at Silverstone, the remainder made up in roughly equal parts by dredge (mixed oats and barley) and oats.[20] More than half the cropped acreage of Silverstone's demesne was devoted to wheat in 1279–80 and 1280–81, with about 40 per cent given over to oats and the remainder to dredge. Other crops, such as peas and beans, were sown on a limited scale.[21] According to the system of classification devised by Campbell, Silverstone may be categorised as 'three-course cropping of wheat and oats', in which wheat comprised the winter course and oats the spring, with all other crops relegated to a comparatively minor role.[22] This farming type was well suited to the heavy boulder clay soils of the Whittlewood area and was probably widely practised. Certainly, at Lillingstone Lovell in 1323–24, wheat and oats were the dominant grains grown, together with smaller quantities of maslin (mixed wheat and rye), peas, beans and vetches.[23] At Potterspury too, in 1326–27, wheat and oats were predominant, although the amounts of barley, dredge and peas sown were not insignificant.[24] Finally, at Leckhampstead in 1279, Richard de Chastilun held stocks of 96 quarters of wheat, 24 quarters of barley, 16 quarters of dredge, 8 quarters of beans and 200 quarters of oats.[25]

The rising demand for grain undoubtedly encouraged lords to clear areas of wood and wood pasture. Most lords in the study area held at least some assarted land before the Black Death, such as William de Dive, who in 1253 was reported to have assarted 13 acres (5 ha) of his wood in Wicken, part of which he sowed with oats and the rest of which was newly ploughed (*friscus*).[26] During the twelfth and thirteenth centuries, hundreds of acres of assarts were added to lords' demesnes in the project area. Extending the area under cultivation allowed more crops to be grown and more to be sold on the market for profit. These assarts, with their stored-up reserves of nitrogen facilitating crop growth, were sometimes worth more than established areas of arable. At Leckhampstead in 1279, for example, Richard de Chastilun held 21 acres (8.5 ha) of assart worth 8*d* an acre, 2*d* an acre more than the rest of his arable.[27] Elsewhere, assarts were worth considerably less. For instance, at Deanshanger 33 acres (13 ha) of ploughed assart were worth 3*d* an acre in 1336, compared to 6*d* an acre for the arable.[28] These differences in value may be attributed to a variety of factors: not only fertility, but also proximity to the grazing grounds of deer, which might damage growing crops, or the price of the crop sown at the time the extent was made. Another contributing factor may have been whether the assart was enclosed and farmed separately by the lord, or whether it was incorporated into the open fields. Assarts which were enclosed may have been worth more because lords could adopt more intensive methods of farming.

In many parts of England, farming more intensively was a calculated response to rising population and the growing demand for food. Attempts were made to increase grain yields on a given area of land by more intensive ploughing, manuring and weeding, by cultivating legumes which fixed nitrogen in the soil, and by alternating between tillage and temporary pasturage which helped conserve and maintain levels of soil nitrogen and other vital nutrients.[29] In the Whittlewood

1100-1250

1250-1400

Leckhampstead, Bucks

Intensification of Manuring

- • 1 sherd
- • 2 sherds
- ● 3-5 sherds
- ⬤ 6-9 sherds

N

0   200   400 m

FIGURE 50.
Increased quantities of potsherds on a field at Limes End in Leckhampstead reflecting increased intensification of manuring between the twelfth and fourteenth centuries.

area the open fields seem to have been more intensively manured after 1250, as demonstrated by the increased amounts of pottery of that date recovered during fieldwalking (Figure 50). Both lords and peasants would have been engaged in the removal of domestic rubbish to the strips and furlongs in dung-carts such as that repaired for the lord of Passenham in 1380–81.[30] Hurdles for folds, bought at Silverstone in 1279–80, enabled the arable to be manured directly by the animals.[31] Other types of fertiliser, such as marl, may also have been used: the traces of what looks like a marl-pit have been identified in Lillingstone Dayrell, located near Marl Pit Field, depicted on a map of 1611. At Silverstone, customary tenants were obliged to weed on the lord's demesne for one day a year, the virgate holders with a helper, according to the custumal of 1288. Additional weeders were hired there in 1275–79.[32] Legumes – peas, beans and vetches – were grown widely in the study area, although in most cases the quantities were small. The fragments of evidence suggest some attempts to employ more intensive methods of farming, but we cannot tell to what extent they were applied. The available yield figures, however, noted by the auditors at Silverstone in 1279–81 and at Potterspury in 1326–27, do not suggest that levels of output in Whittlewood were anything other than ordinary: threefold of wheat, fourfold of barley and dredge, and twofold of oats.[33]

In enclosed assarts concentrations of ceramic-rich manure seem to have been deposited in some places; for example, in Henry de Perie's assart in Whittlebury, which formed part of Luffield Priory's grange of Monksbarn.[34] In general terms, however, the pottery evidence does not indicate that the arable farms established on assarted land – Heybarne, Monksbarn, Stockholt – were intensively manured using domestic supplies. Instead they probably relied more heavily than the open fields upon the stalling and folding of animals and multiple ploughings. At Monksbarn an agreement reached between Luffield Priory and Geoffrey de Insula in *c.* 1216–25 allowed Geoffrey to pasture eight of his demesne oxen there with the oxen of the priory. He was also entitled to pasture all the animals raised on his manor of Heathencote when the assart was fallow and after the third ploughing.[35] On some assarts a form of ley cultivation may have been practised, by which areas of nitrogen-rich pasture were temporarily converted to tillage. In parts of Wicken, place-names with the element 'ley' can be found on an estate map of 1717 (Figure 51). Such an explanation may account for the description of William de Dive's assart, mentioned above, as newly ploughed. One of the meanings of the Latin term *friscus* is ley.[36]

Lords knew how to intensify production, but may have lacked

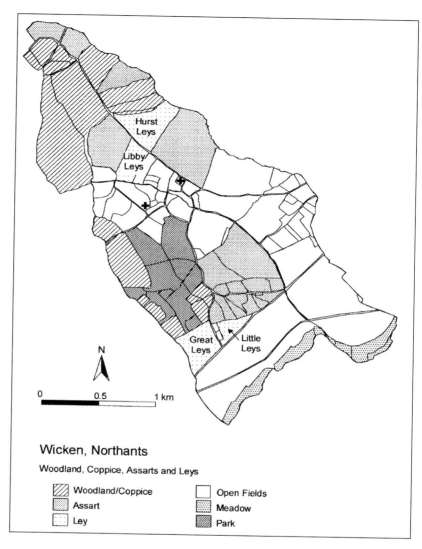

FIGURE 51.
Wicken: woodland,
coppices, assarts and leys.

economic incentive. The ready availability of woodland for conversion into arable encouraged extensive methods of farming. The forest
regard rolls make clear that the holders of assarts generally pursued
the same type of cultivation – three-course cropping of wheat and
oats – which was practised in the open fields, and little attempt seems
to have been made to specialise in a particular crop for sale on the
market. Although demand for grain was generally high in this period,
Whittlewood was remote from major urban centres. Certainly the
area lay outside the provisioning zone for London.[37] Most of the grain
was probably destined for small market towns or was sold locally to
the numerous smallholders and cottagers.

The late thirteenth century may have marked the peak of demesne cultivation. On some manors after 1300 the acreage devoted to crops remained constant or even increased. At Passenham, for example, the arable measured 243 acres (98 ha) in 1278 and 300 acres (120 ha) in 1327.[38] But on other manors there is clear evidence of decline. At Potterspury the area of demesne arable shrank from 340 acres (138 ha) in 1297 to 200 acres (81 ha) in 1301, 123 acres (50 ha) in 1315, and 80 acres (32 ha) in 1325.[39] The partition of the manor following the death of Richard FitzJohn in 1297 probably accounted for much of the initial loss of arable. In addition, some of the land may have been converted to pasture: the manor was said to be without demesne pasture in 1297, but it was recorded thereafter. However, most of the arable was probably leased to free tenants, of whom there were twenty-seven in 1315, paying more than £7 a year in rent. The leasing of the demesne evidently suited the Beauchamp earls of Warwick, who inherited Potterspury in 1297 and were mostly absentee landlords, allowing the manor house of Richard FitzJohn to fall into decay. According to the account of 1326–27, most of the labour services of the tenants were commuted into cash, only a few being retained for harrowing, ditching and enclosing the park.[40]

The scale of demesne cultivation contracted in England in the aftermath of the Great Famine and agrarian crisis of 1315–22. Leasing was an attractive alternative option for lords. Heavy livestock losses from disease-depleted flocks and herds diminished the capacity to fertilise and plough the land.[41] In the study area, demesne and peasant land lay untilled in several parishes according to the tax assessors of 1341: three carucates (approximately 360 acres, or 145 ha) in Stowe; two carucates (240 acres, or 97 ha) in Leckhampstead; a single carucate (120 acres, or 48 ha), described as sterile, in Lillingstone Dayrell. In all three places the paucity of sheep, and thus of a valuable source of manure, was noted.[42] The value of demesne arable in the project area fell, at Potterspury from *6d* an acre in 1297 to *2d* an acre in 1325. Relatively low valuations of *4d* an acre were also found at Wick Dive in 1281 and Passenham in 1327. The value of assarts, such as those at Deanshanger in 1336, was sometimes even lower.[43]

The economic and social changes of the period 1315–75, during which the population was halved, led to a reorientation of arable farming in England. In the Whittlewood area the changes are particularly visible at Passenham, a manor belonging to the duchy of Lancaster. Typical of other manors in Northamptonshire in the late fourteenth century, a high percentage of barley was sown and oats gradually disappeared.[44] Peas increasingly replaced oats as the main fodder crop, especially for sheep, and in addition provided a source of nitrogen for the soil. Barley – used mainly in brewing in the later Middle Ages – was the chief cash crop at Passenham. More than thirty-eight quarters were sold in March 1381, about two-thirds of the harvest (net of tithe).[45] Substantial quantities of dredge were also sold, contributing to the significant bias towards spring-sown crops. This suggests that demesne rotations at Passenham were becoming more flexible and intensive, with peas possibly taking the place of fallows.[46] Yield figures, noted by the auditors in 1382–83, suggest some measure of success: fourfold of wheat, fivefold of dredge and sevenfold of barley, although these were not maintained in later years.[47] However, arable farming was reduced in scale. Between 1382 and 1402 the sown acreage at Passenham averaged only about 150 acres (60 ha), half that recorded in the extent of 1327.[48] High labour costs and falling grain prices encouraged lords to curtail labour-intensive arable husbandry and to convert areas of tillage into pasture.

Pastoral farming

Whittlewood was well suited to pastoral farming, as Domesday's record of numerous pigs shows. In the thirteenth and fourteenth centuries, the lords of Whittlewood kept a wide range of working and non-working animals: cattle, horses, sheep, pigs, goats and poultry. Unlike the rather homogenous arable husbandry of the project area, with its emphasis on wheat and oats, there was a much greater diversity of pastoral farming types. For example, at Silverstone in the period 1275–79 the manor specialised in cattle for dairying: in one year 160 cheeses and 20 gallons of butter were sold for £2 11s 6d.[49] By contrast, at nearby Potterspury in 1326–27, working animals predominated, with only a handful of pigs and poultry contributing to the manor's income.[50] The extensive wood pasture resources of the forest allowed some lords to keep sizeable flocks of goats, often regarded as a destructive browsing animal, at a time when their numbers were falling in more intensively farmed regions. For example, Richard de Chastilun of Leckhampstead held sixty goats at the time of his death in 1279, and Geoffrey de la Lee of Lillingstone Lovell had fifty in 1314.[51]

Lords and peasants alike made use of the common pasture available in Whittlewood Forest which, by tradition, was claimed as recompense for the unhindered access deer were allowed to their own land.[52] In the early modern period a distinction was made between the 'in-towns' and 'out-towns' of Whittlewood. The residents of the six 'in-towns' (Passenham and Deanshanger, Potterspury, Silverstone, Whitfield, Whittlebury and Yardley Gobion) were entitled to common of pasture from 25 March to 1 November, while those of the nine 'out-towns' (Alderton, Grafton, Lillingstone Dayrell, Lillingstone Lovell,

Paulerspury, Slapton, Syresham, Wappenham and Wicken) were limited to the period from 23 April until 25 September. In addition, only cattle and horses were commonable. Sheep, pigs and goats were excluded.[53] These restrictions probably did not apply in the Middle Ages. The records of the forest courts of the thirteenth and fourteenth centuries have almost nothing to say on the subject of illegal grazing. Even goats, which were particularly destructive of young tree growth, were permitted to graze in the forest according to a survey of 1255, although attempts were evidently being made at this time to curtail the practice.[54] At a later inquest, in 1363, the earl of Warwick was fined for allowing goats to enter the forest 'against the assize'.[55] Other restrictions which applied in the Middle Ages included the exclusion of all animals from the forest during 'fence month', the fortnight before and after Midsummer (24 June), when the deer were supposed to be fawning. The king also possessed preserves (*defensis*) in which no one was allowed to common, which may have included newly felled coppices and particular parts of the forest, such as the 'hay' (enclosed woods) of Shrob.[56] On the other hand, Wakefield Lawn was opened for common of pasture in 1253, and in most places animals were allowed to graze freely.[57]

Despite the widespread access to pasture in the forest, there were fears in the thirteenth century that the rapid extension of arable farming into the woods threatened the grazing of livestock. Lords were sometimes compelled to open their newly enclosed assarts, 'after the grain and hay have been carried from the fields', to the animals of neighbouring villages.[58] Both the enclosed land and the open fields were grazed by livestock during periods of fallow, which resulted in the deposition of manure on the soil. In most parts of the study area, a three-field system of husbandry was practised, which was often found in woodland landscapes. The greater availability of permanent pasture enabled communities to support their livestock with only a third, rather than half, of the arable lying fallow each year. However, the number of fields varied considerably, ranging from two to four or more, and some field systems seem to have been reorganised as more land was assarted from the woods. At Deanshanger, for example, the field book of 1566 records four fields of irregular size, ranging from 349 acres (141 ha) in the north field to 87 acres (35 ha) in the south field. Nevertheless, the extent of 1336 shows that the manor's arable was divided into three equal parts. Two parts were sown each year, which were valued at *6d* an acre. The third part lay fallow and was worth nothing because it was always used as common by all the tenants.[59] In such cases, rotations were probably based on groups of furlongs rather than the field as a whole.

In the winter months animals were fed fodder crops, such as the oats grown at Silverstone in 1275–81, and also hay grown in the meadows. Domesday Book records meadow on most manors in the project area in 1086. Nevertheless, it was not always plentiful in the Middle Ages, especially in relation to the arable, and this was reflected in the value of meadow recorded in extents. At Passenham, with its quite extensive meadows, the earl of Lancaster in 1327 held 300 acres (120 ha) of arable worth 4*d* an acre and 70 acres (28 ha) of meadow worth between 1*s* 6*d* and 2*s* an acre. At Potterspury in 1301, there were 200 acres (81 ha) of arable worth 6*d* an acre and just 8 acres (3 ha) of meadow worth 2*s* an acre.[60] The sale of hay often formed a significant part of a lord's income. At Silverstone, for example, hay worth £1 11*s* 9*d* was sold on the king's manor in 1279–80, about 10 per cent of receipts from the sale of produce.[61] Meadowland might also be leased before the hay was mown. At Passenham in 1382–83 an acre of herbage was worth between 1*s* 2*d* and 2*s* 10*d*, although several parcels remained in the lord's hands and were 'mown and carried for the use of the manor because of a want of buyers this year'.[62]

In the fifteenth century sheep farming became widespread. Before the Black Death sheep seem not to have been a predominant element in the forest economy. Some lords maintained flocks: a list of stock at Luffield Priory in 1291–92, for instance, included 341 ewes, lambs and wethers, a number of which were destined for the monks' larder.[63] On Oseney Abbey's manor of Stowe in *c.* 1330–40 the flock comprised 6 rams, 227 wethers, 183 ewes, 80 hoggs and 62 lambs.[64] In 1314 Geoffrey de la Lee held 260 sheep at Lillingstone Lovell.[65] On the other hand, sheep were largely absent from the king's manor of Silverstone in 1275–81, from Richard de Chastilun's manor of Leckhampstead in 1279, and from the earl of Warwick's manor of Potterspury in 1326–27, while they were only intermittently present on the duchy of Lancaster's manor of Passenham in the late fourteenth century.[66] In the fifteenth century, by contrast, following the leasing of the demesnes, sheep were introduced in large numbers and former areas of cultivation were laid down to grass. In an era of high wage costs, sheep farming was relatively inexpensive and wool could profitably be sold to supply England's burgeoning cloth industry. In parts of the study area, as will be seen, these changes in farming had a profound effect on patterns of settlement and landscape.

Demesne agriculture in perspective

The lords of the Whittlewood area, like their counterparts elsewhere in England, extended arable farming in the thirteenth century. Large areas of wood and wood pasture disappeared under the plough, to be incorporated into the open fields or held as closes. The landscape of Whittlewood became more open and new farms and hamlets were founded – at Stockholt and Elm Green, for example – contributing to a more dispersed pattern of settlement. In spite of the somewhat irregular pattern of fields which evolved as a result of assarting and the potential for depredation by browsing deer and hunting parties, a regular three-course rotation was widely adopted, a practice found in many champion districts of the midlands. Furthermore, some attempts may have been made to employ more intensive methods of farming. Paradoxically, however, this was perhaps more common after the Black Death – for instance at Passenham – following a sharp decline in the sown acreage.[67] A considerable proportion of each harvest was sold on the market, although little evidence has been found for specialisation as a result of commercial influences. Most grain and stock was probably sold locally, as discussed more fully below. The plentiful supply of grazing available in Whittlewood increased yet further with a reduction in the arable after the mid fourteenth century. Animals provided both traction and manure. Demesne ploughs were mostly pulled by oxen but a few horses were also kept.[68] Livestock was grazed on the fallow fields and, perhaps more importantly, on assarts, which received little manure from domestic supplies. Lords were able to call on the labour services of their tenants at busy times of the year, such as ploughing and harvest, but for the most part demesnes were worked by hired labour and peasants were left to tend their own crops and stock.

Peasant agriculture

Although free and customary tenants held more cultivable land than lords, their activities are far less well documented. In general terms, most peasants probably followed broadly similar farming practices to those on the demesnes. Thus, before the Black Death, peasants grew large quantities of wheat and oats. For example, in 1332 the taxpayers of Leckhampstead were assessed on crops totalling twenty-nine quarters of wheat, nineteen quarters of dredge, and thirty-two quarters of oats.[69] The predominance of wheat and oats is also suggested by their widespread appearance among the assarts of the forest, whatever the size and location of the newly cleared land. Thus, Ralph de Cheney held an acre sown with wheat and an acre with oats in Furtho during the reign of King John, while half of Thomas de Waleshale's 12-acre (5 ha) assart at Whittlebury was sown with wheat and the other half with oats.[70] Oats were also given in customary payment to the king by the vill of Stony Stratford for rights of common in Whittlewood

Forest in the mid thirteenth century, while the virgate-holders of Deanshanger gave wheat in return for fencing and fuel.[71]

Entries on court rolls provide incidental information about the crops grown by peasants. In an attempt to force an Akeley tenant in 1387 to attend the court, an acre of barley worth 4s was distrained. In 1391 the holding of a tenant who fled from the manor included seven roods of land sown with wheat, which another tenant agreed to farm the following year. A close belonging to Richard Perkins was sown with peas in 1392, when it was depastured by a neighbouring tenant's animals. In 1404 a female servant of John Pollard stole three bushels of malt and a bushel of wheat from other tenants, while in 1406 half an acre of beans was taken by the lord as heriot on the death of John Robert.[72] At Silverstone, too, the court rolls tell us something about the crops grown by the peasantry. In 1403 half a quarter of beans growing on the land of one tenant was consumed by the pigs of another. This led to a tit for tat exchange in which the original perpetrator lost a quarter of barley. In a similar case in 1425 barley was trampled down and consumed by a neighbour's animals, while in another case of trespass in 1433 an acre of oats was destroyed.[73]

Court rolls also contain information relating to the livestock kept by the peasantry. At Akeley in the period 1382–1407 the lord of the manor collected animal heriots comprising five cows, five horses, ten oxen, seven sheep, a piglet and a hen.[74] Heriot was supposedly a render of the best live beast of the deceased tenant. However, tenants might seek to evade the obligation. For example, at Silverstone in 1432 it was argued that a cow seized by the lord's bailiff had been given by the owner to a friend before her death and that the intended heriot was a ewe with lambs, a much less valuable animal.[75] The court rolls suggest that pigs were widely held by the peasantry of Whittlewood Forest. Their supervision appears to have been a problem for the manorial authorities. At Akeley, for example, pigs were found to have uprooted boundary stones separating the land of the rector from one of the tenants in 1388, for which the community was fined. In the following year several tenants, as well as the rector, were fined for having broken a by-law with their pigs, while in 1392 pigs belonging to Richard Dauwes destroyed three bushels of pulses growing in Walter Hawkin's close.[76] Pigs were a nuisance at Silverstone too. In 1390, for instance, four tenants were fined for allowing their pigs to enter the arable.[77] Pannage was collected from peasants throughout the forest, both by the king and other lords, such as the duke of Lancaster, who received 4s 7d at Passenham in 1382–83, implying the presence of fifty-five animals, as the standard payment was usually 1d per pig.[78]

At Leckhampstead in 1332 the villagers liable to tax were assessed on holdings of eighteen oxen, sixteen cows, twenty draught-horses and seventy-two sheep.[79] Sheep were also held by the tenants of Silverstone, where land was leased 'in the fields' to wean 480 lambs in 1279–80.[80] Concerns were expressed at various times about the availability of grazing land. In the fifteenth century, for example, complaints were heard against acquisitive peasants who sought to enclose common land. Thus, at Silverstone in 1444 Geoffrey Webb was fined for appropriating a close out of the common pasture, for which he ignored a stipulation that 'in the winter he ought to have two gates open so that the tenants of Silverstone and Whittlebury are able to have common in the same close without interruption'.[81] In champion areas common pastures were often carefully regulated at an early date by the use of stints. In Whittlewood, however, much land was apparently unstinted, an indication of the widespread availability of adequate grazing. For example, in a dispute at Lillingstone Dayrell in 1272, one of the lord's free tenants was found to be entitled to pasture 'all his beasts apart from goats' on 160 acres (65 ha) of arable at fallow-time and 'with all his beasts' on 80 acres (32 ha) of common pasture throughout the year. Only on a further 12 acres (5 ha) of pasture was he restricted to six oxen and two draught-horses.[82] Stints may have been introduced on some manors at a later date. A by-law at Akeley in 1537 recorded that for each virgate of land a tenant was entitled to pasture six oxen or cows and twenty sheep and no more.[83] Other by-laws sought to limit the number of animals pastured on the common ways and to prevent animals being let loose in the sown fields. Similar stints were imposed at Passenham and Deanshanger in the sixteenth century and at Stowe in the seventeenth century but the antiquity of these arrangements is not known.[84]

Just as there was common pasture, so too were there areas of common meadowland. At Passenham in 1566 the field book demonstrates how this was divided into small parcels, of an acre or more, much as the arable in the common fields was divided into strips. The relative scarcity of meadowland compared to arable, however, meant that not every tenant was able to receive a share on a permanent basis. At neighbouring Deanshanger much of the meadowland was described as 'lottemeade' or 'lottyd', indicating that the meadow was redistributed from time to time among the tenants by casting lots.[85] Some such practice appears to be recorded in a thirteenth-century grant to Snelshall Priory by Henry son of Walkelin of 2 acres (0.8 ha) of meadow belonging to the cotland of Robert Capiun, which were to be divided 'in the same way that the said Robert was wont to divide them each year among his fellows (*sociis*)'.[86] At Stowe, too, the survey of 1633 reveals the presence of 'lott meades', suggesting that the sharing of meadows may have been commonplace in Whittlewood Forest in the Middle Ages.[87]

Medieval peasants were not self-sufficient. They depended on others for a range of goods and services. For example, most peasants probably took their grain to a mill for grinding into flour, rather than attempting to do so by hand.[88] Although some mills fell into decay after the Black Death, many enjoyed long histories: the watermill at Potterspury, called 'Clakke' in late medieval records, operated on the same site close to the church from the eleventh century to the twentieth.[89] Likewise, peasants probably made use of the services of smiths, such as those recorded at Lillingstone Dayrell and Potterspury in the Middle Ages (see above, pages 125–6). Peasant farming was intended not only to supply the subsistence needs of the family, but also a surplus for sale on the market, to raise the cash needed to pay rents, taxes and other dues, and to purchase manufactured goods and other items which the family could not supply themselves. A little evidence survives to demonstrate the links between Whittlewood and nearby market centres.

Town and country

The project area included within its boundaries no medieval town and no market formally licensed by the king. Nevertheless, our parishes lay close to four small towns which flourished in the Middle Ages – Brackley, Buckingham, Stony Stratford and Towcester – the hinterlands of which almost certainly overlapped in the study area and included all of our villages within their spheres of influence. In theory each town should have possessed a hinterland of 10.7 km (6.66 miles), the distance which thirteenth-century lawyers regarded as the maximum for a day's journey to market.[90] Such a figure may well have reflected real trading patterns in the Middle Ages, as indicated by the fact that the theoretical hinterlands of the above four towns lay close to but did not encompass their neighbouring markets. For the inhabitants of the project area, two or even three of these towns lay within a day's journey. To assess which of the markets they were most likely to attend we may turn, in the first instance, to the records of the borough court.

One way of defining a town's hinterland is to examine borough court records for the place of residence of people involved in pleas of debt, detention of chattels, broken contract and trespass.[91] This has been done for Brackley and Buckingham in the sixteenth century; these documents comprise the earliest surviving series of borough

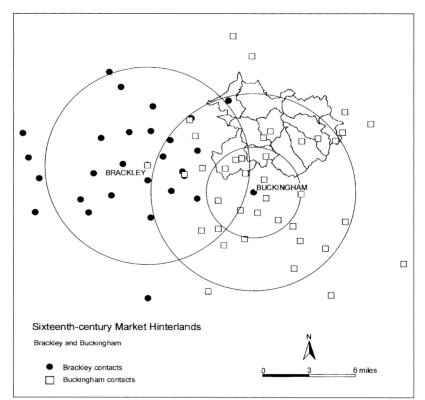

Sixteenth-century Market Hinterlands

Brackley and Buckingham

● Brackley contacts
□ Buckingham contacts

N

0   3   6 miles

court records for the Whittlewood area (Figure 52).[92] In the case
of Brackley, most villages in the immediate vicinity are represented,
the inhabitants of which would naturally have been drawn to the
town to engage in trade. The more distant places tended either to be
neighbouring towns, such as Banbury and Buckingham, or villages
with good communications. As the most distant of the towns from
the project area, it is no surprise that Brackley's influence appears to
have extended no further than Lamport and Silverstone. Furthermore,
although Brackley was a much more important market centre in the
thirteenth century than the sixteenth, when its fortunes had long been
on the wane, the few pieces of evidence surviving from the earlier
period do not suggest that the town had a much wider hinterland in
the years around 1300. For example, the evidence of locative surnames
in the 1301 lay subsidy for Northamptonshire reveals an Adam de
Brackley in Silverstone but the name does not appear elsewhere in
the study area. Likewise, the returns for Brackley suggest immigration
from within the hinterland but not much further: from Radstone,
Whitfield, Cottisford, Croughton, Aynho, Steane near Hinton (which
was deserted by the sixteenth century), Culworth and Sulgrave.[93] Our

mid sixteenth-century market hinterland may thus be a reasonable reflection of Brackley's sphere of influence some 250 years before.

Buckingham appears to have been a more prosperous and busier town than Brackley in the sixteenth century; it may have attracted traders and visitors from a wider area due to its position as the county town. With the exception of Leckhampstead, all the villages in the southern half of the project area were represented in Buckingham's borough court. The town's economic hinterland may also be revealed in a document recording the spread of a rumour about the destruction of Catholic images and objects in 1537. Having traced the rumour to a Buckingham bakehouse, the baker's servant gave the following description of the rumour's spread: 'the said deponent sayeth that he daily carryeth bread from Buckingham to Padbury and three towns more adjoining to Buckingham, and so from town to town to the number of thirteen towns of any side of Buckingham. And now of late ... many persons of the inhabitants of the said towns where he carried bread demanded of him at sundry comings whether Buckingham church was put down or not'.[94] We seem here to have a description of the trading hinterland of a Tudor baker. Although, with the exception of Padbury, these thirteen towns (or villages, as we would call them) remain unnamed, we can on the basis of the court evidence make a fair assumption about where they might be. A total of twelve of the settlements named in the court book lie within 5 km (3 miles) of Buckingham, to which should probably be added Radclive. Assuming the baker delivered to villages all round the town, it seems that we should be thinking in terms of quite a small hinterland for daily or regular contact with the market. For those outside the 3-mile radius contact with the town may have been only weekly or even more occasional, which perhaps encouraged a greater degree of informal trade outside the market place.

A remarkable example of an unlicensed market which grew into a place of considerable size lies within the project area at Old Stratford, at the crossroads of Watling Street and the Buckingham to Northampton road, less than a mile to the north-west of Stony Stratford. The settlement lay on the parish boundary separating Passenham and Cosgrove. The Forest Map shows a total of ten houses on either side of the road, of which several no doubt represent the inns which we know existed there in the seventeenth century (Figure 53).[95] The development of Old Stratford on Watling Street, straddling a parish boundary, mirrors the development of its neighbour Stony Stratford, which originally was divided between the manors of Calverton and Wolverton. The only difference was that Stony Stratford was granted recognition as a market and a borough by the king in the Middle Ages.[96] Very

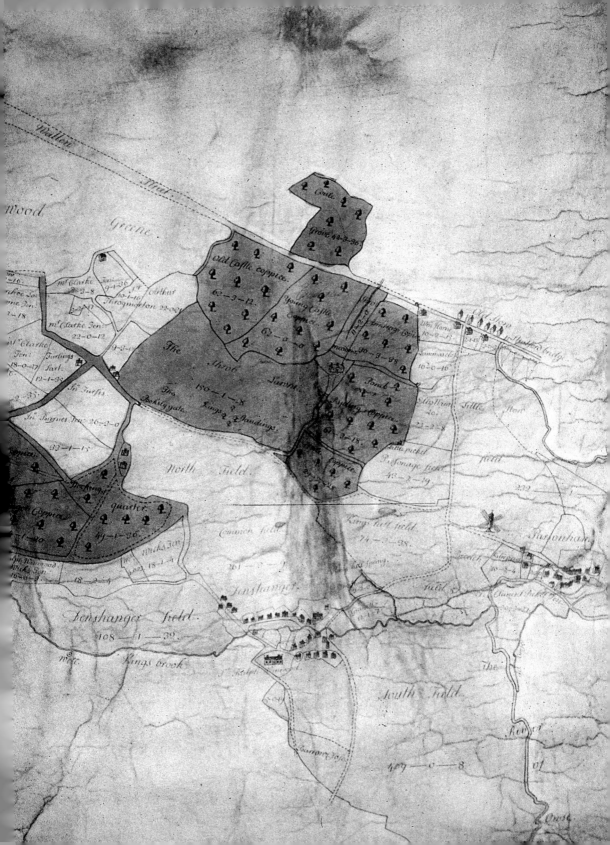

little can be said about Old Stratford in the medieval period – or rather, For Stratford or West Stratford, as it was then known – but it seems likely that some form of trading activity took place there to cater for the needs of the medieval travellers who found themselves at this crossroads. A hermitage established close to the crossroads in the fourteenth century or earlier was probably sited to attract alms from passing traffic.

A good deal of medieval trade probably took place outside licensed markets and towns, at the farm gate, or in unofficial market venues such as a churchyard or other open space. There are a number of references to purchases being made in the project area at places with no official market. For example, in 1380–81 the reeve of Passenham bought two oxen at one of the Lillingstones, either Dayrell or Lovell. Two other oxen were purchased from John Butcher of *Newenton*, possibly Newton Longville, a little over 10 km (6 miles) to the south across the county boundary. The residents of nearby villages likewise travelled to Passenham in order to make purchases; for instance, hay was sold to an inhabitant of Beachampton in 1379–80, and other parcels of hay were sold in 1380–81 to residents of Potterspury and Wicken.[97] Much produce, therefore, never made it to the market place, but was sold at the farm gate. The discovery of a pottery kiln at Silverstone producing a fabric found only in the village also suggests that some trade bypassed official markets and towns. The potter may have delivered his wares directly to the customer, of whom the king's servants at his hunting lodge may have been the most important. Alternatively, there may have been an unofficial market place at Silverstone, perhaps where the roads converge and widen close to the church, as can be seen on the Forest Map (Figure 6).[98] At Akeley, too, the road plan seems to hint at the presence of an unofficial market place. The Square, as it is called, appears to be older than Church Hill, which joins the A413 to the Leckhampstead road. Located opposite the church, at the side of the Buckingham to Towcester road, it is possible that The Square was originally closed at its southern end and functioned as a kind of market place where locals could sell food and drink and possibly other goods to passing customers. Certainly there were appropriate craftsmen resident in Akeley in the Middle Ages, such as John Perkins the shoemaker, recorded in 1387–88.[99]

As well as trading within the project area and in nearby towns, some inhabitants of Whittlewood established links with more distant urban centres. A resident of Lillingstone Lovell was in debt to a draper from Northampton in 1403, while an inhabitant of Deanshanger owed £2 to the prior of the Augustinian friars of Northampton in 1384.[100] An analysis of the locative surnames of townspeople and

FIGURE 53.
Detail of the *c.* 1608 map of Whittlewood Forest, showing Old Stratford on Watling Street and the neighbouring villages of Passenham and Deanshanger.

NORTHAMPTONSHIRE RECORD OFFICE AND HIS GRACE, THE DUKE OF GRAFTON

151

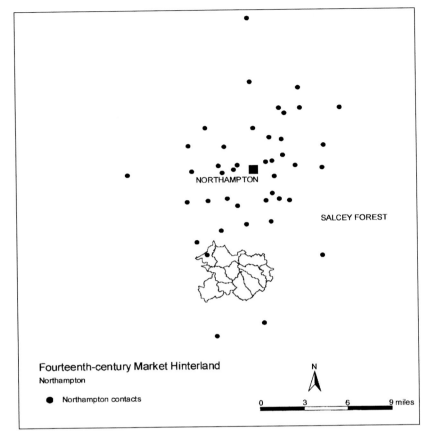

Fourteenth-century Market Hinterland

Northampton

● Northampton contacts

N

0   3   6   9 miles

FIGURE 54.
A fourteenth-century
market hinterland:
Northampton.

food-sellers resident in Northampton in the years around 1300, based
on a detailed rental and an account of purveyance, reveals immigration to the town from a wide region. However, despite the evidence of
the debt cases involving inhabitants of the study area, only Silverstone
is represented among the surnames found in these documents (Figure
54).[101] This is not necessarily indicative of a lack of contact between
Whittlewood and Northampton, only that the town was apparently
less successful at attracting immigrants from the Whittlewood and
indeed the Salcey region, to the south-east of the town, than it was
from areas to the north-east and west. Perhaps the opportunities and
resources available in these woodland areas discouraged migration to
an urban environment.

Contacts between Whittlewood and other towns in the midlands
can be identified from a variety of documents. The 1301 lay subsidy,
for example, records a taxpayer in Potterspury called Geoffrey
de Daventry.[102] The reeve of Passenham purchased a cart-horse at
Banbury in 1380–81, while the Holy Trinity Guild of Coventry

included among its members Thomas de Passenham and his wife.[103] Towns such as Northampton, Oxford and Dunstable received timber from Whittlewood Forest, as a result of grants to religious houses by the king in the thirteenth century.[104] It may well be that the lords of private woods who were given permission to sell timber also looked to the demand from towns to make a profit, although our sources tell us almost nothing about their buyers. While timber was clearly exported from Whittlewood, a good deal of pottery was imported. Much of the pottery used in the study area was sourced locally at Potterspury; however, other kilns were also important. There appears, moreover, to have been a distinct regional distribution of their wares. In the western part of the project area finds of sandy ware from Brackley and Banbury are dominant, while shelly ware, from Yardley Gobion, is more common in the eastern parishes. Assuming that a good deal of pottery was purchased in the market place or sold by itinerant traders operating within a restricted hinterland, we may conclude that the regional distribution of pottery found in the Whittlewood area reflects local trading patterns and the limited economic hinterlands suggested by borough court records, locative surnames and other sources.

To conclude, the inhabitants of medieval Whittlewood had occasional trading contacts over a wide area of the midlands. However, regular trading activity took place much closer to home, in the immediate vicinity of local towns such as Brackley and Buckingham, and at unofficial market places in villages and at the farm gate. The Buckingham baker's daily round of thirteen villages probably took him no further than 5 km (3 miles) from the town, while the distribution of pottery finds shows not only the dominating presence of Potterspury ware but also the favouring of other kilns according to distance. In buying and selling farm produce and manufactured goods, the lords and peasants of the Whittlewood area seem to have been integrated into largely local patterns of markets and trade, reflecting its position on the edge of woodland and champion zones.

Conclusions

Between 1100 and 1350 the landscape of Whittlewood underwent considerable change: former areas of wood and wood pasture were converted to arable, settlements proliferated and grew, and the population expanded. Agriculture was characterised by arable husbandry based largely on wheat and oats, and by more varied livestock farming. Large acreages were cropped by lords, a reflection perhaps of their ability to increase the size of the arable without loss of adequate pasture and the lack of economic incentive to adopt more intensive farming practices. At a time when ploughlands occupied 90 per cent of the territory of some champion villages, there remained large areas of wood and wood pasture untouched by the plough in the parishes of Whittlewood. Even at their height, the open fields of Passenham, Deanshanger and Puxley, for example, probably occupied less than 50 per cent of the area of Passenham parish.[105] Nevertheless, concern was expressed about the loss of common grazing rights as the arable was extended. After the Black Death, similar complaints were heard about the enclosure of land. In the period 1350–1500, as grain prices fell and wage rates rose in the wake of population decline, farming in Whittlewood became more pastoral in its orientation, with a much greater emphasis than before the plague on the raising of sheep. The effects of the fall in population on the settlements of the Whittlewood area are discussed below. In the following chapter, however, we examine the development of the settlement pattern in the period of expansion, from Domesday Book to the Black Death.

CHAPTER EIGHT

Medieval Villagescapes

In Chapter Five we explored the origins of our villages. Over the course of the Middle Ages these settlements grew and their plans changed; it is to these developments that we now turn. The later medieval villagescapes of Whittlewood can be reconstructed with relative confidence. Four villages – Deanshanger, Passenham, Silverstone and Whittlebury – are depicted in their early seventeenth-century form on the Forest Map; others, such as Akeley, Potterspury, Wicken, Dadford and Lamport, were mapped during the eighteenth century before major redevelopment.[1] This information from early maps is complemented by a variety of documents which reveal elements of village topography, such as manorial records and charters. There are fragmentary survivals of late medieval vernacular architecture which reveal the layout and arrangement of individual properties.[2] Of the twelve medieval parish churches, eight preserve much of their pre-Reformation fabric; the others have been demolished or totally rebuilt.[3] To all this, we can add the archaeological evidence, the survival of earthworks marking former settlement zones, and the recovery of building plans and pottery from test-pits and excavation. Taken together, the fortunes of our villages and changes to their medieval morphology can be charted with accuracy.

Discussion of the villagescape should not be restricted to the village core. By the later Middle Ages, settlement was not limited to a single centre in any of the twelve parishes under investigation. Our villages formed part of a settlement hierarchy, comprising hamlets, farmsteads, granges, moated sites and, because of its special forest status, hunting lodges. The term 'villagescape' is used to embrace all these elements, linking settlements to the arable fields, pastures, meadows and woodlands that lay between them, and to the roads and tracks which joined them together. The villagescape, then, is the landscape of the vill, manor and parish. Exploration begins with a reconstruction of the overall pattern of settlement in the later Middle Ages. Then, the morphology of the villages, hamlets and farmsteads present in the late medieval landscape of Whittlewood will be examined. How different village forms developed will be illuminated through a series of individual village studies. Finally, the individual components of the villagescape will be identified in order to establish intra-village relationships (such as the juxtaposition of the manor and church, or the arrangement of peasant tofts and crofts), and to see how different parts of the village articulated with each other.

The late medieval settlement pattern

Throughout the later Middle Ages, champion England was characterised by parishes containing a single large nucleation surrounded by extensive open fields with few outlying hamlets or farmsteads.

FIGURE 55.
Late medieval settlement.

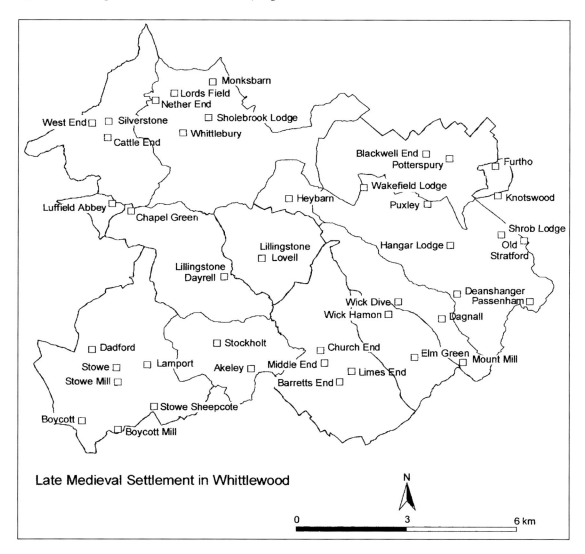

Late Medieval Settlement in Whittlewood

Whittlewood was surrounded by such regions: the Vale of Aylesbury to the south, central Northamptonshire to the east, the Northamptonshire Heights to the north and the north Oxfordshire plain to the west.[4] But examination of the settlement pattern in our parishes reveals that, in addition to a principal settlement area, each parish contained at least one other focus of occupation (Figure 55). In Akeley, for example, the sub-manor of Stockholt was established in the thirteenth century about 1 km (0.5 miles) north-west of the village. At about the same time, a large farmstead called Heybarne was built in the detached portion of Lillingstone Dayrell parish, from which fields were farmed autonomously; and, in the fifteenth century, a chapel dedicated to Thomas Becket was founded in the extreme north-west of the parish, around which the small hamlet of Chapel Green developed.

More than one settlement could be accommodated even in the smallest parishes. In Furtho, a small undocumented hamlet, known as Knotwood, lay close to its southern boundary, remaining active into the late medieval period.[5] In Wick Dive, a hamlet of half a dozen households developed alongside an earlier focus near Dagnall 1.5 km (1 mile) east of the main village. In neighbouring Wick Hamon, the hamlet of Elm Green, perhaps rivalling the main village in size, and associated with a small moated site, thrived until the early fifteenth century. Larger parishes supported even greater numbers of population centres. Although it contained no true outliers, the village of Leckhampstead itself was made up of four fairly substantial and geographically distinct hamlet clusters. Likewise at Silverstone, the late medieval village was comprised of the main centre, together with separate foci in West End, Cattle End and the now-lost Wood End. In addition to the village of Whittlebury, there was sufficient space and resources for a grange of Luffield Priory called Monksbarn to be established in the north-east corner of the parish;[6] and while we have no date for the abandonment of the hamlet of Nether End 800 m (875 yards) north-west of Whittlebury, or its associated moated site at Lords Field Farm, it seems probable in view of the experience shared by other hamlets in the study area that these too remained active into the late medieval period.[7] The largest parishes of all were split into smaller townships. Thus the ecclesiastical parish of Passenham, with the parochial village close to the river Great Ouse, also contained the settlements of Deanshanger and Puxley, each with its own field system, and Old Stratford, which lay on Watling Street.[8] Stowe was similarly divided into four: Boycott, Dadford, Lamport and Stowe itself. While each constituted a separate township, with Boycott and Dadford possessing their own fields, the fields of Stowe and Lamport were shared.[9] A similar situation pertained in Potterspury where, before the splitting of the parish, this larger land unit also included the village of Yardley Gobion, the two settlements possibly sharing a single field system.[10]

At the beginning of the fourteenth century, therefore, an almost universal pattern of multi-nodal settlement within each parish appears to have developed in Whittlewood, marking it out from surrounding areas. But within this pattern, it is clear that there were significant differences in the size, status and autonomy enjoyed by the non-parochial village settlements. At the upper end of the spectrum, there was very little to differentiate, in terms of population, institutions or economic viability, places such as Deanshanger, Lamport, Puxley and Yardley Gobion from the parochial village in whose territory they lay. Elsewhere there were both dependent and independent hamlet clusters, ranging in size from around a dozen households at Elm Green in Wick Hamon to three or four at Knotwood in Furtho. The latest arrivals in the landscape were also the smallest: Heybarne, Monksbarn and Stockholt, established in the first half of the thirteenth century. But even so, there clearly remained sufficient space for expansion. Each of these was able to carve out an estate containing both arable fields and other non-agrarian resources, and to farm these separately from the village community.

Late medieval village, hamlet and farmstead morphology and their development

Given the fragmentary nature of both the historical and archaeological record, any consideration of late medieval village morphology must begin with map evidence. But while these depict the village plan in its totality, our sources are invariably late and must therefore be used with caution if the evidence they provide is to be projected backwards to earlier periods. The Whittlewood area is blessed with a series of maps drawn up before 1750 which show most of our villagescapes before the impact of industrialisation and parliamentary enclosure. Of these, the Forest Map is the earliest, and in showing four of our village plans becomes one of the most useful sources for retrogressive analysis. This map has been examined critically using archaeological techniques and can be shown to be an accurate representation of the early seventeenth-century landscape. Traces of coppice boundaries, for example, are found on the ground along the lines shown on the map. Test-pitting demonstrates a correspondence between early modern pottery concentrations and occupied crofts. Similarly, levels of medieval pottery are highest where buildings are marked on the map and less evident where they are not. From these findings, it would appear that the map presents a faithful picture of those village morphologies that it covers, down to the level of individual houses, and that this represents their state of development not just in the early seventeenth century, but at the end of the Middle Ages.

Of course, all these maps show the Whittlewood villages in the form they assumed following the crises of the fourteenth and fifteenth centuries. As the next chapter reveals, many of these villages shrank, and others were totally deserted. Consequently, for villages such as Lillingstone Dayrell and Lamport, maps of 1611 and 1739 respectively fail to convey a true image of their earlier settlement plan since these had already contracted beyond recognition.[11] Elsewhere, changes to village morphology might have been of lesser magnitude, but nevertheless the resultant plan can be misleading. In the following discussion, consideration of earthwork evidence for former house plots has been critical, where this can supplement the maps. When all the evidence is pieced together, the three basic categories of village described by historical geographers – nucleated, polyfocal and dispersed – can all be identified within our sample parishes.[12] Only four evade categorisation for lack of archaeological or cartographic evidence: Stowe, where eighteenth-century landscaping has erased any evidence of the village beyond the church; Boycott (in Stowe) and Furtho, where farms now occupy the village sites; and Puxley. This leaves thirteen settlements which might be described as villages that can be reconstructed.

Nucleated villages

By the late medieval period, the majority of villages in Whittlewood had assumed a nucleated form, a tight cluster incorporating every element of the villagescape: church and manor house, if these were present, together with peasant tofts and crofts. All exhibited a degree of planning, although the detailed arrangement of each village might be very different.

One of the most developed was Lillingstone Dayrell. The tenth-century core of the village lay 100 m (330 feet) to the west of the parish church. Expansion took place thereafter along the track that still leads to the isolated church, where structural earthworks can be found to its north and concentrations of pottery to its south, the latter associated with limestone scatters. Both mark the location of peasant tofts on either side of the street. Another alignment of limestone concentrations and pottery running parallel and 100 m (330 feet) south of the first street betrays the existence of a second village street, probably laid out during the early twelfth century (Figure 56). The crofts associated with these dwellings ran back off the street frontage to abut those on the south side of the northern street. The eastern end

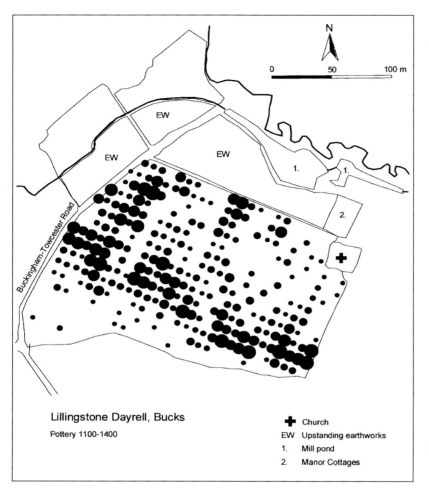

Lillingstone Dayrell, Bucks

Pottery 1100-1400

+ Church
EW Upstanding earthworks
1. Mill pond
2. Manor Cottages

FIGURE 56.
The extent of Lillingstone
Dayrell as shown by pottery
scatters and surviving
earthworks.

of the northern row terminated at the church, with no evidence of occupation to its east, while the southern row ran up to the site of the manor house. These two rows were articulated at their western end by a set of houses fronting on to the main Buckingham to Towcester road, standing opposite further village earthworks on the other side of the road, an area settled by *c.* 1150. By 1300 Lillingstone Dayrell was a village of considerable size. The Hundred Rolls of 1279 record thirty-three households, a threefold increase from its Domesday assessment.[13] As the most compact and regular of all the Whittlewood villages, it bears all the hallmarks of planning as it expanded to accommodate its growing population.

In the late thirteenth century, Lillingstone Lovell was also based on a pair of parallel streets. But just as in the case of Lillingstone Dayrell, this was not a plan laid out from the start, but one that

FIGURE 57.
Schematic plan of
settlement expansion at
Lillingstone Lovell based
on results from test-pitting,
building survey, earthworks
and topography.

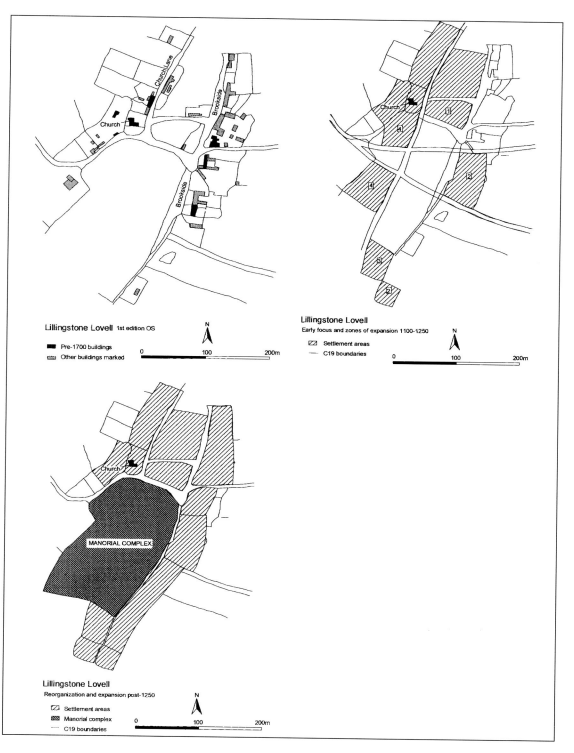

Lillingstone Lovell 1st edition OS

■ Pre-1700 buildings
▨ Other buildings marked

Church Lane
Brookside
Church
Brookside

N

0   100   200m

Lillingstone Lovell
Early focus and zones of expansion 1100-1250

▨ Settlement areas
— C19 boundaries

Church

N

0   100   200m

Lillingstone Lovell
Reorganization and expansion post-1250

▨ Settlement areas
▨ Manorial complex
— C19 boundaries

Church

MANORIAL COMPLEX

N

0   100   200m

developed over 200 years. Around 1100, pottery scatters mark out an area of 2–3 ha (5–8 acres) north of the church which was occupied at this date. Domesday Book records the heads of eleven households at Lillingstone Lovell – eight villeins, two bordars and a slave – split unevenly between two manors.[14] There is no evidence to suggest that these eleven families lived other than in the area around the church, although the precise location of their homesteads cannot be determined. The principal axis of the settlement was probably Church Lane which, at this time, formed just one section of an important cross-country route. The road now terminates at a T-junction immediately to the east of the church, but geophysical survey has detected the continuation of its course across the field to the south, running roughly parallel to the present road to Akeley.

In the 150 years after 1100, archaeological evidence suggests the growth of four main zones of occupation (Figure 57). First, the area immediately to the east of the church was occupied, where earthworks can still be seen today. Secondly, the eastern side of the stream was colonised. Two separate blocks of tenements can be identified to the south of the modern houses. Thirdly, a group of tenements was laid out on the western side of the stream. Finally, a now-obscured area of occupation probably lay to the south of the church, where the southern continuation of Church Lane crossed two roads running parallel to the present main village street. These developments may be linked to a growth of population. The eleven households recorded in Domesday Book increased nearly fourfold in the 200 years to the Hundred Rolls inquiry of 1279.[15]

In the fourteenth century the village underwent another period of reorganisation. In the field to the south of the church are the well-preserved earthworks of a large manorial complex which was probably built in the late thirteenth century. Geophysical surveys and the evidence from test-pitting appear to indicate the foundations of a manor house, barns, dovecote, watermill and five interlinked fishponds (Figure 58).[16] The insertion of this manorial complex into the village plan was almost certainly accompanied by the diversion of the main street through the village on to its present course, forced northwards towards the church in order to avoid the manor. At the same time, the continuation of Church Lane southwards to Akeley was probably cut off and replaced by the surviving parallel path to the east. Any tenants who lived along these roads must have been removed and their houses cleared. Their removal seems to be linked to the infilling of the row on the eastern bank of the stream and its extension both to the north and south, developments which can be dated to the period 1250–1350. On the eve of the Black Death, therefore, the village of Lillingstone

FIGURE 58.
Geophysical survey of manorial complex in Lillingstone Lovell. The dark areas show areas of high resistance in the soil and show the foundations of a rectangular building to the right (*c.* 20 m long). The circular patch above is probably the site of a dovecote, and other partial footprints of large agricultural buildings can be made out in the extreme north of the plan.
RICHARD JONES

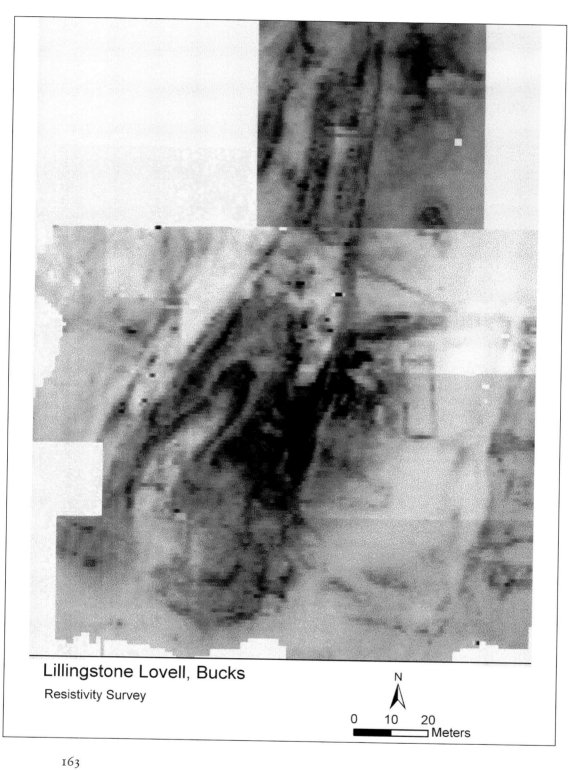

Lillingstone Lovell, Bucks

Resistivity Survey

N

0   10   20
Meters

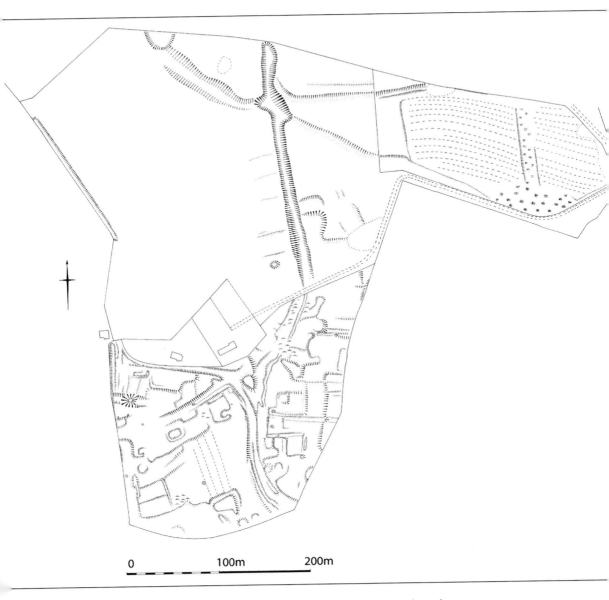

0   100m   200m

Lovell had reached its most developed state. A large manorial enclo-sure, perhaps belonging to the Lovell family, lay at its heart, next to the church, to the north, south and east of which were situated blocks of peasant tenements, linked to each other by lanes.

More common in Whittlewood were linear, rather than grid-based, nucleations, articulated by a single street. Wick Dive is one example. The original kernel of the village probably lay close to the church and manorial complex (Figure 33). Shortly after 1100, a row of equal-sized tenements was laid out over a distance of 300 m (985 feet) on the southern side of the main street. This extension appears to have been sufficient to accommodate immediate population growth, and may even have contained vacant plots that were surplus to initial needs. Additional tenements were only finally occupied on the opposite side of the road during the mid thirteenth century. Other roads appear not to have been settled, the village remaining confined to a single street. In plan, Passenham resembled Wick Dive, the core of the village comprising a double row of tofts and crofts.[17] This was also the form adopted at Dadford,[18] the origins of which remain obscure, and at Lamport too, where surviving earthworks show settlement to have been limited to the north–south through-route, with no buildings on the road to Stowe (Figure 59).[19]

Likewise, Whittlebury developed principally as a simple linear settlement. The origins of the village are obscure: it does not appear in the Domesday survey, possibly because it remained embedded in the estate of Greens Norton, and the earliest mention of its chapel is in 1236.[20] Archaeological evidence, however, establishes that the village began to grow during the late ninth or tenth century in the shadow of the Iron Age hillfort, although what form this settlement took remains hidden from view (Figure 60). During the eleventh and first half of the twelfth centuries expansion took place to the south, with regular plots laid out on each side of the main street, integrally linked to a second row along the road which forked towards Silverstone and led to the church. The church must already have been established by 1100, for burials were taking place within the northern churchyard around this time. A growing population is also reflected in the large 'barn-like' appearance of the twelfth-century church. In a second wave of expansion, the village was developed still further south along the road from Buckingham to Towcester in the mid thirteenth century, producing the plan depicted on the Forest Map. This ordered village plan, with plots abutting one another along the street, is revealed in the documents. Thus, in *c.* 1225–31 the half-messuage which Roger, son of Nicholas of Whittlebury, granted to Philip, then chaplain of Silverstone, was said to lie between the houses of young Aubrey and Hugh Shepherd. At much the same time, a messuage granted to Luffield Priory was stated as being between the houses of Henry Doket and Robert, son of Reginald.[21]

Polyfocal villages

While modern Akeley is a tightly nucleated settlement, this is the result of the coalescence over the last 200 years of two originally separate settlement zones, called Church End and South End in the

FIGURE 59.
The earthwork remains of the deserted village of Lamport. Roads, marked by holloways, meet at a triangular space near the middle of the planned area. The main route seems to be that running from north to south. Numerous banks and ditches mark boundaries between rectangular tofts. Building platforms mark the sites of at least a dozen buildings.
GRAHAM BROWN

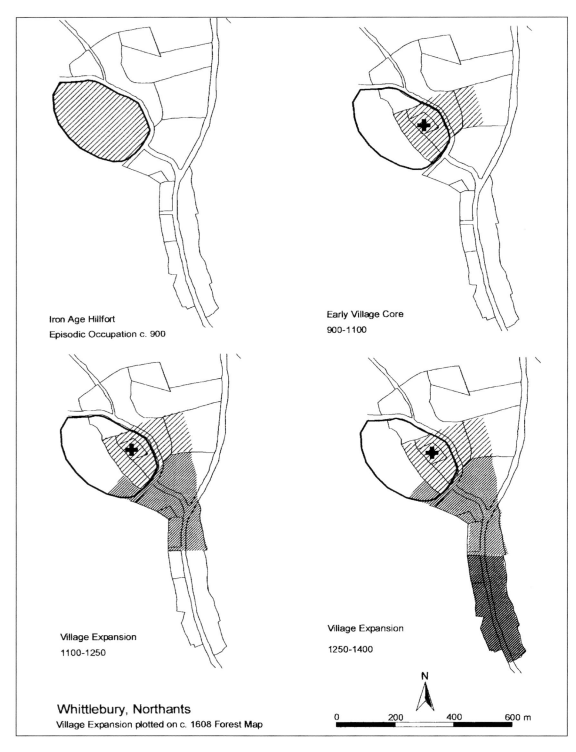

Iron Age Hillfort
Episodic Occupation c. 900

Early Village Core
900-1100

Village Expansion
1100-1250

Village Expansion
1250-1400

Whittlebury, Northants
Village Expansion plotted on c. 1608 Forest Map

N

0   200   400   600 m

seventeenth century.[22] In fact, the origins of the village lie in a single focus close to the crossing of the original course of the main north–south street and an east–west cross-route running on the northern edge of the Great Ouse valley. This site appears to have been abandoned by the mid ninth century in favour of what would become the centre of the modern village, around the church. Although the settlement shifted northwards, it seems to have remained on the periphery of a central space or 'green', the original extent of which appears to be largely preserved in the modern road pattern (Figure 36). Rapid expansion after 1100 altered the village plan. There was growth at the core, where the eastern side of the main street opposite the church was brought under settlement, and a new focus was developed 200 m (655 feet) to the south along the road skirting the green. Settlement on the northern side of this road partially encroached on to the green, but the open space between this new site and the village centre remained. Ceramic finds in this zone indicate a long and regular row of peasant tenements laid out over a distance of some 800 m (875 yards). The manorial farmstead, the foundation date of which is obscure, lay at the eastern end of this row, on the less developed southern side of the road. By 1200, therefore, Akeley had assumed a polyfocal plan, its respective foci the church and the manor house, a plan which appears equally to have been influenced by the need to preserve its central open space.

During the course of the thirteenth century other properties appear to have been established on the same side of the road as the manor. But occupation here seems always to have been sporadic rather than continuous, akin to those settlement patterns classified as 'interrupted rows'. There are good grounds to suppose that stands of woodland survived in this part of the parish into the late medieval period, the new closes perhaps starting life as small assarts cleared as the village population rose. Decisions to cut into the woodland, rather than to develop the more open ground which lay between this part of the village and its main centre, may have been driven by the fact that the area of the original green had by this stage been brought into the open fields. The physical growth of Akeley accords well with known population figures. In 1279 there were twenty-two households, almost a threefold increase since 1086. The location of their messuages is rarely specified, although in 1405 one was said to lie beside the cemetery of the church; the house (*domus*) lay between the barn and a separate chamber.[23]

The village of Potterspury also adopted a polyfocal plan. Throughout the Middle Ages, the lords of the manor were absentees, although a grant of timber to William de Ferrers in 1235 for his hall at Potterspury, together with evidence from inquisitions *post mortem*, attest to a capital messuage presumably located close to the parish church.[24] Development along High Street to the west of the church remains undated, but the preservation of regular tenement boundaries implies that this was laid out as a planned extension, presumably between 1100 and 1300. This linked what would later be called Church End with a western cluster at Blackwell End, although the origins of this part of the village are equally obscure. Whether or not these two clusters were once separate, it is clear that by the late medieval period Potterspury was a single agglomeration, articulated by development along High Street, but retaining its polyfocal appearance.

Dispersed villages

Leckhampstead is marked by the most dispersed pattern of settlement within the Whittlewood project area and contrasts strongly with the more nucleated and polyfocal village forms found elsewhere. At its height *c.* 1300, it comprised four medium-sized clusters, later known as Church End, Middle End, Limes End and Barretts End. There is no evidence to suggest medieval usage of the term 'end', but it is clear that conditions in the Middle Ages encouraged an alternative model of settlement very different from the surrounding nucleations. Of these conditions, high population, divided lordship and large numbers of free tenants may have played a significant role. There were three manors at Leckhampstead in 1086, with a combined population in excess of thirty households. This number more than doubled, to seventy-six, by the time of the Hundred Rolls inquiry in 1279, which included numerous freeholders with their own (unnumbered) subtenants. The largest of the Domesday manors became known as Great Leckhampstead and was held by Hugh de Chastilun in 1279. The two smaller Domesday manors were united in the possession of William de Leaume and were called Little Leckhampstead. This complex tenurial pattern and large population provides a plausible context for the growth of a number of separate settlement and manorial sites. Elsewhere in the midlands, rival property interests in a single parish could encourage the development of several settlement foci, each associated with the manor house of a different lord.[25]

Church End was the largest of the four settlement clusters and should probably be associated with the manor of Great Leckhampstead. In the fourteenth century it comprised a large manorial complex with church, watermill and an orderly arrangement of peasant tofts and crofts on either side of the only street. The mill was located at the western end of this linear settlement, with the manor set back off the road behind the church. The area around the church appears to have

FIGURE 61.
Schematic plan of settlement development at Leckhampstead based on results from fieldwalking and test-pitting.

been the first to be settled. Possibly as early as the late ninth but more probably during the tenth century, settlement was extended eastwards along the north side of the road (Figure 32). These tofts appear to have remained in use throughout the Middle Ages, with others being

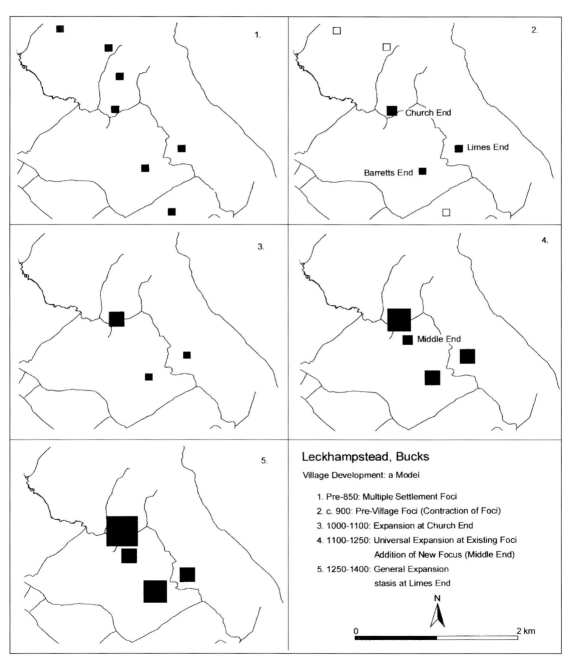

Leckhampstead, Bucks

Village Development: a Model

1. Pre-850: Multiple Settlement Foci
2. c. 900: Pre-Village Foci (Contraction of Foci)
3. 1000-1100: Expansion at Church End
4. 1100-1250: Universal Expansion at Existing Foci
   Addition of New Focus (Middle End)
5. 1250-1400: General Expansion
   stasis at Limes End

N

0   2 km

added to the settlement's eastern end over the following two centuries. The manor of Little Leckhampstead was located 800 m (875 yards) to the south-east, around which another small clustered settlement grew (Figure 61). The site of the manor house almost certainly stood on the natural prominence overlooking the river Leck, now occupied by Weatherhead Farm. Immediately to the north-west fishponds locate the manorial complex. To its south and east, occupation zones are attested by surviving earthworks and large quantities of ceramic finds from fieldwalking. These zones took a coaxial form, based around the junction of two roads. The eastern arm fronted on to the northern side of a holloway leading to the county boundary and the village of Wicken. This row was established well before 1200, and while the detailed layout of plot boundaries has not been recovered, it seems likely that it was originally arranged as a regular line of attached tenements. To the south, the arrangement of buildings and properties seems less regular, squeezed between arable fields and the road leading to the bridge at Thornton.[26]

The remaining clusters at Barretts End and Middle End took the form of linear settlements. Aerial photographs show the survival of house platforms and crofts on both sides of a single street close to Barretts End Cottages.[27] These are coincident with dense medieval pottery scatters dating to the early twelfth century, with tentative evidence for less extensive occupation at an earlier date. At the eastern end of the row, other earthworks to the north of the road point to further occupation. A circular platform 30 m (99 feet) in diameter might be the remains of a windmill mound or an animal pound, while the suggestion of a ditch running into the north-western corner of a depression might have functioned as a leat feeding a valley-side fishpond. If so, this might locate a third manorial site in Leckhampstead. In Middle End, by contrast, there are no signs of a single property of status. Rather, the settlement comprised a regular row of peasant tenements to the south of the road, with further occupation in its western half on the north side. While the overall pattern of settlement at Leckhampstead is very different from that elsewhere, the clusters from which it was constituted shared many morphological traits in common with neighbouring nucleations. In particular, development at each appears to have been closely regulated, perhaps from the outset at Middle End, elsewhere as a result of the reorganisation of earlier, more irregular, pre-village nuclei.

A similar situation existed at Silverstone. When first mapped, Silverstone comprised three separate settlement foci. Archaeological investigation has proved that this settlement model was, like that of Leckhampstead, of long standing. Silverstone appears to have begun

1.

2.

West End

Silverstone Village

Cattle End

3.

Silverstone, Northants

Village Expansion plotted on c.1608 Forest Map

1. Settlement Foci 1000-1100

2. Settlement Expansion 1100-1250

3. Settlement Expansion 1250-1400

Original ?Green or Arable Oval

N

0   0.5   1 km

FIGURE 62.
Schematic plan of
settlement development at
Silverstone based on results
from test-pitting.

as a loose federation of individual farmsteads set around a small oval
of arable land, later known as Woodcrafts Field. Before 1200 settlement extended along High Street and also spread to other areas in the
centre of the village (Figure 62). West End, too, appears to have developed at this time. Here a double row of regular plots was laid out after
1100. Many of the preserved plot boundaries of the eastern row within
the original central oval take a sinuous line, presumably dictated by
arable strips on to which they encroached. Of all the elements of
Silverstone, the origins of Cattle End have been the most difficult to
trace. A settlement may have developed there in the latter part of the

twelfth century, but a date after 1200 is more likely. Unlike West End and the southern parts of the village proper, Cattle End seems to have its origins not in expansion over arable land but in the clearance of woodland. This was an assart settlement. Critical to this hypothesis has been a reconsideration of the Forest Map (Figures 6, 42, 45 and 53). Two important aspects of the map set Cattle End apart from the rest of the village. First, the roads to the south of West End, together with the southern part of High Street, are much wider than their northern extensions, and are very similar to the broad woodland ridings depicted elsewhere on the map. It is probable, therefore, that they were formed in a wooded landscape. Assart names to the south also point to the presence of woodland in the later Middle Ages. By contrast, the northern parts of West End and High Street are much less wide and it is noticeable that both narrow markedly as they enter the central oval. Green Lane, too, is narrow and appears to bear the hallmarks of a road running through interlocking arable furlongs. Thus both Green Lane and West End may originally have followed the headlands of furlongs within an open arable field. Secondly, Cattle End and the area to the south of West End are dominated by small enclosures. These probably represent the piecemeal clearances from woodland, often of an acre or less, which were ditched or fenced and farmed in severalty, and recorded by the king's forest officials in the thirteenth century.[28]

A factor of considerable importance in the village's development was undoubtedly the establishment of a royal hunting lodge in the twelfth century. The lodge was maintained by successive kings, especially Henry III (1216–72), who undertook a major campaign of new building in the years 1247–50, including a new chapel, a new wardrobe for the queen and a new saucery next to the kitchen. Intermittent repairs were undertaken by Edward I (1272–1307), but in 1313 the buildings were considered to be ruinous and the manor was alienated by the king.[29] The location of the hunting lodge has been difficult to pinpoint. The current church may be a successor to the royal chapel, and the earthworks in the churchyard may be the platforms of buildings associated with the house (Figure 63). Pottery made in West End dated c. 1180–1250, thus contemporary with the active life of the lodge, has been found in quantities in this area. Furthermore, the Forest Map reveals an enclosure called 'Hall Yard' in this position. Together with the location of fishponds immediately to the north, this evidence may be sufficient to conclude that the central zone of the village was occupied by the king's house (see above, pages 117–18).

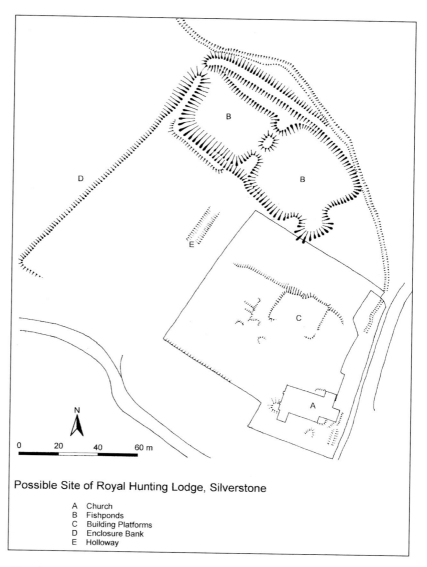

FIGURE 63.
Earthworks at Silverstone.
The building platforms
behind the church may
mark the site of the
medieval hunting lodge.

Possible Site of Royal Hunting Lodge, Silverstone

A   Church
B   Fishponds
C   Building Platforms
D   Enclosure Bank
E   Holloway

Hamlets

The existence of hamlets in the late medieval landscape of Whittlewood is rarely apparent from the surviving historical documents. Only Dagnall is mentioned by name in 1319.[30] Consequently we are almost wholly reliant upon later cartographic evidence and archaeological fieldwork for their identification. Four can be positively dated to the later Middle Ages: Knotwood in Furtho, Dagnall in Wick Dive, Elm Green in Wick Hamon and Nether End in Whittlebury. The evidence for Chapel Green in Lillingstone Dayrell is less certain. Shown as a small cluster of houses around the chapel dedicated to Thomas Becket on an estate map of 1611, little is known about the origins of this small isolated settlement on the parish and county boundary.[31] Other hamlets may have been abandoned at an early date. For example, the settlement associated with the Domesday manor of Wakefield was probably deserted in the twelfth century, to make way for the royal hunting lodge and lawn (see below, pages 211–12).

Those hamlets that we can identify range in size, but all are characterised by uncomplicated morphologies. Knotwood is the simplest. Now destroyed by the plough, aerial photographs reveal a short row of four embanked crofts lying to the south-west of a small holloway.[32] Concentrations of twelfth- to fourteenth-century pottery associated exclusively with these earthworks, and ridge and furrow surrounding them, suggests that this was not part of a larger settlement. The regularity of the row implies a degree of planning. Differences in the size of plot – some have frontages approximately 20 m (66 feet) wide (four perches of 16.5 feet) while others are double this width – might indicate that the community comprised peasants of different status. There is nothing to suggest, however, that this settlement attained any degree of autonomy from Furtho village, with which it must have shared fields and other resources as well as its church.

By contrast, the hamlet of Dagnall farmed its own field system separately from Wick Dive.[33] Nevertheless, its absence from national taxation records, and the lack of a church or chapel, points to its dependence upon the parochial village. The hamlet was laid out in regular fashion on the south side of a single street. Highly degraded earthworks, limestone spreads (the ploughed-out remains of foundations) and concentrations of pottery dateable to 1100–1400 mark the location of tofts set on the street frontage and their crofts, which run back 50–60 m (165–195 feet) to the south. This row extended over a distance of some 200 m (655 feet) and may have accommodated five or six individual plots. At the eastern end of the row was a much larger complex, comprising a subdivided rectangular enclosure containing prominent earthworks (Figure 64). Finds of tenth-century pottery indicate that this was the initial focus of occupation, while the size and nature of the enclosure is suggestive of elevated status. This was the scene of intense activity in the late medieval period, and was presumably the antecedent to the farm which now occupies this position. There was clearly social differentiation within the community at Dagnall, as well as sufficient population early on to carve out and subsequently to maintain its own common fields.

Nether End, 800 m (875 yards) north-west of Whittlebury, for which there is no dating evidence except that it was abandoned by *c.* 1608 when depicted on the Forest Map as a set of vacant closes,

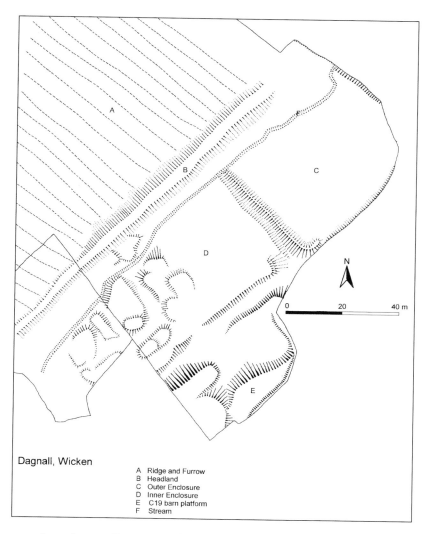

FIGURE 64.
Earthworks at Dagnall.

Dagnall, Wicken

A Ridge and Furrow
B Headland
C Outer Enclosure
D Inner Enclosure
E C19 barn platform
F Stream

may have been of an equivalent or slightly larger size than Dagnall (Figure 45). The principal axis was once again a single street, surviving as a holloway north of Doves Farm. Ploughed-out limestone spreads to the east of this street, and embanked crofts to the west, suggest that both sides of the street were formerly occupied. The settlement appears more dispersed and less regular than that at either Dagnall or Knotwood, although this impression may be misleading. That hamlets might develop in a less planned way is confirmed by the results of an intensive survey at Elm Green in Wick Hamon. This site is defined by dense concentrations of medieval pottery disturbed by modern ploughing, associated with subtle earthworks and limestone scatters (Figure 65). These range over three fields which surround

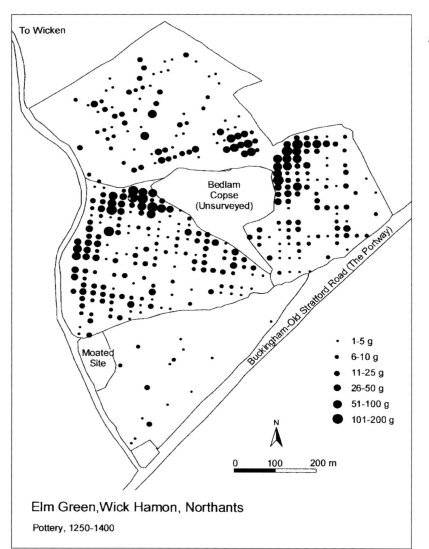

To Wicken

Bedlam
Copse
(Unsurveyed)

Moated
Site

Buckingham-Old Stratford Road (The Portway)

. 1-5 g
• 6-10 g
● 11-25 g
● 26-50 g
● 51-100 g
● 101-200 g

N

0   100   200 m

Elm Green, Wick Hamon, Northants

Pottery, 1250-1400

FIGURE 65.
The dispersed hamlet
of Elm Green, Wicken,
as revealed by pottery
recovered by fieldwalking.

a small wood called Bedlam copse, within which further medieval pottery has been observed in rabbit holes, and which almost certainly covers part of the earlier settlement. The settlement might be loosely defined as coaxial in plan, with houses located on the road which now runs south from Wicken and along a now-lost track which forks from this road to the south-east. Settlement formerly extended over a distance of 400 m (440 yards) along both sides of this track, although the intermittence of the pottery scatters suggests that the hamlet comprised, rather than a sequence of closely spaced crofts, individual plots lacking direct neighbours, in a form commonly labelled an 'interrupted row'. Associated with this hamlet was a rectangular moated site immediately to the south, which lay on the opposite side of a small stream, set slightly apart from the rest of the hamlet.[34] The absence of occupational evidence immediately north of the stream amplifies the impression that space was reserved around this site. The whole settlement covered an area of some 20 ha (50 acres), but even at its height, between 1250 and 1350, it would have contained fewer than a dozen households.

In assessing late medieval hamlet morphology in Whittlewood we must recognize that our sample size is small. Nevertheless, important trends can be detected. First, hamlets might adopt or develop both nucleated and dispersed forms. This may be a product of their creation – more regular forms originating in planned development, more dispersed forms from piecemeal growth – but this cannot be proven. Secondly, differences in hamlet morphology cannot be associated with the timing of their development: both nucleated and dispersed hamlets formed contemporaneously. Thirdly, hamlet plans in no way reflect the form of the parochial village; thus within the territory of a nucleated village such as Wick Hamon, a dispersed hamlet at Elm Green might develop. Similar differences in plan have been observed elsewhere, as, for example, at Anstey in Leicestershire.[35] It would thus appear that decisions made by the promoters of hamlets were made either with little reference to neighbouring settlements, or as the positive choice of an alternative form of communal living space. Fourthly, morphology does not appear to be dependent on size. Certainly, hamlet morphologies are less complicated than those of villages but, large or small, hamlets might adopt regular or irregular plans. Lastly, the most influential factor in the plan of any hamlet appears to have been its social structure. In hamlets where the inhabitants were of the same or similar status, regular planned settlements appear to have been the norm. But where there was social differentiation, and the presence within the community of at least one family of status, the plan appears to have developed with reference to the principal homestead. At both Dagnall and Elm Green, the high-status farmstead and moated site were set slightly apart from the main focus of settlement, probably because restrictions were placed on where other settlements were permitted. Hamlets were thus characterised by a variety of forms; however, the opposite was the case for late medieval farmsteads.

Farmsteads

The largest farmsteads of late medieval Whittlewood were the manor houses and their associated buildings and enclosures. Most lay within or next to the village and formed integral parts of these larger settlements. Often the plots that these farmsteads occupied have been obscured by later development, permitting little to be said about their size, shape and form (see below). Beyond the village, farmstead survival is better, although the sample size is small. The plans of three complete farmstead complexes can be reconstructed from the evidence of aerial photographs and upstanding earthworks. These are the monastic grange of Luffield Priory called Monksbarn, situated in the north-eastern corner of Whittlebury parish; the sub-manor of Heybarne in the detached portion of Lillingstone Dayrell parish; and the home farm at Dagnall, located to the south of Wick Dive. All are remarkably similar in layout. Their basic plan was a rectangular enclosure defined by a shallow man-made ditch on three sides, although their dimensions differ: Monksbarn measured 150 × 90 m (485 × 290 feet), Dagnall 220 × 80 m (710 × 264 feet), and Heybarne 100 × 90 m (330 × 290 feet).[36] In each case the fourth side follows a natural watercourse. At Heybarne there is evidence that water was diverted from the stream using a system of sluices and culverts and fed around the enclosure ditches, and this may have also occurred at the other two sites. At both Monksbarn and Heybarne reservoirs or fishponds were constructed on the stream course, further defining their potentially open side. No such evidence survives, if such a structure ever existed, at Dagnall.

The internal arrangement of the farmsteads was also alike. Each of the large ditched enclosures was divided by a small bank into two halves, of roughly equal proportions at Monksbarn and Dagnall, and more unequally at Heybarne (Figure 66). These areas appear to have been used very differently. Evidence for buildings, revealed by earthwork platforms and geophysical plots of wall foundations, were always restricted to one half, the other half apparently remaining open and free of standing structures. Something of the nature of these buildings can be gained from a description of Monksbarn in 1376, which suggests that at least two large buildings stood within the complex, both set on a north–south axis. They were probably in existence in 1351 when Adam de Cortenhale was said not to be liable to maintain the greater and lesser buildings, and may possibly have served as chambers or barns.[37] Excavation at Heybarne revealed that the surfaces between the building platforms were cobbled. The open halves, by contrast, appear to have been reserved as paddocks or yards, presumably for the corralling of livestock.

The similarity in layout of Monksbarn, Heybarne and Dagnall is striking and can be accounted for in a number of ways. Firstly, the sites were equivalent in status; while they might variously be held in lay or ecclesiastical hands, they were the home farms of the

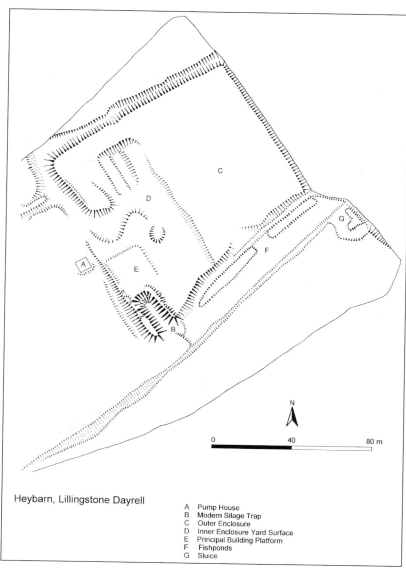

Heybarn, Lillingstone Dayrell

A Pump House
B Modern Silage Trap
C Outer Enclosure
D Inner Enclosure Yard Surface
E Principal Building Platform
F Fishponds
G Sluice

FIGURE 66.
Earthworks at Heybarne.

most affluent and socially elevated members of the local community, serving estates measured in hundreds rather than tens of acres.
Secondly, the economies of these estates were similar, combining both
arable and livestock farming, as discussed in the previous chapter (see
above, pages 134–43). Consequently, the demesne farms required the
same types of buildings: barns to store grain and hay; stockyards
and byres to accommodate livestock; and ancillary buildings where
produce could be processed. Thirdly, they were all of the same period,
having been built during the late twelfth and thirteenth centuries,

and thus were constructed under similar social and economic conditions. Fourthly, they may have been laid out according to some sort of idealised plan fashionable at the time of their construction. Perhaps monastic granges provided the model, or both monks and secular lords followed a similar path.[38] Farmstead morphology may thus reflect the aspirations of their architects as well as providing practical solutions to the requirements of mixed farming.

Village and hamlet components

Manor houses and their complexes

Unlike churches, the sites of early manorial enclosures in Whittlewood were prone to move. Passenham is a good example. In the twelfth century, the manor house appears to have been situated at the east end of the village, on the north side of the main street, close to the river Great Ouse. A rectangular moated site, excavated in 1967, revealed substantial foundations for stone walls, together with pottery dating from the twelfth and thirteenth centuries.[39] This house may have been abandoned in the early fourteenth century, when Passenham seems not to have had a resident lord.[40] A manor house (location unknown) was in existence in 1402 when the king granted to John Cok of Passenham 'the houses of the site of our said manor ... with

FIGURE 67
(*below and opposite*).
Schematic plan of settlement development in Wick Hamon and Wick Dive based on results from test-pitting, earthwork survey, geophysical survey and excavation.

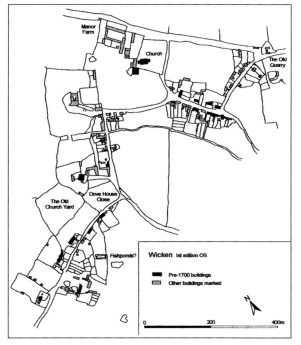

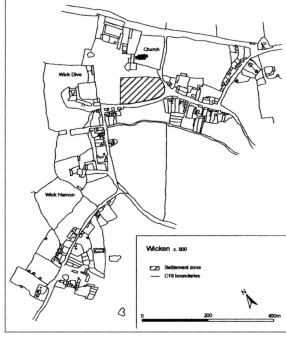

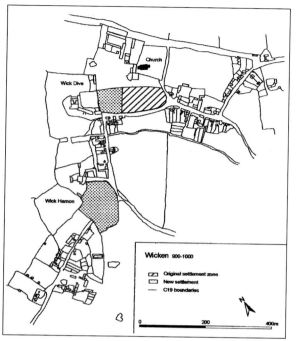

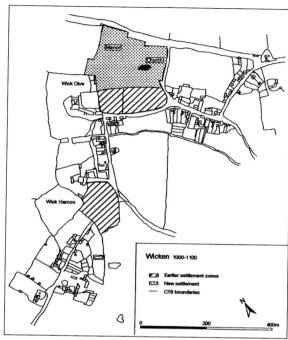

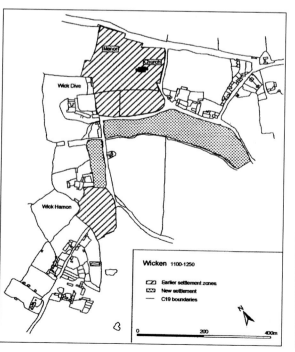

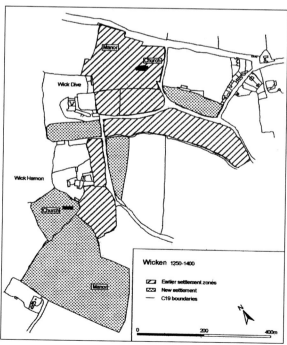

the gardens of the said site together with the demesnes'. This may
have included the 'great chamber at the south end of the hall', which
was repaired in 1383–84. In 1566 the manor house lay to the west
of the church, on the south side of the street – its present location
– although the earliest part of the surviving building dates from the
seventeenth century. This is likely to have been the work of Sir Robert
Banastre, who purchased the manor of Passenham in 1624, and who
seems to have rebuilt the existing structure.[41]

The location of manorial complexes is often based on late evidence,
such as the 1611 map of Lillingstone Dayrell, which depicts the
manor immediately to the south of the church, a plausible location
for an early manorial site, but not one proven beyond doubt by
the pottery gathered from fieldwalking (Figure 78).[42] The surviving
tradition of a manor house in Church End, Leckhampstead, again
immediately to the south of the church, finds support in nearby

earthwork evidence, but it remains unclear when this complex was first established. Manor Farm, Akeley, is today the grandest house in the village. Preserving evidence of a late fifteenth- or early sixteenth-century timber-framed building of some size and quality, this was almost certainly the late medieval manor house.[43] Test-pitting in its vicinity, however, revealed little evidence for earlier occupation. Similarly, at Wick Dive, the identification and dating of a dovecote close to the site of Manor Farm, as illustrated on the tithe map, conclusively places the thirteenth-century manor north-west of the church, but no earlier evidence has been found.

The relocation of a manor site might cause major disruption to the villagescape. The insertion of a manorial complex into the heart of Lillingstone Lovell has already been described. In similar fashion, the capital messuage of Wick Hamon, dating to the 1240s, seems to have been built on a site formerly occupied by tofts of low status which were cleared to make way for the manor (Figure 67). The disruption was often compounded by the sheer size of the late medieval manorial complex. As well as the lordly residence, the manorial complex was also the administrative and economic centre of the estate, comprising farm buildings for the storage of crops and keeping of livestock and birds, and mills, malthouses, brewhouses and bakehouses for the processing of produce. Some of these seigneurial assets are specifically detailed in extents, such as the capital messuage, old hall, two old dovecotes and garden, together with barn, byres and adjoining croft, recorded at Potterspury in 1301.[44] Later extents also mention a water-mill, windmill and fishpond.[45] In the case of Potterspury, the precise location of these structures is not known. But elsewhere, archaeo-logical investigation may reveal the sites of a number of manorial buildings.

In 1280 the manor of Great Leckhampstead was described as a courtyard with enclosure.[46] A prominent bank, defining an area south of the church and encompassing the property known today as Manor House, may mark its extent (Figure 68).[47] The other recorded lordly appurtenances of the manor were fishponds, a three-tiered series of which lies within the proposed embankment, a dovecote, for which no evidence is known, and a watermill. If set on the river Leck rather than the Great Ouse, then a rectangular pond which survives as an earthwork immediately upstream of the manor probably marks the mill's location. Similarly, at Lillingstone Lovell, well-preserved earth-works south of the church include a series of five stepped fishponds, fed from a spring close to the church, as well as other buildings already described (Figure 69) (see above, pages 162–3). It is likely, however, that the windmill to which fourteenth-century documents

FIGURE 68.
Church End,
Leckhampstead.
NATIONAL MONUMENTS
RECORD, SP 7237/5

refer was set apart from this low-lying complex, on higher ground north-west of the church.[48] Windmills are also recorded at Stowe and Passenham, the site of the latter depicted on the Forest Map standing isolated to the north of both village and manor.[49] Inquisitions *post mortem* of the manors of Wick Hamon and Wick Dive record dovecotes, both of which have been found through excavation.[50] At Wick Hamon the dovecote stood between a small fishpond to the south-west and a bakehouse/brewhouse to the north-east, neither of which appear in the written sources (Figure 70). Fishponds in Limes End, Leckhampstead, and south of Hall Farm, Lillingstone Lovell, almost certainly mark the location of other manors.[51]

Taken together, the archaeological and documentary evidence offers a reasonable impression of the late medieval manors of Whittlewood. They might constitute a significant part of the villagescape – in the cases of Leckhampstead, Lillingstone Lovell and Wick Dive, perhaps as much as a third of the total area covered by the settlement of which they were so integral. They appear to have been carefully laid out and their precincts carefully zoned, cordoning off areas for domestic, agricultural and industrial activities. Attention, too, seems to have been given to their aesthetic appearance: the manor house was framed by gardens, perhaps incorporating fishponds in their design or channelling water into surrounding moats, and sight-lines both into and out of the manorial

Lillingstone Lovell, Oxon

Manorial Complex (GPS survey)

N

0   50   100

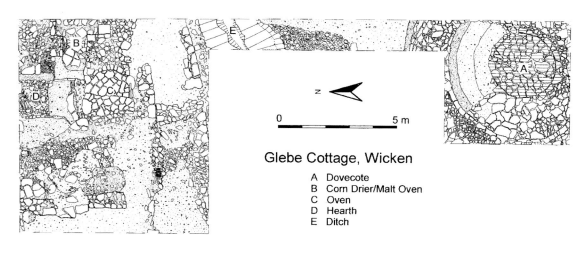

Glebe Cottage, Wicken

A Dovecote
B Corn Drier/Malt Oven
C Oven
D Hearth
E Ditch

0   5 m

enclosure were carefully constructed. The most prominent landmark beyond the confines of the curia was usually the church.

Churches

Of the twelve Whittlewood parish churches, most contain some medieval fabric. Of those that do not, two have been entirely rebuilt in the last 300 years, removing all trace of their earlier form, and two more have been demolished: the church of St James in Wick Hamon in 1619, and the similarly dedicated church at Akeley in 1981.[52] Most were altered in one way or another during the Middle Ages, and many were subject to Victorian restoration. Consequently the reconstruction of their earliest plans relies on the identification of decorative details or architectural anomalies. Nowhere is there clear evidence that the stone churches we see today replaced earlier timber structures, and no excavations have taken place. But as the oldest surviving buildings of our villages and the structures least prone to movement, they offer potentially important insights into our settlements and their development.

The study of the church at Wharram Percy demonstrated the link between the development of the building and the social, demographic and economic fortunes of the village that it served.[53] We might expect that population rise would lead to the enlargement of churches during the medieval period,[54] while churches can equally be read as indicators of 'patronage, piety and wealth'.[55] More recently, an appreciation for the primary function of churches as liturgical spaces has led to a new evaluation of their plans.[56] Changes to the way mass was celebrated or how the dead were venerated are now seen to be significant influences in the design and redesign of the church. Whittlewood may offer up some possible examples of this. For instance, the chancel at Lillingstone Dayrell may have been lengthened 'to accommodate increasing eucharistic ritual ... and to provide burial space for the lords of the manor in the high-status part of the building; the tower was probably added to accommodate the bells which became increasingly important during the thirteenth century; [and the] aisles were added to house side altars and other devotional foci for the ordinary parishioners, reflecting the increased requirements for them as the consequences of belief in purgatory were felt'.[57] These observations thus demand that pragmatic and secular explanations of church development are applied judiciously, since alternative interpretation of the evidence might often be made.

While the churches of Furtho, Lillingstone Dayrell and Stowe now lie in semi–isolation, and the church of Whittlebury stands outside the modern village core, all the Whittlewood churches were once

FIGURE 69.
Global plotting system survey of the manorial earthworks at Lillingstone Lovell, showing fishponds and building platforms.
CONOR GRAHAM

FIGURE 70.
Excavation of the manorial site at Wick Hamon, showing a dovecote to the right and ovens and hearths to the left.
BEN PEARS

integral to their medieval village plans. This is an important contrast to other parts of the country, notably East Anglia, where settlement shift has meant the isolation of many churches.[58] Our villages exhibit more stability, the apparent divorcing of church from village an outcome of late medieval settlement shrinkage or post-medieval settlement desertion. Several interrelated issues stem from this observation. By what stages did this integration occur? Were churches primary or secondary structures in the villagescape? Did the existence of a church encourage the development of the village around it? Were churches built at existing settlement centres which became the foci of later village growth? Or were they inserted into larger settlement cores?

Domesday Book records only one priest in the Whittlewood study area, at Potterspury.[59] The midland section of this source, however, is known to grossly under-record clergy and hence churches in existence by 1086. Surviving fabric and nave dimensions, on the other hand, indicate that many of the Whittlewood churches had been established by 1100 and all by *c.* 1200.[60] Of the pre-1100 churches, Lillingstone Dayrell and Furtho have nave lengths slightly less than twice their width, atypical proportions after the late eleventh century and thus suggestive of origins in the pre-Conquest period, although perhaps not much earlier than 1050. At Potterspury, the unimpressive early stone church, with its nave twice as long as its width, conformed to late eleventh-century archetypes. The eastern half of the nave at Leckhampstead can be dated to before 1160, its proportions consistent with a late eleventh- or twelfth-century construction, and Stowe and Akeley churches can be dated on the same criteria to the same period. Before 1173 it was decided that the church of Akeley was a daughter of Leckhampstead, and that it ought to pay 2*s* a year as a sign of this dependence. The church at Akeley was described in the agreement as a chapel, that at Leckhampstead as the mother church.[61] Only at Passenham, where the nave appears to have been widened, itself an unusual development, does the architecture of the church hint at the replacement of an earlier timber building with stone, and thus an early foundation date. No hard evidence can be offered to substantiate this claim, but some additional support might be found in the church's dedication to the eighth-century Mercian royal prince Guthlac, whose cult was popular in the tenth and eleventh centuries.[62] At Whittlebury, nothing in the fabric indicates a date earlier than the mid twelfth century, but the discovery of securely dated burials in the northern churchyard associated with eleventh-century pottery warns us that there was probably a church on this site by 1100, for which there is no surviving evidence.

All these churches were small, of the size expected to serve a single parish. Given the apparent association that some of the churches have with manorial sites, as at Furtho, Leckhampstead, Lillingstone Dayrell and Passenham, we might assume that these began life as lordly foundations. The exception is Lillingstone Lovell. The thinness and height of the nave indicate a late pre-Conquest construction date. On the north side, there appears to have been a side chapel or porticus-like structure with a narrow entrance from the nave. This suggests a building disproportional to a manorial chapel or parish church. It would seem that this church may have been designed to serve a larger area and thus have its origins in the pre-parochial estate structure. Later documents do not identify any ecclesiastical dependencies which might help in the reconstruction of its possible *parochia*, but it was likely to have been the ecclesiastical centre of the earlier ten-hide Lillingstone estate, which had been divided by 1066. If so, then this provides another context for the construction of Lillingstone Dayrell church, founded in the wake of the fragmentation of this larger polity, and after which Lovell church functioned simply as its neighbouring parish church.

On the balance of the available evidence, and with the warning provided by Passenham and Whittlebury that earlier churches may have totally disappeared from view, it would appear that the majority of those churches for which we can gain some idea of date were founded at existing settlement foci. Our churches are secondary elements in the villagescape. There is every indication, however, that it did not take long before a church was built at these emerging centres. Little time may have elapsed between initial nucleation and the building of the church. At Lillingstone Dayrell, for example, the village appears to have been taking shape by 1000. Perhaps less than 50 years later, the existing church was constructed. This, it would seem, was located just outside the eastern fringes of the settled zone and perhaps hard up against the northern side of the manorial enclosure. At Akeley, the location of the church suggests that it followed, or was contemporary with, the short shift north in settlement position, as it was not left stranded to the south at the original settlement focus. The prominent hilltop position that it occupied may even have been reserved for the church from the outset.

Similar freedom to choose the site of the church is evident at Whittlebury, where it was placed at the centre of the Iron Age hillfort.[63] The growth of the village outside this earthwork would appear to suggest that before the eleventh century settlement either consciously avoided this space or more probably that occupation within it was prohibited. Once the church had been constructed, however, other buildings soon colonised the interior of the enclosure. The permanent settlement of this landmark after 1000, we might tentatively suggest, must have followed a major change in the status, function or tenure that it had previously enjoyed. If we are right in assuming that the hillfort was used as the location of the *witan* of AD 930, are we witnessing the end of royal interest in the site at this period? Continued royal tenure of Greens Norton, on which Whittlebury remained ecclesiastically dependent, might offer further support for this idea: the king released one small part of his estate for the foundation of a daughter church.

The only possible exception to this chronology – village foundation followed rapidly by church building – might be Lillingstone Lovell. Evidence for the occupation of what would later become the village is extremely limited before the second half of the eleventh century and cannot be pushed back any earlier than AD 975 on the grounds of the pottery fragments that have been recovered. These were found in proximity to the church, offering the possibility that there was an already existing small nucleus to which the church was attached. But it might also have been the case that the church was built on an unoccupied site, and that this in turn became the focus of later settlement after estate fragmentation and the loss of its initial super-parochial functions.

If the majority of Whittlewood churches began as simple structures, most were enlarged during the course of the Middle Ages. The phases of rebuilding appear to accord well with demographic trends, lending support to the idea that expansion of their internal space was linked with a growth in members of the laity. These enlarged communities may also have had greater surplus wealth to spend on church building. The nave at Leckhampstead was substantially lengthened in the late twelfth century, and there is more equivocal evidence for similar extensions in the thirteenth century at Akeley and Passenham. The addition of aisles also increased the body of the church; Potterspury's north aisle was built in the late twelfth century and its south aisle during the thirteenth. Two new aisles were also added at Whittlebury *c.* 1200, and at Lillingstone Dayrell during the early or middle part of the thirteenth century. These might subsequently be widened, for which there is evidence in the north aisle at Leckhampstead, and at Whittlebury, dating to the first half of the fourteenth century. Such causal links between the size of community and the scale of building must be used with caution: aisles also provided additional space for devotional foci and altars, and might have been built specifically for this purpose rather than for the provision of further standing room for the congregation. Where the evidence is available, however, it does seem that the size of the Whittlewood churches was largely commensurate with known medieval population levels. One possible exception is Whittlebury, where the twelfth-century church appears to have been larger than was required. Whittlebury, however, also served the neighbouring community at Silverstone, retaining burial rights into post-medieval times, offering an explanation for its capacious internal dimensions.[64]

Peasant tofts and crofts

The villagescape is most clearly defined by the houses of its inhabitants. They must be present in sufficient numbers to differentiate between villages and hamlets; how they were set out denotes whether the settlement can be considered nucleated or dispersed, regular or irregular, planned or unplanned. Most holdings comprised a toft or homestead, set within a larger plot, or croft.[65] In clayland areas, the boundaries of these tenements were generally marked by ditches, which have left little trace on the ground, although under certain conditions they can show as soil or crop marks; or they were embanked, elements of which might survive as earthworks. The size and shape of individual plots might vary considerably, affected by topography, existing features in the landscape and, most importantly, by the status of their inhabitants. In regular villages, measurement of plot frontages apparently reveals that tenants, such as bordars or villeins, were provided with properties of equal size according to rank.[66] Regardless of the status of their occupiers, plots tended to be laid out, if unobstructed, with narrow street frontages, the croft extending back often over a considerable distance. In places the crofts terminated at a back lane, offering alternative access into these properties or out to the surrounding fields.

The best evidence for the detailed arrangement of tofts and crofts in Whittlewood comes from metrical analysis of tenements shown on early cartographic sources and surviving boundary banks. The basic unit of measurement in medieval England was the rod or perch. While the standard perch of 5 m (16.5 feet) was most commonly used, its length might vary from 4.5 m to 7.5 m (15–25 feet). The longer perch was often associated with forest areas. There are clear indications that more than one perch length was used in Whittlewood. For instance, a grant of 4 acres (1.5 ha) of wood in Akeley in 1228 states that this was measured 'by the king's perch', implying that this differed from the local perch.[67] The length of the Whittlewood perch is not recorded in surviving texts – it may have been 6.5 m (21 feet) mentioned in an agreement of 1309 – but where metrical analysis of the frontages of tenement plots is possible, it is clear that the standard 5 m was normally used.[68] The narrowest tenements in Dadford, which

FIGURE 71.
The medieval (left) and
modern (right) village of
Dadford with ridge and
furrow surviving in the
fields beyond.

NATIONAL MONUMENTS
RECORD, SP 6638/4

can be reconstructed from a map drawn in 1739, appear to measure in the region of 20 m (66 feet), or four perches of 5 m. This is also the unit of measurement which appears to underlie property layout in Leckhampstead, Lillingstone Lovell, Silverstone and elsewhere.

Both Domesday Book and the Hundred Rolls reveal that the inhabitants of Dadford were, with the exception of four free tenants in 1279, all bordars or cottagers.[69] We might expect that cottagers would be allotted plots of equal size commensurate with their social status. If these plots were indeed 20 m wide, then to accommodate

190

FIGURE 73.
Church Cottage,
Leckhampstead.
FRAN HALSALL

locally available timber. Fragmentary survival of cruck frames in properties in Akeley, Leckhampstead and Whittlebury attests to the use of this late medieval building tradition in Whittlewood. Examination of parts of the roof structure at Bridge House, Lillingstone Lovell – albeit a house of some status – suggest that this had been crafted from fast-growing timber, in all probability grown locally specifically for use in building construction.[75] Internally, the buildings might be provided with clay or mortar floors, such as those encountered in test-pits in Whittlebury and Wick Dive, or, where conditions allowed, as in Wick Hamon, the naturally-occurring limestone was utilised.

Areas immediately to the side and to the back of the house were often cobbled.[76] Rough limestone surfaces have been found during test-pitting in all the villages that have been examined, such as that in Church End, Leckhampstead, on the surface of which was a smashed glazed Potterspury jug, and below which was found the skeleton of a dog. Almost all of these surfaces appear to have been laid down in the thirteenth century, sealing earlier material below them, but nowhere is there evidence that they replaced older surfaces. They therefore attest to an investment in, and improvement of, property at this period. For the most part, however, the croft must have been put to horticultural use or left open for the keeping of domestic animals such as pigs or fowl. Within the croft, large build-ups of soil containing quantities of pottery sherds, its dark colour revealing that it was rich in organic matter, point to the regular spreading of domestic material on to these plots and conscious efforts made to improve soil quality in order to achieve maximum return from the kitchen garden. For cottagers, holding no land in the open fields, this must have provided a valuable source of food and occasional income if surplus produce or stock could be sold. For villeins, the croft supplemented their other holdings, although the contribution of the croft to the local economy can only be guessed at.[77] Nor should it be overlooked that crofts also provided space for other activities. Earthworks in Barretts End suggests that the southern crofts of the row were organised into crewyards, for the overwintering of animals.[78] Likewise, the location of medieval pottery kilns in Potterspury indicate that most potting workshops were to be found within crofts, akin to the rival Rockingham Forest industry based at Lyveden and Stanion.[79] A late twelfth-century small pottery manufactory, of which its waster heap of discarded sherds was found in West End, Silverstone, was likewise located at one end of the peasant row, and perhaps within one of its individual tenements.

Standard plot sizes, similar house plans and the ubiquitous uses to which the croft was put identify a highly regulated local society, which in many ways reflected the orderly organisation of individual holdings in the fields. As such, the forest villages of Whittlewood closely resembled contemporary settlements in the surrounding champion regions. Almost all exhibit some signs of planning, not simply restricted to the nucleated villages, but found in the various elements of its dispersed settlements and hamlets. Such organisation, however, arrived relatively late in Whittlewood: certainly, it does not appear to be a pre-Conquest phenomenon. But once embraced, most subsequent development was undertaken in similar fashion. There is little evidence for the piecemeal addition of properties to the village core: rather, extensive areas appear to have been designated for settlement extension, over which several plots of equal size, or of a size appropriate to status, were laid out in a single concerted action. But how did these areas articulate with other parts of the village?

Intra-village relationships: manor, church and peasant tofts

The majority of late medieval villages contained a finite number of elements that together produced the village plan. Amongst these might be included industrial and agricultural buildings, or 'public' open spaces such as greens. But the three that were most commonly present, and came in some degree to define the character of nucleated villagescapes, were the manor house, the church, and peasant tofts and crofts. These might articulate in different ways but detailed exploration of the various spatial relationships that existed between manor house and church, manor house and peasant tofts, and church and peasant tofts, reveals a number of common associations. The regularity with which the same internal arrangements of the villagescape can be found is striking. Repeating patterns seem to betray the careful use, allocation and definition of space within the villagescape. But it is by no means easy to identify either how such village plans developed, or what hidden structures, processes and chronologies they conformed to or were created from.

The pattern which is repeated time and again regionally is the siting of manor house and church close to one another. Within a 16-kilometre (10-mile) radius of Whittlewood, the manor house and church pairing can be seen in over half of all villages, an arrangement which pertains across all the English regions where nucleated settlements predominate. In Whittlewood, this juxtaposition can be identified at Furtho, Lillingstone Dayrell, Passenham, Potterspury, Wick Dive and Church End in Leckhampstead. The same association may have originally existed at Stowe, Whittlebury and Wick Hamon, although in these cases the evidence is equivocal. The proximity of these two buildings must reflect the fundamental link that formerly existed between them. What archaeological evidence we have from Whittlewood indicates that churches were generally built at existing settlement foci and, perhaps with one notable exception, were not themselves the primary structure around which later settlement grew. In places such as Furtho, Lillingstone Dayrell and Wick Hamon, the original village nuclei were likely to have been lordly residences created in the aftermath of the fission of earlier larger estates. Here, churches that would later serve a parish were primarily founded as manorial chapels. Certainly the small and simple ground plans of the churches at Furtho and Lillingstone Dayrell accord with their beginnings as private chapels. In similar fashion, but at a later date, there are good grounds to support the notion that the parish church at Silverstone started life as the chapel serving the royal hunting lodge. Designed to provide ecclesiastical provision to a single household, and financed by it, these chapels were invariably sited close to or even within the curtilage of the capital messuage, giving little regard to the broader pastoral needs of the community. Indeed, in some cases their foundation may have preceded the main growth of settlement. Importantly, then, the grouping of manor house and church reveals the dependence of the ecclesiastic building on the centre of secular power, and their construction during an early but nevertheless secondary phase of settlement development.

In our villages, and again in accordance with trends visible in a broader survey of settlement plans, the built environment can be seen to have been manipulated to maintain or even exaggerate social differentiation. Manor house complexes were usually not surrounded by peasant tofts and crofts, but were located on the periphery of the village core. The original site of the manor house at Passenham, for example, lay just south of the main village. The manorial farmstead at Akeley was located on the south-eastern fringe of the occupied zone. At Lillingstone Dayrell, while the manor was integral to the nucleation, it lay on its extreme eastern edge and looked out upon open countryside. Even within the smaller hamlets, the same positional traits can be seen. At Elm Green in Wick Hamon, the moated site was located outside the main settlement centre, while at Dagnall in Wick Dive, the principal residence was sited off one end of the hamlet's regular row. So both village and hamlet plans reveal regulation underlying their physical development. The peasantry were not free to choose where their tofts and crofts could be established, but were directed to some areas and denied others. By so doing, lords were able to imprint the realities of social order, and their privileged position within it, in the form that they allowed settlement to assume. It might be argued that, far from seeking any articulation between manor house and the village core, lords sought to dissociate themselves and their property from it by reserving space around the capital messuage. This might also explain the location of the more remote moated sites, such as Lords Field Farm, Whittlebury, 800 m (875 yards) north of the village, or the moat on Watling Street, an outlier of Puxley and perhaps the residence of the keeper of the forest.[80]

One of the most common methods deployed by lords whose residence lay within larger settlements, and yet who wished to remain apart, appears to have been to use the church as a screen. At Potterspury, Wick Dive and Church End, Leckhampstead, the manor house was to a large extent hidden from the main settlement by its positioning behind the church. This is a device that can be seen in other villages in the locality, as at Greens Norton, Helmdon, Slapton and Sulgrave, for example.[81] Of course, as the private manorial chapels became parish churches, serving the needs of the wider community as well as their lords, such a spatial arrangement reflected the church's role as a link between manorial curia and village core. But it need not have been planned that way from the outset. Whatever the original intentions of the first architects of the village plan, by the later Middle Ages in both Whittlewood and beyond, many had developed variations on the linear sequence of peripheral manor, church and village core.

Village plans which do not conform to this model are equally informative, and help to distil other factors which may have led to the development of manor, church, core village in some places, and alternative morphologies elsewhere. In Whittlewood, a case in point is Akeley. Here the close spatial relationship between manor and church does not exist. Rather these two critical elements of the villagescape are set in two separate settlement foci: the manorial farmstead on the south-eastern edge of the village, and the church in a northern cluster. Moreover, in the villages that we have already examined, churches tended to be liminal features of the village, perhaps because of their association with the manor which sought to remain semi-divorced from the main centre of population, but in Akeley the church appears to have been surrounded by peasant tofts and crofts. Why should this very different settlement plan have developed at Akeley and not else-where? Perhaps the principal reason was the absenteeism of the lord: after the Conquest Walter Giffard's principal residences lay elsewhere, and later the manor was transferred first to the abbey of Longueville in Normandy, and finally to New College, Oxford. Without a resi-dent lord there was no capital messuage or seigneurial presence to promote the construction of a private chapel in its shadow. We might conjecture that the church, known to have been dependent on the neighbouring church of Leckhampstead, may have been financed and constructed by the local community, hence its position at the heart of the village and away from the demesne farm.

The location of the church at Lillingstone Lovell and its articula-tion with the other components of the village seems to follow that of Akeley. Again the church is set amongst surrounding peasant tofts and crofts at the centre of the village. While a close association with the manor house had been established by the late thirteenth century, this appears to have been the product of the late insertion of a new manorial complex into the village and may not have been the original association. Two possible tentative explanations can be proposed for this arrangement. The first might relate to the nature of lordship. Although lords were resident, the manor of Lillingstone Lovell was already by 1086 split between a number of lords and would remain divided throughout most of the Middle Ages; a neutral position may have been selected away from the individual capital messuages if the church had been sponsored by two or more lords. Secondly, the archi-tecture of Lillingstone Lovell church supports the idea that it did not begin as a simple manorial chapel. Was it in fact positioned to serve a larger territory than its later parish, and thus perhaps without reference to other settlement features? Is this indeed a rare instance when an originally isolated church, lacking any associated settlement, later became the focus of occupation, with the village growing up around the church and manorial interests remaining on its periphery?

The examples of Lillingstone Lovell and Akeley only serve to emphasise that clues to settlement development and the agencies and structures that lay behind it appear to be preserved within the villagescape. In particular, the ways in which the different elements of the village articulate with one another seem to express where power and authority lay within the local community. Strong, resident and undivided lordship would produce one idealised form of settlement. Weak, absentee and divided lordship, on the other hand, could lead to village plans that diverged from the norm. Village form also appears to reflect the chronology of development. Where secular centres of power represent the first phase of settlement establishment, the position of the church and peasant dwellings seems to have been predetermined. Where the church preceded settlement growth, alternative developmental paths might be followed.

CHAPTER NINE

Ends:
Village Decline and Desertion

Population grew and settlement expanded in the twelfth and thirteenth centuries. The countryside of medieval England, and of western Europe, was at its most crowded in the years around 1300. By contrast, the fourteenth and fifteenth centuries witnessed the widespread abandonment of holdings, the contraction of settlement and, in some places, the complete desertion of villages. Deserted medieval villages have attracted the attention of scholars since the 1940s. They provide material evidence for the changes in the countryside after 1350 because the sites of many are still visible as earthwork remains of streets, houses and property boundaries, preserved in pasture fields. Others are marked by pottery scatters.[1] In recent years, attention has also turned to the fate of hamlets and individual farmsteads, and to changes in the landscape, studies which have begun to reveal the true extent of settlement decline and abandonment. In the period 1400–1600, it has been estimated that 20,000 hamlets either contracted to one or two surviving farms, or were entirely deserted. During the same centuries, a million acres of arable were laid to grass and about 10 per cent of common arable land was enclosed by agreement.[2] The desertion of settlements and changes in land use can be found throughout the country, although levels of abandonment and the ways in which the countryside was remodelled varied from region to region. Desertion was most apparent in areas where nucleated villages dominated the rural scene, in particular within the Central Province. It was here, too, that the open fields were replaced by fields enclosed with hedges.[3]

With the failure of so many different settlement types, set in a variety of landscape contexts, individual places have an unsurprisingly diverse history. Some were abandoned by their inhabitants, in search of a better life elsewhere; others were killed off by their lords. Some declined gradually over many decades, while others succumbed more quickly. Despite the prominence given to such settlements, however, they were far from typical. Most villages and hamlets experienced shrinkage to varying degrees in the fourteenth and fifteenth centuries, but they survived and many still exist today. A conclusion reached in France applies equally to England: 'il est bien difficile de tuer un village'.[4] These successful villages are more difficult to investigate archaeologically than those which failed because they continue to be occupied, but their study is of equal, if not greater, importance. If we can understand why settlements survived, even thrived, at a time when neighbouring villages were being abandoned, we can perhaps gain a better understanding of the factors which shaped the pattern of settlement in earlier centuries.

Crisis and innovation

At the beginning of the fourteenth century, the settlement pattern of medieval Whittlewood reached its most developed state. From small beginnings – the pre-village nuclei – large settlements flourished, some having been in existence for 500 years or more. The period 1100–1300 also witnessed the formation of other settlements, including hamlets and farmsteads, which lay away from the principal villages. Contained within our twelve parishes at this time were over forty different population centres of varying size (Figure 55). Settlement was at its most dense in the middle ground, up off the flood plain of the Great Ouse and down from the watershed of the Great Ouse and Tove. In this area villages, hamlets and farmsteads were found at intervals of less than 2.5 sq km (1 square mile). On the higher ground and in the valley bottoms, the density of settlement was considerably less, but even here the average was about one every 7.5 sq km (3 square miles).

The population of medieval England peaked *c.* 1300. Precise calculation is not possible, but here it will be assumed to have been about 5 million.[5] Thereafter, a series of natural disasters conspired to place the population, and ultimately farming regimes and settlement patterns, under great stress. In 1315–17 about half a million people, around 10 per cent of the total population, were killed by the Great Famine, after which crisis population continued to rise in some places, while falling back in others. Outbreaks of murrain and rinderpest, which decimated sheep flocks and cattle herds in 1315–17 and 1319–21, added to the hardship.[6] The impact of the Black Death of 1348–49 was even more devastating. Perhaps half of the English population died, and the onset of endemic plague and other diseases ensured that no sustained population recovery was possible until the sixteenth century. In 1377 the poll tax returns imply that the population had stabilised at about 2.5 million, at which figure it remained with only minor variations until *c.* 1550.[7]

The impact of these events was felt everywhere in England. Population decline led to a shortage of labour and high wages. Arable farming was the first to succumb to the effects of the crisis, in the decades after 1370, when scarce and expensive manpower led to a decline in productivity and output.[8] Moreover, with fewer mouths to feed, grain prices began to fall, leading many farmers to convert their former ploughlands to pasture. With arable husbandry on the wane, both lords and peasants looked to alternative uses for their land. In some places, profits were sought in fish-farming, the rearing of birds, the construction of rabbit warrens, and deer parks. Numbers of cattle and sheep rose with the increase in pasture, while new crops were introduced.[9] Innovations in farming practices were further encouraged by changes in social and tenurial structure. Low profits from cereal crops, growing rent arrears and increased wage bills for hired hands led many lords to lease out their demesnes, which were mostly taken up by peasants. Acquisitive peasants increased their holdings further by acquiring vacant plots in the villages and fields, in a process of engrossment. Society became increasingly polarised as ambitious peasants amalgamated formerly separate holdings into large blocks of land. If those possessing more than 20 ha (50 acres) were rare before the Black Death, one estimate has placed their number at around 50,000 in the middle of the sixteenth century, perhaps one in eight of rural landholders.[10] The engrossment of holdings and the conversion of tillage to pasture threatened the economic base of many village communities, encouraging migration and in some cases leading eventually to desertion.[11]

Although widespread, the extent of these changes varied from region to region. Whittlewood provides a particularly interesting case-study because of the mixed pattern of settlement and landscape. The area offers the opportunity to examine a range of deserted, shrunken and surviving settlements. Open-field farming continued in some places, but some land was enclosed early and arable converted to pasture. The amount of woodland also increased. A combination of archaeological and documentary evidence may be used to illustrate these developments, which are examined in this chapter under two headings: settlement shrinkage, and settlement desertion and landscape change.

Settlement shrinkage

In the Whittlewood area, both archaeological and documentary evidence suggests that at least one settlement began to contract even before the crises of the fourteenth century. At Lamport (in Stowe), the failure to find the ubiquitous Potterspury ware in the large quantities observed elsewhere appears to indicate that at least part of the village was in decay before the end of the thirteenth century. The area around Lamport was experiencing agrarian problems and a decline in grain-growing at the time of the inquests of 1341. The parish of Stowe was particularly badly affected, with three carucates (360 acres or 145 ha) lying unploughed, an indication perhaps of falling population and settlement shrinkage before the onset of plague.[12] It may also be significant that, on the very eve of the Black Death in 1348, one of the lords of Lamport sought unsuccessfully to avoid payment of a rent of 6s 8d for part of his land which he held of Luffield Priory.[13] The surviving earthworks at Lamport reveal that the medieval inhabitants occupied a row of properties regularly spaced along the major north–south valley (Figure 59).[14] Tenements were abandoned on the east side of the main street and at the southern end by c. 1300. Nevertheless, the village at Lamport survived, recorded figures of about sixteen households in the sixteenth century indicating a settlement of comparable size to others in the region.[15] In this case, and others, the evidence supports ideas of long-term reduction in the size of settlements.

After 1350, signs of contraction can be found in all the villages and hamlets that have been investigated. In some cases the retreat was severe. At Lillingstone Dayrell, for example, the amount of post-1400 pottery recovered during fieldwalking suggests that the village had shrunk to about a quarter of its former size. All the tenements along the southern row seem to have been abandoned, the remaining inhabitants clustering around the original nucleus of the settlement, 100 m (330 feet) west of the parish church (see above, pages 61, 159–60). The loss of whole parts of the village plan was uncommon in the Whittlewood area before 1400, but Lillingstone Dayrell was not unique. At Akeley, the northern row along the Leckhampstead road was also abandoned at about this time (Figure 74). More often, the Whittlewood villages suffered only piecemeal contraction, albeit sometimes on a large scale. At Wick Dive, for example, about half of the tenements which produced evidence for occupation between 1250 and 1400 showed no signs of activity in the fifteenth century, leaving those that did flanked by vacant plots. A taxation schedule of 1489 reveals a 26 per cent reduction in Wicken's assessment since 1334, a greater fall than in any of the other villages of the Whittlewood project area.[16] At West End in Silverstone, and along Brookside in Lillingstone Lovell, individual houses were abandoned but the framework of the original rows was preserved.

The manorial complex at Lillingstone Lovell, which was inserted

FIGURE 74.
Schematic plan of settlement contraction at Akeley based on results from test-pitting.

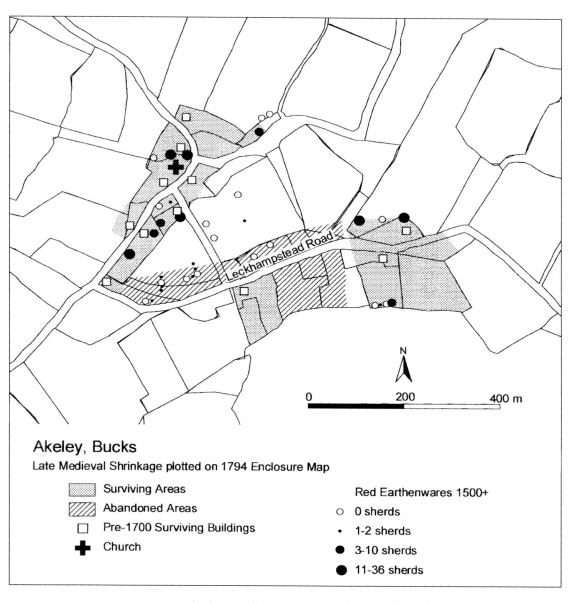

Akeley, Bucks

Late Medieval Shrinkage plotted on 1794 Enclosure Map

	Surviving Areas
	Abandoned Areas
□	Pre-1700 Surviving Buildings
✚	Church

Red Earthenwares 1500+

○	0 sherds
·	1-2 sherds
●	3-10 sherds
●	11-36 sherds

into the heart of the village, south-east of the church, in the thirteenth century, was apparently abandoned soon after 1400 (Figure 75) (see above, pages 160–4).[17] At about the same time, a number of peasant tenements along Church Lane were also deserted; their remains survive as a series of house platforms and closes. Nevertheless, sufficient quantities of fifteenth-century pottery have been found in this area to indicate some continuing occupation. Contraction here was evidently piecemeal in the later Middle Ages. A similar picture emerges from

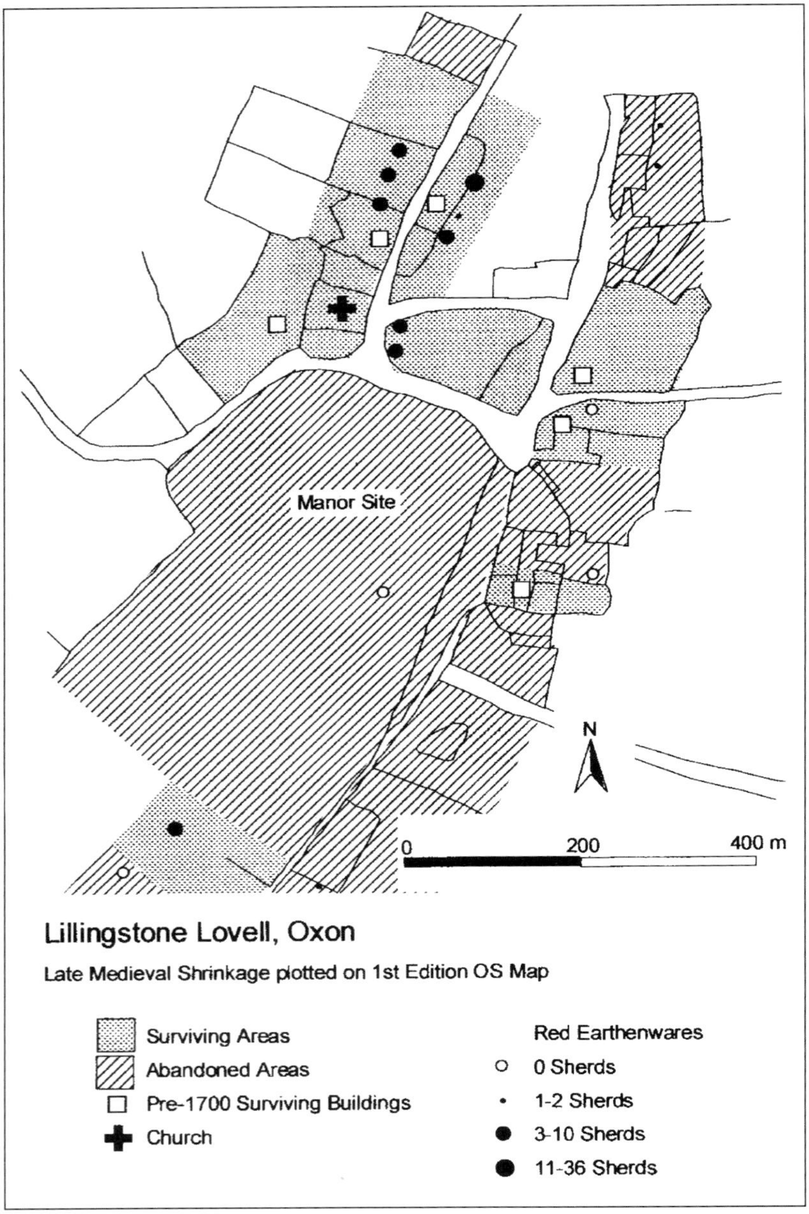

Lillingstone Lovell, Oxon

Late Medieval Shrinkage plotted on 1st Edition OS Map

- Surviving Areas
- Abandoned Areas
- □ Pre-1700 Surviving Buildings
- ✚ Church

Red Earthenwares
- ○ 0 Sherds
- · 1-2 Sherds
- ● 3-10 Sherds
- ⬤ 11-36 Sherds

FIGURE 75.
Schematic plan of
settlement contraction at
Lillingstone Lovell based on
results from test-pitting.

investigation of the properties along Brookside. In the southern part
of the row, the earthworks of croft boundaries are clearly visible under
pasture; ceramic evidence indicates that some, if not most, of these
houses were abandoned in the fifteenth century. Further north along
the stream, in an area still occupied today, some properties were likewise abandoned after 1400, but others survived and the framework of

regular-sized plots making up the row was largely preserved. Evidence of the engrossment of holdings is perhaps limited to the site of Bridge House, a timber-framed open-hall house of four bays built around 1500, and its associated outbuildings. Although not the manor house, the construction and carpentry of the building are of high quality, suggesting an owner of considerable wealth.[18] The house was probably owned by one of five landholders in the village with more than 100 acres (40 ha) of land in 1699.[19]

The contraction at Lillingstone Lovell can also be recognised in the documentary evidence of population decline after the Black Death. The number of households recorded in surveys and tax records for Lillingstone Lovell can be estimated to have been about forty in 1279, more than fifty in 1327, and twenty-five in 1377, so the population probably halved during the fourteenth century, just as it did in England as a whole.[20] The number of inhabitants was unlikely to have recovered during the fifteenth century, to judge from the archaeological evidence of contraction, and may have fallen still further. Thereafter, there may have been growth. A total of eleven surviving houses in the village were built during the sixteenth and seventeenth centuries.[21]

The extent to which settlement shrinkage was the direct result of mortality caused by plague is difficult to determine. The dramatic reduction of population caused by the Black Death of 1348–49 and subsequent outbreaks of plague in 1361, 1369, 1375 and sporadically throughout the later Middle Ages, undoubtedly led to the contraction of settlement in many parts of England. However, most historians would argue that few villages and hamlets – or, indeed, individual streets – were permanently deserted as a direct result of the mortality caused by disease. The pioneering work of Beresford and Hoskins in the 1950s, and many subsequent studies, have played down the role of plague as the sole agent of desertion, instead laying greater stress upon migration.[22] Thus in some parts of England signs of settlement shrinkage are few, and there may even have been growth. These places were not unaffected by plague, but they were able to attract migrants to take the place of the dead.[23] Elsewhere, the movement of people contributed to settlement decline, but migration was not necessarily coincident with, or directly connected to, mortality caused by plague. There may have been social, economic or environmental reasons for the desertion of particular settlements or parts of settlements, which were related to changes in land use, farming and community organisation. Some villages, for example, were replanned in the late fourteenth century.[24] Very few desertions in fourteenth-century England can be demonstrated to have been a direct consequence of the effects of disease; an exception frequently cited, however, is Tusmore in Oxfordshire, about 16 km (10 miles) south-west of Whittlewood.[25]

Evidence of growth in the Whittlewood area in the period 1350–1500 is apparently non-existent, although we might expect that large villages with numerous trades and crafts, such as Potterspury and, possibly, Deanshanger, were able to attract considerable numbers of migrants. Notably, the church at Potterspury was extensively rebuilt in the fifteenth century, enjoying a higher level of investment than all other churches in the Whittlewood area.[26] By contrast, the degree of settlement shrinkage in the study area after 1400 was most extensive in the smaller hamlets and in some of the 'ends' that made up the dispersed villages. For example, the hamlet of Elm Green (in Wick Hamon) was apparently reduced from around a dozen households to just two or three. Dagnall (in Wick Dive) reveals a similar level of contraction, and so too do Cattle End in Silverstone and Barretts End in Leckhampstead.[27] These smaller settlements were scarcely likely to have been more severely affected by plague than their larger neighbours. More likely is the suggestion that plague reduced these places to a perilous level of existence, causing population to fall below what was viable to allow the community to function. Settlements which were small before the Black Death were more likely than those with larger populations to lose a greater proportion of their inhabitants in the general movement of people which characterised the later Middle Ages.[28] Perhaps the surviving residents of the Whittlewood hamlets and 'ends' seized the opportunity to occupy vacant tenements in the nearby villages, thereby exacerbating the decay of the hamlets, and allowing the villages to survive. Alternatively, they may have been pushed out by their wealthier neighbours who wanted to engross their holdings and enclose the land. At Dagnall, for example, two farms were created following the contraction of the settlement, the annual rents of which were worth together about £22 in 1630, and which were sold by the lord of the manor for £1,050 in 1641.[29]

Perhaps the villages which experienced less severe shrinkage were better able to attract inhabitants from other settlements to take up abandoned holdings. At Whittlebury, for instance, the row of peasant houses on the east side of the main street seems to have survived largely intact, with only two vacant plots marked on the Forest Map. Piecemeal abandonment also occurred on the path which now leads to the southern porch of the parish church. Four buildings have been identified from geophysical survey and test-pits, two of which were abandoned before 1400, a third by *c.* 1550, while the fourth survived to be mapped in *c.* 1608 (Figure 45). This evidence suggests that the village's contraction was neither extensive nor rapid. References to tofts – deserted house sites – do occur in the documents and they were consolidated into the hands of particular individuals. The court rolls also, however, reveal only a few tenements standing vacant, and an apparently thriving community of tenants engaged in a variety of domestic, agricultural and communal activities.[30] A comparison of the number of taxpayers recorded in the village in 1301 and 1524 indicates a reduction in the population of about a third, by no means a dramatic decline, especially when compared with villages elsewhere in the county which were later deserted.[31] Whittlebury may well have been able to attract migrants to take up vacant holdings; for example, the court rolls of the manors of Whittlebury and Silverstone regularly record the swearing-in of new tenants into tithings, some of whom may have been outsiders, including perhaps from the nearby deserted hamlet of Nether End, where a row of peasant tofts survives as earthworks and which was depicted on the Forest Map as a series of irregular closes.[32]

The period after 1400 may also have witnessed the internal reorganisation of some villages, even in the absence of migration from outside. The archaeological evidence for the abandonment of large parts of Akeley, for instance, is at odds with the picture that emerges from the court rolls of 1382–1422 of relatively little engrossment and few vacant plots remaining in the lord's hands.[33] However, if the occupants of the Leckhampstead road moved into the vacant plots in the village core around the church, and their abandoned tofts were quickly cleared and the land converted to pasture (the field in which the row lay was called 'The Leys' in 1794), rather than standing unoccupied and falling slowly into ruin, then the physical and documentary sources are once again in agreement (Figure 74). Moreover, the architectural evidence suggests a period of rebuilding in the later Middle Ages, with at least two cruck-framed buildings surviving in the main part of the village.[34] The possible reorganisation of late medieval Akeley may account for the relatively small reduction in its mid fifteenth-century tax assessment: only 13 per cent, compared to 15 per cent at Stowe, 20 per cent at Leckhampstead and 21 per cent at Lillingstone Dayrell.[35]

The abandonment of house plots not only provided opportunities for migration and village reorganisation, but also for the engrossment of holdings by acquisitive tenants. This process may have begun soon after the Black Death, but it is hidden from us in the documentary record until the fifteenth century. For example, in a rental of Luffield Priory's lands in Whittlebury in 1468, five tofts were listed, of which one was stated to be 'formerly a cottage', and two others were held by William Hall 'beside his messuage'.[36] The empty plots depicted on the

Forest Map probably represent the engrossment of late medieval tenements, although some rebuilding and infilling may have taken place by the early seventeenth century.[37] At Silverstone, too, buildings fell into disuse as the remaining inhabitants accumulated holdings. Thus, when John Hempman died in 1423 he held a messuage and a virgate called Hygonnes, a toft and a virgate called Smartes, and a toft and half a virgate called Bondes. The virgate called Smartes was formerly held by John Smart, one of thirty-seven tenants listed in 1403 who owed suit to the manorial court at Silverstone belonging to Burnham Abbey. He was probably a descendant of William Smart, who paid tax to the king in 1301. The list of 1403 was periodically updated, and John Hempman was recorded as John Smart's successor. John Smart's buildings were probably abandoned and his messuage reduced to a toft during the years 1403–23.[38] Other buildings also fell into decay at this time, in spite of repeated injunctions made in the manorial court to the contrary, together with the provision of timber to tenants by the lord in order to keep houses in good repair.[39]

In the absence of large-scale excavation, the process of engrossment is difficult to detect archaeologically. For example, it might be expected that the former external boundaries of tenements, in cases where they became internal to new larger holdings, would be filled in or taken down, evidence for which would probably be recovered if investigated. What can be said, however, is that once the regular rows of houses began to break down as plots were vacated, the buildings were rarely reoccupied and were most likely removed. Certainly, most vacant plots in the study area produce little ceramic evidence dating to the period 1400–1600. Almost certainly, these holdings were amalgamated with others, becoming part of a large open croft, thereby diminishing the likelihood of future redevelopment. This pattern is seen most clearly at West End in Silverstone, a village in which the court rolls suggest that engrossment was underway in the fifteenth century. The Forest Map depicts tenements in the western row of West End two or three times wider than the standard frontages of 20–30 m (66–99 feet)

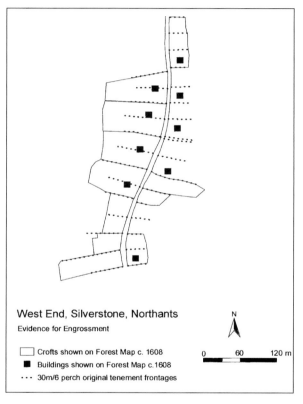

West End, Silverstone, Northants

Evidence for Engrossment

☐ Crofts shown on Forest Map c. 1608
■ Buildings shown on Forest Map c.1608
··· 30m/6 perch original tenement frontages

N

0   60   120 m

FIGURE 76.
West End, Silverstone:
evidence for engrossment.

found in earlier periods, suggesting that these plots were constructed out of the smaller units which preceded them (Figure 76).

Mortality and migration in combination most likely led to the shrinkage of villages and hamlets in the Whittlewood area. If we can assume that all types of settlement were equally affected by the Black Death and subsequent outbreaks of plague, their survival or failure ultimately depended on their ability to retain their surviving inhabitants and attract incomers. Antisocial behaviour such as the overburdening of commons with livestock, against which by-laws were issued in a number of villages in the study area, may have encouraged some residents to leave. Such disputes were common at Wicken in the 1580s, and were partially responsible for the depopulation of Stowe in the early seventeenth century (see above, page 146).[40] However, the critical factor was probably the settlement's pre-Black Death population level. Long-established villages with large populations were better able to support a halving of their numbers while remaining economically and socially viable. By contrast, the small number of residents in many of the hamlets made these places vulnerable to changing economic conditions and the encroachments of lords and wealthy tenants, who took advantage of the breakdown in communal arrangements to introduce farming practices detrimental to the survival of the settlement.[41] Nevertheless, with few exceptions, the villages, hamlets and farmsteads of the Whittlewood area survived the natural disasters of the fourteenth century. Desertion of settlements was largely a phenomenon of the fifteenth, sixteenth and seventeenth centuries, when other agencies brought about their final demise. Inevitably, those most weakened during the fourteenth century were the first to succumb. But formerly vibrant communities, too, might be erased from the map.

Settlement desertion and landscape change

Desertion was not the product of a particular age; settlements succumbed to internal and external pressures throughout the Middle Ages and beyond. An early desertion in the Whittlewood area occurred at Wakefield. The origins of the settlement at Wakefield probably lay in the formation of a new post-Conquest manor held in 1086 by Alan, count of Brittany. Earthworks, comprising perhaps half a dozen tenements, mark its site, while nearby ridge and furrow suggests that for a brief period the community cultivated its own fields. Records indicate that the king regained the manor in the twelfth century, leading to the abandonment of the settlement. Its demise should probably be associated with its location in the heart of the forest. By the 1120s

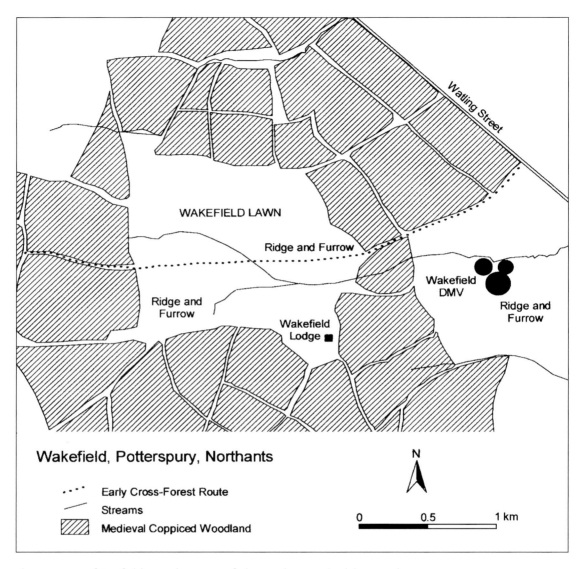

WAKEFIELD LAWN

Ridge and Furrow

Ridge and
Furrow

Wakefield
Lodge ■

Wakefield
DMV

Ridge and
Furrow

Watling Street

Wakefield, Potterspury, Northants

···· Early Cross-Forest Route

— Streams

▨ Medieval Coppiced Woodland

N

0   0.5   1 km

those parts of its fields to the west of the settlement had been taken out of use and laid down to grass to form Wakefield Lawn (Figure 77). The king may have built his hunting lodge there at the same time, although its existence is first recorded in 1170–71.[42]

The impact of the forest on the growth and development of settlement has already been discussed (see above, pages 117–18). But was the continued enforcement of forest law after 1350 responsible for the desertion of any settlements in the Whittlewood area? The farmstead at Heybarne originated in the assarting movement of the thirteenth century and was first mentioned in 1250, when Simon de Patishulle

FIGURE 77.
Wakefield, Potterspury.

was caught poaching in the surrounding woods.[43] Pottery from the site likewise suggests that the farmstead was built in the second half of the thirteenth century. The land surrounding the site was ploughed before the Black Death, but in 1369 the manor's low valuation was said to be 'because it lies in the forest of Whittlewood and is destroyed by the king's deer'. By 1391 the arable had fallen out of cultivation – the destructive actions of the deer were again cited – and in 1418 Heybarne was no longer described as a manor but a toft and carucate called 'Heybernefeld'.[44] The farmstead was almost certainly deserted by this time, a suggestion supported by pottery finds with a terminal date no later than 1400. The protection afforded under forest law to wandering deer clearly had an adverse effect on farming at Heybarne and this may have been a factor in hastening the abandonment of the site.

In other cases of desertion, the role of forest law cannot be established with any certainty. For example, the hamlet of Knotwood, comprising three or four houses on the edge of the forest in Furtho parish, was probably deserted by 1400, to judge from the lack of fifteenth-century pottery fabrics discovered during fieldwalking. However, no documentary evidence survives to establish whether the inhabitants, like those of Heybarne, were harassed by the actions of the king's deer (or forest officials). Both Knotwood and Heybarne were among the smallest settlements in the project area, and both were located on the heavy clays away from the preferred limestones, sands and gravels. It is tempting to associate their demise with their small size and unfavourable location. Many of the hamlets and farmsteads established during the colonisation of the woods and wastes in the twelfth and thirteenth centuries were located on the claylands and, as in other periods of settlement retreat, such as the post-Roman era, these sites were often the first to be abandoned. But just as in the early Middle Ages, the later retreat from the claylands in the Whittlewood area was not complete, and the farmsteads of Monksbarn and Stockholt, as well as the hamlets of Dagnall and Puxley, survived, albeit in a severely shrunken state. Such places continued to attract inhabitants throughout the fifteenth century; for example, the monks of Luffield Priory were able to find a series of lessees for their property at Monksbarn, although its rental value appears to have declined from £1 10s in 1424 to 10s in 1478 and a derisory 2s in 1499–1500. By this time the buildings at Monksbarn were almost certainly deserted and the land given over to grazing.[45] In other parts of the study area, too, the retreat of settlement from the claylands after 1500 was probably more extensive than in the first 150 years after the Black Death. One of the reasons for this change may have been the need to find more grazing ground for sheep at a time when arable husbandry was beginning to recover.

The shrinkage of settlement and the weakening of village communities in the late fourteenth and fifteenth centuries made many places, especially in the midlands, vulnerable to enclosing landlords, or even tenant farmers, who wished to graze sheep on former arable fields.[46] Contemporary complaints against the depopulation of villages were in no doubt that the expansion of sheep farming was to blame. Thomas More wrote in *Utopia* (1516) that sheep 'consume, destroy, and devour whole fields, houses, and cities'. Nor were areas of woodland spared this transformation: 'when the great forests' dwelling was so wide, and careless wood grew fast by the fires' side, then dogs did want the shepherd's fields to keep; now we want foxes to consume our sheep'.[47] Sheep farming was attractive to lords and tenants in the later Middle Ages because labour costs were low and wool was in demand to supply England's cloth industry, but there were fears – proved right in 1482/3 – that grain growing was so much in decline that people would go hungry in the event of a poor harvest.[48] In the Whittlewood area, sheep grazed former settlement sites, including perhaps Monksbarn, and landholders were encouraged to enclose former arable land and convert it to pasture.

A number of early maps depict ancient piecemeal enclosure in Akeley, Deanshanger, Potterspury, Puxley, Silverstone, Whittlebury and Wicken.[49] Some of these closes had been in existence since the era of assarting in the twelfth and thirteenth centuries (see above, pages 118–22), but others were more recent developments. Complaints against the enclosure of arable fields were heard in a number of villages at the time of the government enquiry of 1517–18. For example, it was claimed that Richard Empson, lord of the manor of Little Leckhampstead, in 1492 enclosed 20 acres (8 ha) of arable which he converted to pasture. Empson was a notorious depopulator, responsible for the destruction of the nearby village of Easton Neston. Other landholders in the parish followed Empson's lead, putting twelve householders out of work and bringing about the effective abandonment of the settlement at Little Leckhampstead.[50] At about the same time, Thomas Grey, marquess of Dorset, converted 40 acres (16 ha) of ploughland in Wicken to pasture, to the detriment of four workers. In 1512 John Spencer, another notoriously acquisitive lord, who had purchased the estate the previous year, removed a further 40 acres (16 ha) of arable from the open fields of Wicken which he used to enlarge the medieval park.[51] At Puxley, a landscape of open fields in the late fourteenth century was transformed into one that was fully enclosed by the time of the Forest Map. Part of the change occurred in 1500, when Sir Thomas Green enclosed 20 acres (8 ha) of arable, thereby displacing six tenants. The settlement at Puxley survived, but only just; in the 1720s Bridges described it as 'an hamlet of four mean houses ... formerly a much greater number'.[52] In all these places, houses and arable were sacrificed for grass.

One of the largest villages in the project area to be deserted was Lillingstone Dayrell, its final demise occasioned, once again, by an expansion of grazing. In 1491 Thomas Dayrell, lord of Lillingstone Dayrell, engrossed eight peasant holdings of 20.5 acres (8.25 ha) each, thereby displacing forty people from their homes and leading to the abandonment and ruin of seven messuages and four cottages. In total, 164 acres (66 ha) of previously cultivated land were given over to pasture, on which the lord's sheep were set to graze.[53] The village was almost totally deserted, creating the dispersed settlement pattern in the parish which was depicted on the estate map of 1611 (Figure 78) (see above, page 204).[54] A similar fate befell the village of Furtho, at which only three taxpayers were recorded in 1524. Almost certainly, Furtho was largely deserted by this date; the responsibility for this rested with the lords of the manor, the Furtho family, who began to consolidate their demesne and convert arable to pasture in the fifteenth century. The process was probably completed by Thomas Furtho, who stopped up the principal highway through the village in 1571–72, leaving the settlement isolated and off the beaten track.[55] By contrast, the village of Stowe was large and relatively prosperous in the fifteenth and sixteenth centuries, the community investing in public buildings such as the parish church and a church house.[56] However, the decision taken by Sir Peter Temple in 1637 to enclose common land in order to expand his deer park sounded the death knell for the village, the inhabitants of which were probably moved to the neighbouring village of Dadford, immediately outside the Stowe estate.[57]

The villages of Lillingstone Dayrell and Furtho were seriously weakened by the mortality and migration of the post-Black Death era and, as such, were easy prey to resident lords who saw an opportunity to make money from the wool trade in the changed economic conditions of the late fifteenth century. Little Leckhampstead and Puxley probably suffered similar fates.[58] By contrast, at Wicken, whatever the intentions of the lord, the village was too large to be entirely removed.[59] The same might have been said about Stowe. However, its demise was sealed by the ambition of one of the wealthiest and most powerful lords in the region, who took advantage of the fact that he employed many of the villagers on the estate at Stowe; they were in no position to refuse when he took the decision to remove the village and extend his deer park.[60] Lordship was thus a key factor in the desertion

FIGURE 78 (*overleaf*). Lillingstone Dayrell estate map, 1611. The church and manor house are marked in the bottom left-hand corner, above the millpond and beside the warren, the site of the deserted village.
BUCKINGHAMSHIRE COUNTY COUNCIL

A Copy of a Large Plan

"Off a Description of the Manor House
"of Sillingston Dayrell in the County of Bucks
"with the Lands & Woods unto the same
"belonging - as it was taken in the Year 1611
"by order of Sir Thos. Dayrell Knight
"The Original Survey being much defaced
"this Copy (meaning the large measure)
"was taken in the year 1700. as well as
"could be discovered from the said Original
"& supplied by the direction of Pr. Dayrell Esqr.

The Spots markd thus ▪ were Houses anciently
The Spots markd thus ▪ are modern habitations
The Part of Wood within the Red lines are now
Pastures - the whole being formerly Wood
The Red Lines in the most of the
Grounds - mark the present
alterations made in them
since the old Plan

Mounds,

The Black Lines are
the Ancient form of
the Lands —

Plan of the Manor House
in Sr. Thos. Dayrells Time
near as could be discoverd

Rueth Field
The House Close 24.

Rueth Field 1. 3. 5.

Great Rueth Field
101 Aer
Scott

50 Aer
Rueth Field
53 Aer

Dry Lees

Rueth Field

Pale Close 7. 3. 0

Corn Field

Warren

14 Aeres

7 Aeres

Spinney

Alders Close

Adders Close

Teggs Field

Nether Teggs fields

Mill

Moory Clot 7. 0.

Part of Sillingston Lovell

Woodlands of which many are
over which are turned out Pasture

Lower Tile House Wood Lord Trees 38, 1, 4
The Tile House Wood — D° 26, 3, 8
Caunewell Wood Trees 15, 3, 7. D° D° 18, 3, 6
Dead Rich ...... D° 32, 1, 2 ... D° 25, 1, 8
Postern Copse ...... D° 29, 3, 0 ... D° 35, 1, 1
Three Radesment N Birch Lane D°. 28, 2, 0 ... D°. 33, 3, 5
Middle 3 Slades ...... D°. 19, 1, 1 ... D°. 58, 2, 5
Little 3 Slades ...... D°. 28, 2, 0 ... D°. 33, 3, 5
Both Broadnels ...... D°. 25, 2, 3 ... D°. 30, 1, 5
Hatch Hill ...... D°. 67, 0, 6 ... D°. 99, 3, 8
Upper Shrines ...... D°. 31, 2, 0 ... D°. 37, 2, 0
Lower Shrines ...... D°. 31, 2, 1 ... D°. 37, 2, 1

Wood about Acr. 457, 1, 12
Lands about by an old survey 840, 0, 16
Total abt. Acres 1297, 1, 28
or 1300 Acres

Part of Whittlebury Forest

Rich. Dayrell delin° 1701

217

of villages in the Whittlewood project area. For the most part, lords (and tenants) were only able to remove settlements which had, to some extent, been abandoned by their inhabitants in the 150 years after the Black Death. Many of these, such as Dagnall, Heybarne, and Puxley, had developed on the claylands after the Norman Conquest and had always been small. In the case of long-established villages, or parts of villages, such as Lillingstone Dayrell and Little Leckhampstead, it is more difficult to be certain why they contracted so dramatically between 1350 and 1500, but their final demise was clearly the result of intervention by lords who seized the opportunity to convert tillage into pasture. Only at Stowe was an apparently thriving village removed to satisfy the ambitions of the landowner. Elsewhere in the study area, rural depopulation was a more protracted process which continued into modern times. At Lamport and Passenham, for example, population failed to recover to the levels achieved at the end of the thirteenth century, and these formerly large and significant villages are now severely shrunken.

The enclosure of former arable land for conversion to pasture in the later Middle Ages was undertaken by tenants as well as lords. For example, at Passenham, the field book of 1566 reveals that some tenants, in particular the demesne lessees, had begun to consolidate their holdings within the open fields. A furlong of 29 strips measuring 9.75 acres (4 ha) was in single ownership, while smaller pieces of land were enclosed with a ditch and hedge. A few years later 60 acres (24 ha) of open-field land in Parsonage Field (marked on the Forest Map) was enclosed by a freeholder, Francis Flower.[61] Likewise, at Lillingstone Dayrell in 1530, two closes in the former open fields, called 'Baronfeld', were granted to a yeoman, Henry Baker. The document does not make it clear whether the name refers to the closes or the field, but in either case it does not appear in the survey of 1611.[62] At some point prior to the early sixteenth century the three open fields of Lillingstone Dayrell, recorded for perhaps the only time in a survey of 1288–89, had been replaced by the enclosed landscape depicted on the 1611 map, and much of the arable converted into pasture (Figure 78).[63] A similar process, at about the same time, probably took place at Puxley, where the open fields, which were created largely by assarting in the twelfth and thirteenth centuries, had been completely enclosed by the time the Forest Map was compiled *c.* 1608.[64]

The extension of arable farming which characterised the centuries before the Black Death was thus reversed in the fifteenth and sixteenth centuries, with an increase in the numbers of stock kept. The former ploughlands at Heybarne, for example, which had suffered from the depredations of the king's deer, reverted to rough pasture following the desertion of the farmstead and, in 1550, were leased to a tanner from the nearby village of Abthorpe, who no doubt used the land to graze cattle.[65] Although sheep were introduced widely into the study area in the later Middle Ages, at Furtho, Lillingstone Dayrell, Little Leckhampstead, Puxley and Wicken, some of the land converted to pasture may have been used to graze cattle and other animals, such as pigs. For example, at Wicken the by-laws were careful to specify the animals most likely to cause damage to the grain growing in the fields: cattle, pigs and (especially) sheep.[66] Deer also benefited from the widespread reversion to grass. At Stockholt, for example, the arable fields assarted from the waste in the thirteenth century were added to the lord's deer park in 1412.[67] At Wicken, too, the deer park encroached on former ploughlands, and the same occurred on a larger scale at Stowe after 1600.[68] However, the conversion of arable to pasture and the enclosure of fields ought not to be exaggerated. Arable husbandry remained extensive throughout the study area in the later Middle Ages and the open fields of many of our villages, such as Akeley, Deanshanger, Potterspury, Silverstone, Whittlebury and Wicken, survived until enclosed by agreement or act of parliament in the eighteenth and nineteenth centuries.

By 1600, therefore, the landscape of the Whittlewood area was mixed in character. More land was enclosed than had been the case before the Black Death, but in many places the wide expanse of the open fields survived to be depicted on the earliest maps. In addition, the number of settlements, especially dispersed settlements, had fallen from the forty or so recorded when the medieval population was at its height *c.* 1300, to about thirty-two. Places such as Elm Green, Heybarne, Monksbarn and Nether End were no more than a series of closes by the seventeenth century. No single explanation can account for these changes. Although there was a retreat of settlement from the claylands, this was not a universal phenomenon. Farmsteads at Dagnall, Puxley and Stockholt, for example, remained inhabited. Resident lords at Furtho, Lillingstone Dayrell, Little Leckhampstead and Stowe depopulated houses, enclosed land and converted arable to pasture, but these places were vulnerable for other reasons, as we have already discussed, and lords living elsewhere in the study area were either unwilling or unable to pursue a similar course of action. The ability of individuals to alter established patterns of farming and transform the landscape depended on a variety of factors which are often difficult to identify. It is by no means clear why the sixteenth-century demesne lessees at Passenham were able to consolidate their holdings in the open fields, while their counterparts in neighbouring Deanshanger apparently found this an inappropriate course to take.[69]

Documents relating to the leasing of the demesnes do not survive in any numbers for the Whittlewood area, and details about the farming practices adopted by lessees are not generally recorded. Likewise, changes in landownership following the dissolution of the monasteries were not necessarily followed by similar transformations of villages and fields. Thus, while the sale of Oseney Abbey's former manor of Stowe allowed the Temples to begin altering the landscape there, fewer changes can be detected at Silverstone, where the Throckmortons were granted the lands of Luffield Priory and Burnham Abbey.[70]

One aspect of the landscape which changed little in the period 1350–1600 was the woodland. The clearance of woodland and waste to extend arable farming ceased abruptly once plague struck in 1348–49. Indeed, woodland may have been allowed to regenerate over former assarts. The extension of the deer park at Stockholt, for example, may have been accompanied by woodland growth across the ploughlands of 'Homfeld' which adjoined the wood called 'Kyngesshrobfeld'.[71] Likewise, the small settlement at Knotwood, which was deserted before 1400, lay under woodland at the time of the Forest Map. The copse, measuring 23 acres (9 ha), was leased with underwood of nine years' growth in 1588.[72] For the most part, however, the extent of the woodland depicted on the Forest Map was probably much as it had been immediately before the Black Death. Nor is there evidence to suggest that the woodland shown on the map of Lillingstone Dayrell in 1611 was very different from that in existence 300 years before. A survey of Whittlewood Forest in 1571 reported that the woods were 'never in better order', and that the deer were untroubled by poachers.[73] Nevertheless, the woodland remained a valuable resource for the inhabitants of the surrounding villages. The woodwards of Silverstone, for example, were kept busy presenting offenders who felled trees and branches in copses, such as Hicks, Cheese and Wildwood, which are marked on the Forest Map as belonging to the lord of the manor, Sir Arthur Throckmorton.[74]

Conclusions

The decline and desertion of so many rural settlements between the fourteenth and seventeenth centuries stands in such contrast to their growth and development during the previous 500 years that this downturn has come to be seen as representative of the age. However, it would be wrong to lose sight of the fact that the great majority of settlements survived in some shape or form. In the study area, survival rates were four out of five. The reduction in population caused by the Black Death did not account immediately for a single desertion. Lords may have prevailed in the struggle for the depopulation and enclosure of a number of villages, but not necessarily without a fight. In the case of Stowe, Peter Temple was challenged by various of his tenants in what has been described as 'a violent theatre of honour'.[75] Both nucleated villages and dispersed settlements proved capable of survival, with dispersed settlements perhaps, on balance, out-performing their nucleated neighbours. Villages such as Leckhampstead and Silverstone may have lost individual elements of their plans, but they retained their basic form and continued to farm their open fields. Nucleated villages such as Lillingstone Lovell and Wicken lost their cohesion, their regular rows degraded into interrupted rows, but they did not break apart completely. In many senses both the pattern and hierarchy of settlement in the Whittlewood area remained intact. These communities continued to farm the land and find by-employments in the woods. The village institutions proved sufficiently robust to maintain their open-field systems, often until parliamentary enclosure, and to protect their common rights until the disafforestation of Whittlewood in 1853. How ironic, then, that the first documented use of the term 'end' to describe part of the settlement pattern in the study area occurs in the fifteenth century, at a time of desertion, when in most cases this term was applied to places for which there was no end, and which still survive today.

CHAPTER TEN

Implications and
Wider Perspectives

....

The study of medieval rural settlement in England currently finds itself at a crossroads. National surveys of settlement patterns have revealed broad regional trends, while local case-studies have produced detailed examinations of individual sites. Yet there remains little agreement as to why, when and how nucleated villages and more dispersed patterns of settlement formed in different parts of the country. In particular, doubt can be cast on many of the current models explaining nucleation, and it might be questioned how applicable these are beyond the localities on which they have been based. And beyond the Central Province, much work remains to be done to explore more fully dispersed settlement patterns. Those studies that have been undertaken reveal that no two villages follow exactly the same route or chronology to the adoption of their final plan. Their desertion, where it happened, has been more easily explained, occurring in a better-documented world which enables the agencies that lay behind their failure to be identified. In this, but nowhere else in what is a vast subject, do conclusions drawn 40 years ago still remain valid today.[1]

The aim of this book has been to examine settlement patterns at a regional scale, and thus to provide a bridge between the national overviews and local exemplars. While its focus has necessarily been restricted to the twelve parishes subjected to close analysis, its primary ambition has been to explore from this base why the more general settlement pattern of medieval England should have been so diverse. The area selected for investigation is difficult to categorise; it was chosen specifically for this reason. It is a landscape that lies within the broad central belt of England dominated by nucleated villages, yet contains within it the full range of medieval rural settlement types, with compact villages lying alongside multi-nodal villages, hamlets and farmsteads. It is a hybrid, combining elements of the 'land of villages' and the 'land of hamlets', terms used by earlier historians to express the basic divisions that exist between different parts of England;[2] until recently, however, they have masked the more subtle variations of settlement form that they are now seen to contain. Defining the study area as we have has permitted the detailed exploration of the full range of medieval settlement types to be undertaken side-by-side for the first time. This comparative method has exposed the similarities and differences that might exist not only between settlements of very different form, but also between settlements whose plans suggest they shared much in common.

The conclusions that are presented here have been framed by four oppositions. These have emerged from this study and embrace its three central themes of landscape, settlement and society. They are: culture versus economy; stability versus instability; lord versus community; and dispersion versus nucleation.

Culture versus economy

Taking the long view of the development of the Whittlewood landscape reveals its versatility. Its woodland resources, lush pastures and nutrient-rich soils were all exploited at one time or another. Long cycles are visible. Woodland was cleared, only to regenerate before being cleared again. Likewise, the extent of pasture and arable has varied, long periods of intensive cultivation giving way to equally extended periods when the area was largely laid to grass before being ploughed up once more. But never did one land use become so dominant as to eradicate all others, a fact which perhaps accounts for the apparent ease with which successive generations of farmers switched their emphasis between alternative farming systems. The close symbiosis between man and environment is certainly evident, and might encourage advocates of physical determinism to identify a self-regulating macrocycle, dictated by the condition of the soil, which demanded that those who sought to exploit it to rotate between periods of intensive and non-intensive agriculture. Of course, shifts in the uses to which the land was put were linked to many other factors: rising and falling population levels, variations in the market, new agricultural technologies and changes to the organisation of individual or grouped farming units all had major roles to play.

This was a reality for much of the English midlands. Nature guided, but farmers in the end decided how the land would be worked for economic return. Its development was not constrained in the same way by climate, topography or poor soils as was that in the areas which surrounded it, but even here farmers chose within the parameters of a more restricted range of options. In peripheral regions pastoral farming and dispersed settlement came to predominate.[3] Midland farmers might have competed favourably with these economies had they turned to animal husbandry as their principal activity. But where the midland soils and gently rolling countryside held clear superiority over these peripheral zones was in their capacity to grow cereals. By the end of the thirteenth century, large parts of the midlands had been developed as extensive corn belts, with nucleated villages surrounded by open fields occupying up to 80 per cent of each individual farming territory.[4] The creation of these landscapes was driven by subsistence needs and the market. That Whittlewood did not follow the same trajectory suggests that other, more localised, controls on the use of the land competed here against the tendency towards monoculture, restricting the growth of the arable landscape and preserving tracts of pasture and woodland.

The most identifiable counter to the formation of an arable-dominated landscape in Whittlewood was its designation as a royal forest, a political and cultural institution imposed at a critical stage in the area's medieval development. There can be little doubt that the crown's successful defence of core blocks of pasture and woodland as hunting grounds provided the principal local barrier to the spread of cultivation during the late medieval period. Without the forest, Whittlewood may well have more closely resembled the champion landscape that surrounded it.[5] Yet it is far from clear how areas of royal forest were selected. Rarely were they simply bad land incapable of supporting agriculture. The forests of Rockingham (Northants.) and Wychwood (Oxon.), as well as Whittlewood, all reveal that these later forest zones had been intensively cultivated and densely settled during the Roman period.[6] But despite their arable pedigree, there are good grounds to suggest that, far from representing an unprecedented departure, the application of forest law after the Norman Conquest may simply have formalised long-standing royal and common rights over these areas that had originated during the post-Roman centuries. Royal forests, it might be argued, perpetuated how those areas that now fell within their compass may have already been viewed; as places on the outside (the term forest deriving from the Latin *foris*, meaning outside), or at least on the margins, of political and economic units created several centuries earlier. This is implicit both in the name of the Oxfordshire forest of Wychwood, 'the wood of the Hwicce', and in its location on the edge of this tribal territory.[7] Rather than leading to changes in how these areas were exploited, forest status may simply have ensured that the traditional, albeit post-Roman, uses to which these blocks of land had been put, as valuable areas of intercommoned pasture and woodland on the edge of new administrative divisions, were perpetuated.

The origins of Whittlewood Forest are more elusive than those of

Wychwood. Nevertheless, three strands of evidence might be presented which point to its early establishment, and possibly its active promotion and preservation, as a peripheral landscape offering essential woodland and pasture to be felled, hunted and grazed from more distant centres of power. The first is the extensive and long-established royal interest in the area, most of Whittlewood falling within the orbit of six estates held by the king in the pre-Conquest period: Kings Sutton, Greens Norton, Towcester, Passenham, Buckingham and Kirtlington. What was it about Whittlewood that meant that successive kings were reluctant to relinquish direct control over it? The answer may lie in the second piece of evidence, the detached manors within Whittlewood over which these royal estate centres exerted control: Lillingstone Lovell and Boycott from Kirtlington, and Silverstone and Whittlebury from Greens Norton. These links appear to predate the creation of hundreds and shires, suggesting that before these administrative units were established, Whittlewood provided resources unavailable elsewhere, the rights and access to which were carefully guarded despite later political and administrative reorganisation. That multiple interests in the area might have arisen from the exploitation of Whittlewood as an ill-defined zone of intercommoned land on the edge of several polities finds further support in the final piece of evidence: place-names.

Whittlewood contains a cluster of names in -*feld* (Whitfield, Tiffield, Luffield and Wakefield), a concentration not matched elsewhere in Northamptonshire, and in Buckinghamshire only in the Chilterns.[8] Interpretation of this element is complicated since the meaning of the term changed over time.[9] Generally rendered simply as 'open country', its earliest usage appears to have applied to areas of common pasture, only later becoming associated with common arable land. In other parts of the country, clusters of -*feld* names have been found to be coincident with county boundaries (e.g. Herts./Mx), or the borders of the early English kingdoms (e.g. Windsor Forest (Berks.), dividing the territories of the West and Middle Saxons). It has been suggested that here the grouping of these names derived from the exploitation of these liminal spaces as areas of intercommoned pasture. In the same fashion, Whitfield, Luffield and Wakefield all lie on the Northamptonshire/Buckinghamshire border; the elements *tig* (perhaps 'meeting place') in Tiffield and *waca* (more certainly 'festivities') in Wakefield suggesting their use as group assembly points (Figure 26).[10] It is entirely possible, therefore, that the passing of the later shire boundary through these places represented an attempt to divide equitably an area over which estate centres, that now found themselves within different administrative regions, once shared rights.

In Whittlewood, early medieval tribal divisions cannot be traced with certainty. Yet for the reasons just outlined we may suspect that it lay 'on the edge', divided among a number of territories, as it had been in the Iron Age and Roman period. Boundaries may only have been formalised with the creation of the hundreds and shires in the tenth century, and perhaps only tightly defined in the post-Conquest period. While perpetually located away from centres of authority, the development of its landscape was nevertheless carefully managed by those who held power and who wished to exploit its primary assets, woodland, pasture and game; its later forest status was simply a new expression of this enduring reality. Consequently, while Whittlewood was an integral part of a wider economy, providing resources that were not available elsewhere, its development was clearly culturally determined. Its farmers were denied the freedom afforded to their counterparts in the champion regions to extend arable cultivation, despite its soils being able to support such a farming regime. It is this that explains the creation and survival of an alternative midland landscape in medieval Whittlewood, one that contrasted so markedly from those that surrounded it.

Stability versus instability

Villages and hamlets have always been part of the rural settlement pattern of England.[11] Depending on time and place, these either became the dominant form of settlement in a particular region, or remained a rarity, a communal cluster in a sea of individual farmsteads. In many senses, therefore, the medieval villages and hamlets of Whittlewood, which have been the focus of this study, represent the continuation of a settlement tradition stretching back into prehistory. Indeed, the area has produced evidence for early agglomerations, such as the Iron Age settlement at Old Tun Copse, or the large Roman settlements at Lillingstone Dayrell and Briary Copse. But such discoveries, often made well away from later population centres, are also reminders that while the basic forms of settlements have remained constant, their locations have not. Moreover, individual farmsteads, the third component of the medieval rural settlement pattern, have tended to exhibit even greater instability, coming and going, reappearing and relocating, at all periods.

Indeed, it would appear from the numerous surveys that have now been undertaken across the country that most early settlements, and particularly those formed during the sub-Roman centuries, were either short-lived, their sites abandoned in favour of new locations, or drifted across the landscape in regular short-range shifts. Evidence for settlement mobility has not only been found across south-east England, West Stow (Suffolk) and Mucking (Essex) being prime examples of the 'wandering settlement', but also in north-west Europe, where the term *Wandersiedlung* was first coined.[12] There are notable exceptions – that is, early-established, long-lived and stable communities occupying the same location over centuries – such as Catholme (Staffs.). But these are still commonly regarded as failing to conform to the normal life-cycle of other contemporary settlements.[13] For Christopher Taylor, settlement mobility was a universal experience, a reality not simply confined to earlier periods, but one that underpinned the process of village nucleation in the midlands, or helped to explain the isolation of medieval churches in East Anglia as they were left marooned by the later movement of the settlements they served.[14]

Similar instability might also be suggested for the territorial division of the landscape. While claims that later administrative units, such as parishes, might have preserved, for example, the structure of Roman estates, this has nowhere been proven categorically.[15] Other studies have shown how the multiple estates of the early medieval period might grow or contract, subdivide or coalesce.[16] The fragmentation of these large estates and the creation of smaller manors and vills similarly represents another stage in this process of constant reorganisation. Consequently, the layout of the authoritative landscape was regularly changing, rarely remaining the same over time. Within those landscapes, individual landholdings were equally subject to such dynamism, seen no more clearly than in the champion regions, in the move from the farming of discrete blocks in severalty to the intermixing of strips in the common fields. These were changes paralleled in later periods too, as manors continued to divide or join together, and land was reparcelled during the process of enclosure.

Instability in Whittlewood is not difficult to find. The settlement pattern has continued to change from the Iron Age, when it can first be mapped, to the present day. Its administrative divisions have been realigned on numerous occasions, both in the Middle Ages and more recently: for example, the division of Foxley Hundred in the tenth century to create the hundreds of Greens Norton and Towcester; or the complex administrative geographies of Passenham and Potterspury, which were not finally settled until 1951.[17] Patterns of farming and landholding were also permanently in flux. But, as the study of Whittlewood has shown, such instability was controlled, contained within defined structural parameters which were themselves inherently more stable. While the Roman settlement pattern differed from that of the Iron Age, it built upon it, up to a quarter of all sites exhibiting signs of continuity of occupation across several centuries. Just as

Roman *civitates* preserved earlier tribal territorial divisions, there are indications that the central functions of the hillfort at Whittlebury were transferred to the town of Towcester, ensuring that the local administrative network remained largely intact. In turn, it would appear that the early medieval estate centre at Greens Norton perpetuated these structures, long-standing arrangements perhaps echoed in the association of *Witela* with both the prehistoric fortification and the wider area.

In contrast to surrounding areas, the medieval settlement pattern of Whittlewood was also characterised by stability. The identification of pre-village nuclei lying under later settlement foci extends the occupancy of particular sites back before AD 850. Perhaps as much as half of the early medieval settlement pattern was preserved by the later villages, their origins seemingly not reliant upon the mass abandonment of dispersed farmsteads. On these sites, villages and hamlets might grow and contract but, barring failure, they were places from which they would never subsequently move. And in the wider landscape too, radical reorganisation also appears to have been conducted within an established framework. The discovery of pre-medieval boundary ditches lying below some headlands in the open fields suggests that, rather than being laid out with no regard for what had gone before, the ways in which they were arranged and subdivided were in part influenced by earlier systems. On many levels, then, the Whittlewood landscape can be demonstrated to have extraordinary temporal depth, resulting from the successive borrowing of physical, mental and administrative structures from the past. It is stability rather than instability which should be seen as the decisive factor in its development, and as such Whittlewood joins a growing number of other local studies which are beginning to demonstrate similar developmental trajectories.[18]

Lord versus community

At various stages in the development of what we have termed the 'villagescape', the guiding hand of lordship is clearly visible. It is at its most obvious in the creation of private parks or the depopulation of villages such as Lillingstone Dayrell or Puxley, where local lords engrossed and enclosed holdings during the later Middle Ages. It can also be seen in earlier reorganisations of the village plan: at Lillingstone Lovell, for instance, the insertion of a manorial complex into the heart of the village appears to have displaced the resident population, leading to the laying-out of new tenements in areas which had previously been outside the settlement; and in Wick Hamon, a capital messuage was developed on the edge of the village in the middle of the thirteenth century, apparently requiring the clearance of a small number of peasant holdings, leading to the creation of another new row of tenements. The actions of these resident lords were, equally, constrained by a higher level of overlordship. Royal interest in the forest ensured that lords and communities were unable to develop the types of extensive arable landscapes seen elsewhere in the champion midlands. The crown successfully defended its rights, preserving large tracts of land, particular along the Great Ouse/Tove watershed, under wood pasture, or dividing them into defined coppice compartments.

But the strength of the community at large, and its influence over the development of settlements and their wider landscapes, should not be underestimated. Again, evidence is most forthcoming in later periods, as seen in complaints raised by those affected by seigneurial attempts to increase their holdings or to parcel up and grass down areas of former common field. Indeed, the survival of the greater part of the open fields until parliamentary enclosure might be taken as a clear sign of the wider community's capacity to defend its interests against enclosing lords. At Stowe, the community was investing in the village fabric in the fifteenth century, purchasing a plot of land close to the church and constructing a church house. Surviving cruck-framed buildings in villages such as Akeley, Leckhampstead and Whittlebury indicate a peasantry still actively developing their tenements at the end of the Middle Ages. Furthermore, court rolls for Silverstone record the peasant engrossment of village and field holdings. In earlier periods, there are further signs of general improvement to living areas, with hard surfaces been laid around peasant houses during the thirteenth century. Beyond the village, despite the significant deterrents that faced them, the peasantry can be seen to have been active in the assarting movement, breaking new land and bringing it under the plough, either to be incorporated into the open-field system, or to be farmed in severalty. In Wick Hamon, there are indications that the community took advantage of a vacuum of power, brought on by the minority of one of its lords in the late thirteenth century, to once again plough land that had previously been emparked.

In periods when the archaeological evidence is supplemented by the written record, therefore, it emerges that the separate actions of either lord or community could lead to significant changes in the built environment and the remodelling of the landscape. Records of fines for assarting or complaints against engrossment provide unequivocal testament to the conflict that might exist between these two factions, or between local lords and the king, as all parties sought to make the best use of the land. Manorial court rolls also bear witness to other tensions, this time within the community, between members of the same social standing. Disputes amongst neighbours commonly resulted in grievances being brought before the court. There are examples of crops destroyed by the animals of another tenant or the illegal breaking of hedges. Nor was infighting amongst lords unknown, as the eruption of violence between the Chastiluns and Leaumes in Leckhampstead in the 1330s and 1340s shows. All medieval village societies were to some extent divided. Social differentiation, and the opposing interests of the various groups present in the community, meant that the potential for open conflict was never far away.[19] Villages might be considered as fragile institutions, constantly on the verge of social or economic disintegration. So it may be wondered whether this was compounded in Whittlewood by the limitations imposed by forest law. Did the forest provide further grounds for tension?

In other royal forests, perennial poaching and periodic confrontations with forest officials provide a clear impression of the disdain in which forest law might be held by those who lived under its restrictions. But if forest law could prove potentially divisive, pitching lords against the king, and the interests of farmers against those of the hunter, records of concerted action taken against it by whole villages suggest that it might equally have encouraged social cohesion, providing a common cause around which individual communities or groups of communities could rally. This was certainly the case in Kinver Forest (Staffs.) in 1358, when 100 men from a number of villages attacked the forest regarders.[20] The attitudes of the inhabitants of Whittlewood to the forest are difficult to gauge. If the forest promoted resentment, this either rarely surfaced or remained unrecorded. An absence of open rebellion, however, might suggest that life in medieval Whittlewood was largely characterised by the peaceful coexistence of hunter and farmer. A balance was seemingly struck which permitted the accommodation of these two competing interests. The growth and survival of Whittlewood's villages suggest that in this context, too, a sense of cooperation and perhaps compromise prevailed, ensuring that, despite inevitable minor flash-points, both lords and peasants were able to negotiate a mutually acceptable, and perhaps beneficial, place within a strongly integrated society. Far from being weak, the Whittlewood villages, like their equivalents beyond the forest, ultimately proved to be resilient solutions to the problem of communal living.

In attempting to understand why villages formed, and why different settlement forms were adopted, it is important neither to overplay the role of lordship, nor underplay the role of the community. Throughout this book we have been careful to acknowledge that, where positive proof of the authority that directed the development of Whittlewood's settlements and landscape is lacking, sufficient uncertainty exists to permit three alternative explanations of the evidence. Lords might act in isolation, imposing change on the community. Alternatively, the community, acting together, might be sufficiently powerful to bring about change without lordly consent. In both cases, change may have been positively embraced by both parties, or forced by the powerful upon those unable to mount a challenge to unwelcome change. Finally, change might result from consensus, lords and communities acting in unison, a scenario less likely to prompt resistance or complaint. No document survives, if one ever existed, to inform us of the processes involved in the making of a village, nor who initiated such reorganisations. Nevertheless, the apparent ease with which villages were later remodelled suggests that a degree of mutual cooperation must have existed within them. If lord and community could work together to redevelop their settlements, often along radically new lines, the possibility that they might both have participated in their formation clearly cannot be dismissed. Nor was the major role played by the community restricted to the village; consensus between lord and community seems even more evident in the creation of the open fields, an undertaking with far-reaching implications, and one which was, potentially, immensely disruptive in the short term to the economic well-being of its stakeholders.

Dispersion versus nucleation

There is a temptation, perhaps, to view the nucleated village and its open fields, so typical of the English midlands, as one of the great medieval achievements of the lower orders, leaving a lasting legacy no less significant than the castles, cathedrals and parks of the social elite. In replacing a more primitive form of settlement pattern, comprised of small hamlets or isolated farmsteads dispersed across the landscape, and by altering how the land was managed and exploited, the village could be said to represent a new and elevated level of social and economic organisation, one characterised by planning and order. If this is accepted then it necessarily follows that those areas where nucleated villages rarely or never developed must be viewed as somehow backward. Here communities could be accused of either failing to grasp the opportunities nucleation offered or of being in no position to act upon them.

In the early years of medieval rural settlement studies, scholars were certainly inclined to interpret dispersed settlement patterns as largely unchanged survivals from a 'Celtic' past.[21] Now it is universally accepted that areas of dispersed settlement experienced equally dynamic change as those areas in which nucleated villages developed. Recent studies have conclusively shown that while the framework of dispersal might be perpetuated in some places, the actual location of the individual sites which made up the overall pattern might vary considerably over time and might often be punctuated by periods of abandonment, followed by recolonisation. This was certainly the case for settlement on the claylands of east Suffolk and north-west Essex between the Roman and late Saxon periods.[22] Where evidence for the development of dispersed settlement patterns from the late Saxon period through to the early fourteenth century have been found, commentators have tended to stress how such settlement, driven by demographic pressure, was attracted or forced towards primarily marginal areas, such as green-edges, roadsides, uplands, woodlands and waste, or was later required to colonise on to arable land.[23] Because dispersed settlement appears to lack an overarching strategy, and often involved the breaking of peripheral and unattractive land or the surrendering of previously agriculturally-productive areas, and because the settlement forms themselves tended towards the irregular and unplanned, a persistently negative aura still surrounds their development. This contrasts with nucleation, where the positives of maximising land potential, creating an equitable division of landholdings, and offering opportunities for cooperation and the pooling of resources are regularly cited, and where the advantages of this form of communal living are so clearly accepted as outweighing any possible disadvantages.

The pros and cons of dispersion
This rather disparaging view of dispersed settlement can be questioned. Take, for example, the ubiquity of this form of settlement. Unlike nucleated villages, dispersed settlements can be found in every part of the country. In the Middle Ages, they comprised the dominant settlement form in many areas, and in the Central Province they coexisted with nucleations.[24] Clearly, then, dispersed settlement archetypes proved both remarkably resilient and flexible. This form of settlement, the community it housed and the economy it supported were able to develop and survive within every environmental, economic and social niche. Because of their adaptive qualities and their ability to thrive everywhere, dispersed settlements far outnumbered clustered centres. Consequently, in absolute terms, the majority of the medieval rural population continued to reside in individual farmsteads or within small hamlets rather than in nucleated villages. And for most, the decision to do so was apparently a matter of choice; some advantage

in retaining or developing a dispersed settlement pattern must have been perceived by their inhabitants.

This offers up the possibility that it was positive rather than negative stimuli that lay behind these settlement models. The attraction of a dispersed settlement pattern is not only clear in its adoption to the near exclusion of all other settlement forms in earlier periods, but also in the continued development of non-village communities throughout the so-called 'village moment'. It seems to find similar expression in the early modern world: it is perhaps indicative that, once freed from the shackles of nucleation and the open-field system by parliamentary enclosure, dispersed farmsteads immediately recolonised the new landscape of the English midlands. It might even be concluded that given a free evolutionary route, dispersion would always be preferred over nucleation: in ecological terms, it is dispersed and not nucleated settlements which represent the natural climax state. These observations provide a new context within which dispersed settlement, as it developed in the Middle Ages, can now be explored, a task helped by a growing body of evidence generated by the relatively recent intellectual shift away from nucleated villages towards other forms of rural settlement.[25] But we are most especially aided by the evidence from Whittlewood, a project which has sought from its outset to address this particular question of dispersion.

The medieval settlement pattern in the Whittlewood area was mixed, comprising both nucleated villages and dispersed settlements. Most of the larger settlements of the area were relatively compact, and may be described as nucleated villages. These villages had a variety of forms, which may be classified more precisely in terms of rows (e.g. Passenham) or grid clusters (e.g. Lillingstone Dayrell). But they all shared the general characteristic of containing relatively little open space within the built-up area. By contrast, two of our larger settlements were more dispersed in character and may be called 'dispersed villages': Leckhampstead and Silverstone. These villages possessed three or more distinct areas of settlement (called 'ends'), which were separated from each other by fields of arable and pasture, and linked by lanes. The question remains, therefore: why, given the similarities of topography and landscape shared by these communities, did people in one place live in large nucleations, while in others they lived in hamlets and farmsteads? And why, when and how did these differences between the nucleated and dispersed villages of Whittlewood emerge?

Across the Central Province, it is argued, centripetal forces were at work in the eighth, ninth and tenth centuries, encouraging the movement of people away from their scattered hamlets and farmsteads towards a central nucleated settlement.[26] This movement, it is suggested, was the result of pressure from lords and tenants to facilitate the more efficient exploitation of the restricted arable and pasture in a period of population growth and estate fragmentation. The arable was extended over former inhabited areas and, in some cases, pasture and woods. The fields were divided into strips and shared among the villagers, and livestock was pastured in common on one of these fields while it lay fallow. The upheaval involved in such a transformation of the countryside was considerable and the decision to undertake this change must have been made after careful deliberation of the advantages and disadvantages. The benefits of change at those places in the vanguard of the movement would have been noted by settlements nearby and the adoption of a nucleated pattern of settlement and open-field farming may have spread by emulation. Nucleation may have begun as a response to practical problems of demography and farming, but we should not underestimate the importance of cultural factors in encouraging its spread: the village may have become an ideal, to be preferred over the hamlet or farmstead. Yet such hypotheses have failed to engage fully with the reality of dispersion. The comparative investigation of nucleated and dispersed villages in Whittlewood has provided a unique insight into the development of both settlement forms, and has demonstrated that some of the assumptions made in previous models can no longer be substantiated.

The influence of earlier settlement patterns and pre-village nuclei

One critical relationship that we have been able to observe is that between the emergent medieval settlement pattern and that which existed before AD 850. Underlying both, it would appear, is a fully dispersed pattern of isolated farmsteads spread across the landscape. Of course, this landscape was not without variation, but we can confidently conclude that the routes later medieval settlements took towards nucleation and dispersion were not predetermined by earlier arrangements. For instance, the number of dispersed elements occupying the later village territories neither presaged nucleation nor caused dispersion. So a nucleated village such as Wick Dive or Lillingstone Dayrell might develop from a sparsely populated landscape of small farmsteads, while the basis of similar developments in central Northamptonshire, at settlements such as Brixworth, Irthlingborough, Higham Ferrers and Raunds, would appear to have been a dense pre-850 settlement pattern.[27] Following a contrary trajectory, the dispersed Buckinghamshire village of Leckhampstead appears to have grown from just such a dense base of farmsteads, while at Silverstone later dispersion appears to find few immediate precedents.

Thus, one of the cornerstones of the nucleation hypothesis, that it represents a solution to an overcrowded countryside, beset by internal boundary disputes, problems associated with movement and access to resources such as pasture and woodland, or the need to provide sufficient grazing against the expansion of arable, finds little support in Whittlewood. Nucleation need not be born of crisis, and nor need dispersion develop only where such pressures were absent.[28]

Secondly, it has been possible to demonstrate that certain places exhibit a level of continuity between the pre-850 settlement pattern and that which was to follow. These earlier settlements have been called pre-village nuclei. They are represented by spreads of pottery no greater in extent than those found on the sites of abandoned farmsteads later covered by the open fields, and consequently should probably be interpreted in much the same way. Pre-village nuclei have been found to lie below both later nucleations, as at Whittlebury and Lillingstone Dayrell, and dispersed villages, such as Leckhampstead. In each case occupation, albeit on a small scale, can be dated to before AD 850. In other places, such as the nucleations of Lillingstone Lovell, Wick Hamon and Wick Dive, the pre-village nucleus appears to find its origins in the period 850–1000, the very date at which other dispersed elements, such as Dagnall in Wicken, also establish themselves. In their earliest stages, these too probably represent the dwellings of only one or two households, and could certainly not be considered fully-fledged hamlets. Few correlations can therefore be drawn. It is impossible to differentiate between pre-village nuclei which would either fail or grow. For those that did survive, it is equally impossible to identify why some should develop into nucleated villages while others would become simply one part of a more complex dispersed settlement pattern. Nor does the chronological dimension help, since both early and late pre-village nuclei might subsequently develop along different lines. Again, therefore, there appears to be little prede-termination of settlement form. Whether a single pre-village nucleus or many nuclei developed into a nucleation or a multi-nodal village, a hamlet or farmstead, seems to rest in the critical phase of transition which has become known as the 'village moment'.

Of course, the physical layout of these early foci may have exerted some influence over the type of settlement that would emerge. The only difference, perhaps, between a polyfocal nucleation and a dispersed village might be the original distance between their pre-village nuclei. At Akeley, for instance, outward growth from two centres eventually led to their coalescence and the formation of a single nuclear settle-ment. In neighbouring Leckhampstead, growth was experienced at all the pre-village nuclei, but since they were located at considerable distances from each other, outward expansion and infilling remained at a scale insufficient to create a built-up area uninterrupted by fields. A similar pattern may be seen in the parish of Stowe. Here there were four discrete areas of settlements, all of which may be called nucleated villages: Boycott, Dadford, Lamport and Stowe. These were even more widely spaced than the ends of Leckhampstead; the inhabitants of Boycott and Dadford, for example, were able to develop their own field systems. But in many ways, these four settlements may be likened to 'ends' and probably grew in much the same way from pre-village nuclei. But instead of forming a single dispersed village, the parish of Stowe would be divided into four separate townships. It is likely, however, that the routes to dispersion and nucleation were in reality far more complex than simply the chance location of their earliest centres.

Nucleation and dispersion: end-products of the same process

There can be little doubt that both nucleations and dispersions were the end-products of *processes* rather than unique *events*. In Whittlewood, perhaps in contrast with other parts of the midlands, there is almost no evidence to support the idea that nucleation took place rapidly, or that it involved those living in outlying farms being moved or moving voluntarily to a new centre.[29] Rather, our nucleations appear to find their origins in slow growth out from earlier settlement foci, perhaps coupled with the infilling of vacant plots. Currently we have no knowledge of the actual decisions by which individual houses were sited or how the early inhabited area was divided by gift, purchase and inheritance into messuages, curtilages and crofts. Nor is it known whether these villages initially grew organically or by planned stages. But if the details are hazy, the general trend for expansion from an original core is clear in many of the Whittlewood villages. In the same way, the small hamlet clusters comprising our dispersed villages also seem to have developed around and grown from very similar nodes. Whatever the processes at play, however, the Whittlewood data clearly stand in opposition to any claims that dispersion simply reflects stasis, the survival of an earlier and more primitive settlement pattern. Dispersed settlement developed as a consequence of dynamic change.

What appears to emerge from the evidence is that nucleated and dispersed settlements were in fact end-products of very similar, if not identical, processes. This view finds some support, for instance, in the chronology of their development: both nucleated and dispersed villages formed over the same prolonged period from AD 850. So the basic framework of the dispersed village of Leckhampstead might have already been in place by AD 850, but this was supplemented in the post-Conquest period by the addition of another distinct hamlet cluster, Middle End. At Silverstone, dispersion appears to have occurred over a period of 250 years, during which time first West End and later Cattle End were added to the main village. Likewise, in Wicken dispersion was sequential, with the addition of hamlets such as Elm Green and perhaps Wick Hurst to the three earlier centres at Wick Hamon, Wick Dive and Dagnall. But elsewhere, seemingly oblivious to the explosion in the number of settlements now in the landscape immediately surrounding them, places such as Lillingstone Dayrell and Whittlebury developed as examples of single-centred settlements. This common chronology and the interconnected process of outward growth from earlier centres appears to imply that many of the socio-economic influences and agencies that lay behind both developments were shared by the two forms of settlement.

If there were no fundamental differences between nucleation and dispersion, there were clearly subtle and important distinctions which, at a local level, resulted in one settlement form being favoured over another. The decision to nucleate or to disperse may have been made communally and consciously, but equally it may have begun almost imperceptibly. A tiny shift in emphasis at any point in the development of a settlement might have started a chain reaction with enormous and perhaps unpredictable consequences for settlement morphology. The decision of just one farming unit, for instance, to relocate to the vicinity of another might be sufficient to begin an irreversible process of nucleation which would ultimately affect the whole community. And the converse may also have been true: a conscious move away from a central place could stimulate a larger movement towards dispersion. In sociological terms, it is well-attested how the micromotives of an individual or small group of individuals can quickly escalate into a pattern of communal macrobehaviour, a developmental model best exemplified by Schelling's 'segregated city', otherwise known as the 'tipping theory'.[30] But what might drive the initial moves? And why should it result in distinct regional preferences towards either nucleation or dispersion rather than the blanket adoption of a single settlement form?

Christopher Taylor's observation that the boundaries between zones of nucleation and dispersion cannot be correlated with topography or geology, the amount of arable, woodland or pasture, social structures, patterns of lordship or tenure, or areas of high or low population, is a warning that no single cause is likely to explain their distribution.[31] Far from being insignificant, however, it is probable that all had a part in the conscious or unconscious decision-making of rural communities, and other scholars have made fine cases for the overriding importance of one or more of these causes in the development of regional settlement patterns, while recognising the complex interplay between these and other factors.[32] Ultimately, however, decisions were made at local level, by people making a living off the land: by lords wishing to maximise their incomes through the extraction of tribute, services, taxes and rents from their tenants; and the peasantry itself responding to these demands and seeking to produce surpluses for sale at the market. What the land could offer in terms of the farming systems it might support, and how this land was organised, must, therefore, have been of primary significance to all communities, and must have been a fundamental influence upon how the land was settled. This relationship has long been recognised, of course, its most obvious expression the link between largely arable economies and nucleation, and pastoral communities and dispersed settlement.

But beyond the few specialist farming zones where topography, soils and climate dictated that animal husbandry and dispersed settlement was the only viable economic option, in most places medieval agriculture was mixed, combining the raising of stock with the growing of crops. In these areas, there was no overriding economic or practical necessity for settlements to take either a nucleated or dispersed form. Yet in certain regions one type eventually came to predominate. One reason may have been changes in their economic focus. In mixed but biased farming regimes, which strongly favoured either arable or livestock, small changes in the ratio of these activities were unlikely to force settlement change. This might be likened to warm water cooling by a few degrees but remaining in liquid state. But under more equitable regimes, small shifts might inexorably tip the balance in favour of one form of farming over another, with fundamental consequences for settlement form, akin, in this case, to cooling water crystallising into solid form as a result of miniscule changes in temperature around freezing point. This moment of transition, which may have been effected consciously or have resulted from global changes, might equally have arisen from small events, perhaps the failure of a single crop, or an isolated outbreak of animal murrain, or a small fluctuation in the local market. If of this kind, then it is unlikely that the seminal moments in settlement development will have left any trace in either the historical or archaeological record. Such invisibility might help to explain why it has so far proven impossible to be categorical about the underlying factors which led to nucleation and dispersion. Where did such equitable farming regimes flourish in the ninth and tenth century? The answer lies in the Central Province and, particularly, in the southern and eastern midlands. Could it be that small shifts of farming emphasis towards more extensive arable cultivation, perhaps affecting only a handful of individual communities in this core zone, led to the first nucleations, a concept that then fairly rapidly spread as the new cereal belt was expanded?[33]

That nucleated and dispersed forms of settlement might form organically in accordance with natural laws perhaps offers a new way of thinking about this subject. It finds a ready-made home in the growing acceptance of the theory of complexity, current in both the physical and social sciences, which acknowledges the role of self-organisation in the development of composite structures.[34] Complexity has provided a valuable model to explain, for example, the tendency for industries of similar type to agglomerate in certain areas, often away from their principal sources of raw materials; or the transition from weakly to strongly integrated systems, such as the shift from a local to global market, or indeed from water into ice. All these models provide close analogies for the development of medieval rural settlement of all types.

Choosing dispersion over nucleation

But there are clear indications that some types of medieval settlement did not simply happen, but were purposely conceived, encouraged and promoted in preference to other forms of communal living. This, of course, has long been accepted as a contributory factor in the process of nucleation, but there is now a substantial body of information to suspect that it lies behind dispersion too. Why, for example, in Wick Hamon around 1100 was a previously unoccupied part of the parish, lying 2.5 km (1.5 miles) south of the main village, developed into the hamlet of Elm Green, when there appears to have been ample scope for further expansion of the existing village core? Who or what guided or motivated people to congregate around what appears to have been a single farm at Dagnall in the neighbouring parish of Wick Dive, again in the first half of the twelfth century, in preference to the parochial village itself? What prompted the development of the proximal, but geographically distinct and tenurially dependent hamlets of West End and Cattle End around Silverstone or, in a similar move, the hamlet of Middle End in Leckhampstead, when their populations might equally have been accommodated in the principal existing centres? These questions are placed in sharper relief by other developments in the vicinity. Around 1100, new rows of peasant tofts were being laid out and extended from the village cores of Akeley, Lillingstone Dayrell and Wick Dive. A century or so later, a similar village extension was executed at Whittlebury, and in the middle of the thirteenth century also at Lillingstone Lovell. Those that chose nucleation or dispersion thus did so with full knowledge of alternative settlement templates.

This fact alone indicates that both forms of settlement developed as a result of positive choice. Whether the advantages of one form of settlement over another were real or simply perceived, they were sufficient to guide neighbouring communities towards different settlement models.

The advantages of nucleation have been well rehearsed and have been mentioned briefly above. There were disadvantages too. Primarily, the concentration of human and agricultural resources in one place divorced farmers from their land, extending the distance over which men, animals and ploughs had to be transported or vital manure carted. This time/distance deterrent was especially exaggerated in the midlands by the division of landholding units across the open fields. Against this must have been weighed the opportunities to extend the areas available for arable cultivation, the ease with which communal resources such as ploughs and carts could be pooled, and the more efficient management of the agricultural cycle, particularly with regard to the harvesting and ploughing of the demesne. But with the exception of exclusively monocultural arable farming regimes, of which there were very few, equal if not improved efficiency could have been achieved from a dispersed settlement pattern. The distance between the furthest furlongs and the nearest centre of population would have been reduced, producing a more cost-effective method of farming which reduced the time spent travelling to and from the fields. This may perhaps explain the hamlet creations of Dagnall and Elm Green, new satellites which allowed further areas of arable to be created in those parts of the parish furthest from the principal village. If a dispersed cluster reached a critical mass of around half a dozen households, problems of pooled resources also seem to disappear, for it is likely that these too would have been able to supply at least enough oxen for a single communal ploughteam. Co-aration then need not have necessitated total nucleation.[35] Indeed, the farming of typical midland demesnes, characteristically dispersed amongst the peasant strips in the open fields, during the agricultural year's two 'bottlenecks', often cited as a driving force for nucleation, would have been made less not more efficient where it demanded the assembly of ploughteams at a single centre. Dispersed settlements would have offered a choice of rendezvous, which might be chosen advantageously to fit the cycle of field rotation or the individual strips that required work. Where space was not at a premium, where the significance of arable cultivation to the local economy did not demand that every available acre should be devoted to cereal cultivation, in these places, one might expect dispersed settlement patterns to be preferred over nucleated models.

The disadvantages of nucleation for more pastoral economies are even easier to identify. Animals not only require access to pasture, but also demand greater and more regular consideration than arable crops. Daily care is required for milking herds, while at a number of other critical points in the year – for example, shearing, calving and lambing in the spring, or folding during the autumn and winter – much time and energy was required to be expended on the herd or flock. On modern mixed farms, the greater attention demanded by livestock over arable manifests itself in the almost universal arrangement of permanent pasture around the farm and arable fields on the estate edge. Nucleations may have offered small public spaces such as greens, on which the community's livestock could be folded or overwintered, but private space within crofts was restricted. Livestock farming thus demanded a dispersed settlement pattern. It is probably here that the link between settlement plan and economy is seen most clearly. For, elsewhere, the relationship is far less clear: as we have seen, arable farming did not demand nucleation to the extent that animal husbandry required dispersal. Often, however, nucleation was a consequence of attempts to maximise arable production.

In many ways, it seems that the problems associated with living in both large nucleations and, at the other extreme, in isolated farmsteads could be resolved by the development of the hamlet cluster or small nucleation: particularly so if a number of these small foci were bound together administratively, rather than geographically, to form a more sizeable community. In such situations, households remained close to their land, had space for expansion, for the cultivation of vegetables and for the keeping of livestock, and had neighbours upon whom they could call. They avoided the deprivations of a solitary lifestyle, while also avoiding the restrictions imposed by larger settlements. When a number of these hamlets worked in unison, they could provide the levels of manpower and equipment to work the land efficiently, and could expect to sustain an economy which would challenge the largest nucleations. Dispersed settlement models must have offered strong competition to the nucleation model. In the end, perhaps for the smallest of reasons, one settlement type might be chosen over another. What precise considerations lay behind the critical decisions made by individual communities either to develop new geographically distinct nodes, to continue to develop pre-existing centres whatever their number, or to concentrate growth at a single centre may never be understood. But these choices need not have been profoundly different in order to produce very different forms of settlement. If the nucleated village was one medieval rural ideal, for others the dispersed village model, comprising a number of small settlement

clusters, must have been equally attractive. We might see the community at Leckhampstead carefully preserving this arrangement, and the
communities of Silverstone and Wicken actively creating such a settlement pattern, in the four centuries straddling the Norman Conquest.
If it can be entertained that the model of nucleation proved so popular
that it spread by emulation, there is perhaps no reason why the model
of the dispersed village might not have been disseminated and copied
in the same fashion.

Conclusions

Historians, archaeologists and geographers who seek to understand
past landscapes are only too aware of the fragmentary nature of the
evidence on which they must base their conclusions. Much of this
book has been concerned with revealing the physical structure of
a small part of midland England, the uses to which the land was
put, and how it was settled. Our view of medieval Whittlewood has
either been obscured behind more recent agricultural developments,
or totally erased by them. However, extensive archaeological investigation, rich documentary sources and the targeted exploration of the
palaeoenvironmental record, the built environment and place-names,
have ensured that the historic landscape can be reconstructed with
some accuracy. The shifting location of settlements and changes in
their form can all be charted over time, as can the arrangement of
fields, pasture and woodland. Inevitably, the picture that emerges
of more remote periods is not as full. Yet even so, the fundamental
stages through which the landscape passed to produce that of the
early Middle Ages, the landscape within which villages began to form,
can still be identified.

There are no landscapes without people. What led one particular
group of medieval inhabitants, the Whittlewood villagers, to adopt
and develop new forms of settlement and to introduce novel systems
of farming has been the focus of this book. Their testimony has been
hard won. No document chronicles the moment of village creation,
nor indeed any subsequent reorganisation of their plans. Similar
silence surrounds the laying-out of the open fields and the parcelling
of woodland into enclosed coppices. But these people have left an
imprint on the surface of the land, in the surviving shape of their
villages, earthworks of abandoned settlement sites, woodland banks,
ridge and furrow and scatters of pottery, all of which help to define
the extent of settlement and agriculture. Together with echoes of
earlier arrangements preserved in later documents, these have been
used to explore the agencies that lay behind fundamental change in

the Whittlewood countryside between AD 800 and 1400, together with the ways in which the land was perceived, divided, organised and exploited. Critically, answers have been sought to how and why different communities developed alternative forms of communal living: the nucleated village, the dispersed settlement, the hamlet and the farmstead. Despite its title, much of this book has necessarily been concerned with the 'middles' of these settlements, not just because it is here that the historian and archaeologist can combine forces most easily, but because it is also here that clues to their beginnings and ends invariably reside.

Notes to the Chapters

Notes to Chapter 1: Studying Medieval Villages and Landscapes

1. Fox, 'Adoption of the midland system', 94–8.
2. Mynard *et al.*, *Great Linford*.
3. Taylor, *Village and Farmstead*, 15; Lewis *et al.*, *Village, Hamlet and Field*, 49–51; Taylor, 'Polyfocal settlement'.
4. Roberts, *Rural Settlement*, 82–4.
5. Maitland, *Domesday Book and Beyond*, 38–9.
6. Roberts and Wrathmell, *Atlas of Rural Settlement*; Roberts and Wrathmell, *Region and Place*.
7. Thorpe, 'Rural settlement', 360–1; Roberts, *Rural Settlement*, 16; Lewis *et al.*, *Village, Hamlet and Field*, 4.
8. Beresford and Hurst, *Deserted Medieval Villages*, 66.
9. Dyer, 'Mapping rural England', 7.
10. Roberts and Wrathmell, *Region and Place*, 1–2.
11. Rackham, *History of the Countryside*, 4–5.
12. Everitt, 'Country, county and town', 16. See also Thirsk, *Rural England*.
13. Phythian-Adams, 'Introduction', 9–23.
14. Roberts and Wrathmell, *Region and Place*, 8, 10, 64.
15. Taylor, 'Dispersed settlement in nucleated areas'.
16. Roberts and Wrathmell, *Region and Place*, 54–6, 180–1.
17. For a recent study, see Gelling and Cole, *Landscape of Place-names*.
18. Taylor, *Village and Farmstead*, 109–10; Williamson, *Shaping Medieval Landscapes*, 9–10; Gray, *English Field Systems*, 411.
19. Thirsk, 'Common fields'.
20. Rippon, 'Landscapes in transition', 57–8.
21. e.g. Oosthuizen, 'Origins of Cambridgeshire'.
22. Hinton, '"Scole-Dickleburgh" examined'; Williamson, '"Scole-Dickleburgh" revisited'.
23. Oosthuizen, 'Prehistoric fields into medieval furlongs?', 151.
24. Hesse, 'Field systems in south-west Cambridgeshire'; Harrison, 'Open fields and earlier landscapes'; Oosthuizen, 'Roots of the common fields'.
25. Rippon, 'Landscapes in transition', 49, 51, 56.
26. Oosthuizen, 'Prehistoric fields into medieval furlongs', 151.
27. Brown and Foard, 'Saxon landscape', 73.
28. Upex, 'Landscape continuity', 99.
29. Losco-Bradley and Kinsley, *Catholme*, 15–20, 123–9.
30. Taylor, 'Saxon settlement at Quarrington'.
31. Rippon, 'Landscapes in transition', 58.
32. Lewis *et al.*, *Village, Hamlet and Field*, 76–7.
33. Brown and Foard, 'Saxon landscape', 71.
34. Jones and Page, 'Characterizing rural settlement', 66.
35. Rippon, 'Landscapes in transition', 55–7.
36. Dark, *Environment of Britain*, 134–56.
37. Wright, 'Woodland continuity and change'.
38. Branch *et al.*, *Whittlewood project*.
39. Taylor, *Village and Farmstead*, 131.
40. Hall and Martin, 'Brixworth'; Shaw, 'Discovery of Saxon sites'; Brown and Foard, 'Saxon landscape', 73–6.
41. Brown and Foard, 'Saxon landscape', 77–82; Lewis *et al.*, *Village, Hamlet and Field*, 193.
42. Brown and Foard, 'Saxon landscape', 82–92.
43. Aston and Gerrard, 'Shapwick project', 29.
44. Oosthuizen, 'Ancient greens'.
45. Oosthuizen, 'Medieval settlement relocation'.
46. Dyer, 'Power and conflict', 11; Lewis *et al.*, *Village, Hamlet and Field*, 177–9.
47. Aston and Gerrard, 'Shapwick project', 29.

48. Aldred and Dyer, 'Medieval Cotswold village'.
49. Lewis *et al.*, *Village, Hamlet and Field*, 151; Oosthuizen, 'Prehistoric fields into medieval furlongs', 151.
50. Harvey, 'Initiative and authority', 43.
51. Brown and Foard, 'Saxon landscape', 90–2.
52. Taylor, *Village and Farmstead*, 131.
53. Taylor, *Village and Farmstead*, 12–15; Hamerow, 'Settlement mobility'; Lewis *et al.*, *Village, Hamlet and Field*, 13–16.
54. Williamson, *Shaping Medieval Landscapes*, 155.
55. Ibid., 173–4.
56. Williamson, *Shaping Medieval Landscapes*, 181; Lewis *et al.*, *Village, Hamlet and Field*, 143–5, 148.
57. Williamson, *Shaping Medieval Landscapes*, 192.
58. Taylor, 'Nucleated settlement', 53–4.
59. Lewis *et al.*, *Village, Hamlet and Field*, 200; Taylor, 'Nucleated settlement', 54.
60. Lewis *et al.*, *Village, Hamlet and Field*, 201–2; Taylor, 'Dispersed settlement in nucleated areas'.
61. Taylor, 'Nucleated settlement', 55.
62. Lewis *et al.*, *Village, Hamlet and Field*, 172–82, 191.
63. Williamson, *Shaping Medieval Landscapes*, 198–9.
64. Harvey, 'Initiative and authority'; Lewis *et al.*, *Village, Hamlet and Field*, 198–201; Brown and Foard, 'Saxon landscape'.
65. Morris, *Churches in the Landscape*, 248–74.
66. Taylor, *Village and Farmstead*, 133–47.
67. Ibid., 146–7, 151–2.

Notes to Chapter 2: Whittlewood: An Introduction

1. Hoskins, *Making of the English Landscape*, 14.
2. NRO Map 4210; Brown and Roberts, *Passenham*, 229–30; cf. Mastoris and Groves, *Sherwood Forest*.
3. Finch, 'Fox-hunting'; Thirsk, *Alternative Agriculture*, 230.
4. Linnell, *Old Oak*, 3.
5. Neeson, *Commoners*.
6. *VCH, Northamptonshire*, V, 13.
7. Beckett, *Rise and Fall of the Grenvilles*, 283–4; *VCH, Northamptonshire*, V, 15, 35–6, 215, 303, 305–6, 418–19.
8. Pevsner and Cherry, *Northamptonshire*, 377.
9. Private collection: Ministry of Health clearance order, 22 October 1936 (we owe this reference to the kindness of David and Christine Jackson); *VCH, Northamptonshire*, V, 15–16.
10. *Akeley: Past Times* (2001); *Potterspury: The Story of a Village and its People* (2001); *Silverstone: An Historical Mosaic* (2001).
11. Lewis *et al.*, *Village, Hamlet and Field*.
12. Lewis and Mitchell-Fox, 'Leverhulme project'; Dyer, 'Whittlewood project'.
13. Jones, 'Signatures in the soil', 162; Gerrard, 'Misplaced faith?'.
14. For an exception, see Hall, 'Woodland landscapes'.
15. e.g. Foard, 'Systematic fieldwalking'.
16. For the Whittlewood area, see RCHME, *Southwest Northamptonshire*.
17. Jones, 'Luffield Priory grange'.
18. Riley, *Stowe Park*.
19. Bridges, *Northamptonshire*; Baker, *County of Northampton*. See also Stamper, 'Northamptonshire'.
20. *VCH, Northamptonshire*, V.
21. Elvey, *Luffield Priory Charters*; Pettit, *Royal Forests*; Hall, *Open Fields*.
22. Steane, *Northamptonshire Landscape*.
23. Brown and Roberts, *Passenham*.
24. Linnell, *Old Oak*.
25. Willis, *Buckingham*; Lipscomb, *County of Buckingham*; Sheahan, *History and Topography of Buckinghamshire*; Bolton, 'Buckinghamshire'.
26. Reed, *Buckinghamshire Landscape*; Clarke, 'History of Stowe'.
27. Reed, 'Seventeenth-century Stowe'; Bevington *et al.*, *Stowe Landscape Gardens*.
28. TNA:PRO E179/155/31, E179/161/8–10; Chibnall, *Early Taxation Returns*, 39–41.
29. Fenwick, *Poll Taxes*.
30. Raftis, *Assart Data*, 97–156.
31. Illingworth and Caley, *RH*, II, 338–41, 835–6.
32. TNA:PRO SC6/759/31; SC6/1089/6, 16–18; SC6/1120/10; DL29/324/5303–4, 5306, 5311–12; DL29/325/5316–19, 5321.
33. TNA:PRO SC6/949/2, SC6/1123/4; BLO, Oseney Rolls 94.
34. NCO 4084–5; NRO Misc Ph 1682, XYZ 1390; WAM 27769–79.
35. BL Harleian MS 4714; Elvey, *Luffield Priory Charters*; Salter, *Oseney Abbey*, V.

Notes to Chapter 3: Inherited Landscapes

1. Hamerow, *Early Medieval Settlements*, 52–4, 93–103.
2. Waterbolk, 'Patterns of the peasant landscape', 30–3.
3. Roberts and Wrathmell, *Atlas of Rural Settlement*, 28–34; Finberg, *Roman and Saxon Withington*; Taylor, 'Whiteparish'; Phythian-Adams, *Continuity, Fields and Fission*.
4. Sumbler, *London and the Thames Valley*, 118–22.
5. Toulmin Smith, *Itinerary of John Leland*, I, 10–11; II, 35.
6. Martin and Hall, 'Brixworth'; Phillips, *Mesolithic in Northamptonshire*, 5.
7. Walker, *Towcester retail development*.
8. Branch *et al.*, *Whittlewood project*.
9. Healy *et al.*, 'Excavations of a Mesolithic site', 71–2.
10. Evans, *Environment of Early Man*, 94.
11. Fyfe *et al.*, 'Mesolithic to Bronze Age vegetation change', 179.
12. Phillips, *Mesolithic in Northamptonshire*, 2.
13. Mellars, 'Fire ecology', 35–6; Innes and Blackford, 'Ecology of late Mesolithic woodland', 191–2.
14. Healy *et al.*, 'Excavations of a Mesolithic site', 72.
15. Simmons, *Environmental Impact*, 148–9.
16. Branch *et al.*, *Whittlewood project*.
17. Pers. comm., Lynden Cooper, University of Leicester; Hall, 'Survey work in eastern England', 32–3.
18. Evans *et al.*, 'Upper Kennet valley', 187.
19. Brown and Meadows, 'Environmental analysis', 188–9.
20. RCHME, *South-west Northamptonshire*, 34, 171.
21. Pers. comm., Northamptonshire Archaeology.
22. RCHME, *South-west Northamptonshire*, 118.
23. Green, 'Early Bronze Age burial', 100, 126–9; Green, 'Stacey Bushes', 11–16.
24. Malim, 'Ritual landscape'.
25. Green, 'Early Bronze Age burial', 130–6; Parker Pearson, *Bronze Age Britain*, 91.
26. Malim, 'Ritual landscape', 81–2; Parker Pearson, *Bronze Age Britain*, 91–2.
27. Grimes, *Excavations of Defence Sites*, I, 245–7.
28. Knight, *Late Bronze Age and Iron Age Settlement*, 304.
29. Ibid., 271, 280.
30. Northamptonshire Archaeology, *A43 Towcester to M40 dualling project*.
31. Knight, *Late Bronze Age and Iron Age Settlement*, 324.
32. RCHME, *South-west Northamptonshire*, 168.
33. Meek, *Salcey Deanshanger*; RCHME, *South-west Northamptonshire*, 188.
34. Meek, 'Settlement site at Potterspury'.
35. RCHME, *South-west Northamptonshire*, 41.
36. Ibid.
37. Ibid.
38. Ibid., 118.
39. Ibid., 168.
40. Chapman, 'Crick'; Hughes, *Covert Farm*; Thomas and Enright, 'Excavation at Wilby Way', 61–6.
41. Knight, *Late Bronze Age and Iron Age Settlement*, 324–9.
42. Ingle, 'Quernstones from Hunsbury hillfort', 31–2.
43. Jackson, 'Settlement and activity around Hunsbury hillfort', 37, 44–6.
44. Foster, 'Late Iron Age/early Roman Northamptonshire', 131–3.
45. RCHME, *South-west Northamptonshire*, 112.
46. Jackson, 'Settlement and activity around Hunsbury hillfort', 37, 44–6; RCHME, *South-west Northamptonshire*, 12; Brown and Taylor, 'Settlement and land use in Northamptonshire', 88–9.
47. Vaughan-Williams, *Archaeobotanical remains*.
48. Meadows, 'Wollaston'; Ovenden-Wilson, *Grange Park*; Thomas, *Grange Park*; Foster, *Changes in the landscape*.
49. e.g. Taylor and Dix, 'Iron Age and Roman settlement at Ashley'; Williams and Zeepvat, *Bancroft*; Quinnell, 'Villa and temple at Cosgrove'; Friendship-Taylor, 'Piddington'; Neal, 'Stanwick villa'; Jackson and Dix, 'Late Iron Age and Roman settlement at Weekley'; pers. comm., Stephen Young, University College, Northampton, regarding Whitehall.
50. RCHME, *South-west Northamptonshire*, 41.
51. Following Gaffney and Tingle, *Maddle Farm Project*, 220–3.
52. Ibid., 220.
53. Parry *Raunds*, 76.
54. Branch *et al.*, *Whittlewood project*.

55. Meek, 'Settlement site at Potterspury', 195.

56. RCHME, *South-west Northamptonshire*, 41.

57. Kron, 'Roman ley-farming'.

58. Marshall, *Bourbon Fields*; Wainwright, *Fallow deer park*.

59. RCHME, *South-west Northamptonshire*, 150–6.

60. Rivet and Smith, *Place-names of Roman Britain*, 347–8, 382–3.

61. RCHME, *South-west Northamptonshire*, 41.

62. Meek, 'Settlement site at Potterspury', 196–7.

63. Parry *Rounds*, 80–1.

64. Branch *et al.*, *Whittlewood project*.

Notes to Chapter 4: Authoritative Landscapes

1. Faith, *English Peasantry*, 1–11; Hooke, *Landscape of Anglo-Saxon England*, 39–54.

2. Hamerow, *Early Medieval Settlements*, 103.

3. Hooke, 'Early units of government', 48.

4. RCHME, *South-west Northamptonshire*, 109–10.

5. Jones and Page, 'Characterizing rural settlement', 66; Taylor, *Village and Farmstead*, 116.

6. RCHME, *South-west Northamptonshire*, 151.

7. Branch *et al.*, *Whittlewood project*.

8. Dyer, *Making a Living*, 26–9; Britnell, *Britain and Ireland*, 59–61.

9. Hooke, 'Early medieval estate and settlement patterns', 10–12; Fox, 'People of the wolds', 87–9.

10. Davies, *Vikings to Normans*, 147–9.

11. TNA:PRO SC6/HenVIII/6033, m. 3.

12. Whitelock, *English Historical Documents*, 427.

13. *VCH, Oxfordshire*, VI, 3.

14. Coates, 'New light'.

15. Swanton, *ASC*, 102.

16. Jones, 'Signatures in the soil', 164, 184.

17. Watts, *Place-names*, 357, 583, 644; Clarke, 'History of Stowe', 214.

18. Hadley, 'Multiple estates'.

19. Bailey, 'Early Anglo-Saxon territorial organization', 133–5.

20. Foard, 'Administrative organization of Northamptonshire', 193–200.

21. Bassett, 'Origins of Anglo-Saxon kingdoms', 24.

22. Rippon, 'Landscapes in transition', 49.

23. Brown and Taylor, 'Settlement and land use in Northamptonshire', 89.

24. Taylor, *Village and Farmstead*, 41; Foard, 'Administrative organization of Northamptonshire', 197.

25. Bradley, 'Time regained'.

26. Pers. comm., David Parsons and Paul Cullen, University of Nottingham; cf. Kitson, 'Anglo-Saxon personal names', 125.

27. Young, *Royal Forests*, 2.

28. Page, 'Extent of Whittlewood Forest', 25.

29. Dyer, *Making a Living*, 30–3; Faith, *English Peasantry*, 168–9.

30. Langdon, *Mills*, 182–5.

31. Lewis *et al.*, *Village, Hamlet and Field*, 140–1; Jones, 'Signatures in the soil', 165–6.

32. Lewis *et al.*, *Village, Hamlet and Field*, 135–6.

33. Faith, *English Peasantry*, 209.

34. Harvey, 'Initiative and authority', 36–43.

35. Blair, 'From minster to parish church', 7–8.

36. *VCH, Northamptonshire*, V, 234.

37. Salter, *Newington Longeville Charters*, no. 16.

38. Barnwell, *Medieval churches*, 8–10.

39. Reynolds, *Kingdoms and Communities*, 81; Faith, *English Peasantry*, 167.

40. Taylor, *Village and Farmstead*, 124; Watts, *Place-names*, 583.

41. Blair, 'From minster to parish church', 8–9.

42. Barnwell, *Medieval churches*, 16; *VCH, Northamptonshire*, V, 77, 127–9.

43. James, *Britain in the First Millennium*, 223–4.

44. Mawer and Stenton, *Place-names of Buckinghamshire*, 49–50.

45. Dumville, 'Treaty of Alfred and Guthrum', 1–23; Davis, 'Alfred and Guthrum's frontier'.

46. Swanton, *ASC*, 102–3.

47. Campbell, *Anglo-Saxons*, 172; Loyn, *Governance*, 133–6.

48. Steane, *Northamptonshire Landscape*, 85; Stafford, *East Midlands*, 139.

49. Reed, *Buckinghamshire Landscape*, 77–9.

50. Blair, *Anglo-Saxon Oxfordshire*, 102.

51. Swanton, *ASC*, 100.

52. Phythian-Adams, 'Introduction', 9–18.

53. Hooke, *Landscape of Anglo-Saxon England*, 66–7.

54. Whitelock, *English Historical Documents*, 429–30.

55. Douglas and Greenaway, *English Historical Documents*, 517–20.

56. Loyn, *Governance*, 140–6.

57. Gover *et al.*, *Place-names of Northamptonshire*, 38, 96; Gelling, *Place-names of Oxfordshire*, I, 196.

58. Meaney, 'Hundred meeting-places'.
59. Franklin, *Minsters and parishes*, 314–15, 329.

60. Gelling, 'Stôw', 194; Klingelhöfer, *Manor*, 84–91, 103–12.

Notes to Chapter 5: Beginnings: The Origins of the Village

1. For a recent survey of the period, see Davies, *Vikings to Normans*.
2. e.g. Hall and Coles, *Fenland Survey*; Higham, *Frontier Landscape*; Rippon, *Transformation of Coastal Wetlands*; Van de Noort, *Humber Wetlands*.
3. Lewis *et al.*, *Village, Hamlet and Field*, 191–204.
4. e.g. Seebohm, *English Village Community*; Homans, *English Villagers*; Dyer, *Making a Living*.
5. Roberts, *Making of the English Village*, 6–7.
6. Rippon, *Historic Landscape Analysis*, 8–14.
7. Above, Chapter 1 n.18.
8. Gray, *English Field Systems*, 403–18.
9. Homans, *English Villagers*, 92–101.
10. Baker and Butlin, *Studies of Field Systems*, 624–5.
11. Thirsk, 'Common fields'.
12. Foard, 'Systematic fieldwalking'.
13. Brown and Foard, 'Saxon landscape', 82–92.
14. Harvey, 'Origin of planned field systems', 185–91.
15. Hall, 'Origins of open-field agriculture', 34–8.
16. Hall, *Open Fields*, 133–5.
17. Brown and Foard, 'Saxon landscape', 76–7, 89–92.
18. Lewis *et al.*, *Village, Hamlet and Field*, 191.
19. Ibid., 198–202.
20. Williamson, *Shaping Medieval Landscapes*, 182.
21. Ibid.
22. Hall, 'Late Saxon countryside', 100–1.
23. Hey, *Yarnton*, 28, 30, 37.
24. Branch *et al.*, *Whittlewood project*; Jones, 'Signatures in the soil', 164, 184.

25. Hey, *Yarnton*, 86–91.
26. Brown and Foard, 'Saxon landscape', 76.
27. Hall, 'Late Saxon countryside', 101.
28. Brown and Foard, 'Saxon landscape'; Williams, *Pennyland*; Hey, *Yarnton*; Millett, 'Cowdery's Down'; Losco-Bradley and Kinsley, *Catholme*; Powlesland, *West Heslerton*; Steedman, 'Riby Crossroads'.
29. Jones, 'Signatures in the soil', 165, 167.
30. Ibid., 167–9.
31. Hall, *Open Fields*, 131–5.
32. Fowler, *Landscape Plotted and Pieced*, 235–6.
33. NCO 4467.
34. Williamson, *Shaping Medieval Landscapes*, 173–7.
35. Faith, *English Peasantry*, 179–80; Carpenter, *Struggle for Mastery*, 79–80.
36. Faith, *English Peasantry*, 180–1.
37. Dyer, *Making a Living*, 85; Carpenter, *Struggle for Mastery*, 82.
38. Dyer, *Making a Living*, 88; Faith, *English Peasantry*, 216–17.
39. Lewis *et al.*, *Village, Hamlet and Field*, 149–50.
40. Illingworth and Caley, *RH*, II, 339–41.
41. Faith, *English Peasantry*, 201–44.
42. Bishop, *Medieval Nottinghamshire*.
43. Millett, 'Cowdery's Down', 247–9; Warner, *Origins of Suffolk*, 123–7.
44. Hey, *Yarnton*, 86–91.
45. Mynard *et al.*, *Great Linford*, 16–17.
46. Cooper and Priest, 'Great Easton'; Liddle, *Anglo-Saxon Leicestershire*.
47. Lewis *et al.*, *Village, Hamlet and Field*, 81.
48. cf. Taylor, *Village and Farmstead*, 131.

Notes to Chapter 6: The Forest

1. Poole, *Domesday Book to Magna Carta*, 34.
2. Bartlett, *England under the Norman and Angevin Kings*, 674.
3. Poole, *Domesday Book to Magna Carta*, 35.
4. Dyer, *Hanbury*, 48.
5. Rackham, *History of the Countryside*, 131–8.
6. Gilbert, *Hunting*, 10–12.
7. Jones and Page, 'Characterizing rural settlement', 61, 63–6.

8. Branch *et al.*, *Whittlewood project*.
9. Gelling and Cole, *Landscape of Place-names*, 220, 237.
10. Ibid., 230.
11. Mawer and Stenton, *Place-names of Buckinghamshire*, 41; Gover *et al.*, *Place-names of Northamptonshire*, 2, 45–6.
12. VCH, *Northamptonshire*, I, 304; Foard, 'Rockingham Forest', 44–5.

13. Rackham, *Ancient Woodland*, 114. The calculation is as follows:
(4x12) × (3x12) × 10 × 0.7 = 12,096.

14. Elvey, *Luffield Priory Charters*, I, 162–7, 174–5, 215–16; II, 80–1; TNA:PRO E32/108, m. 2; Jones, 'Luffield Priory grange'.

15. Rackham, *Ancient Woodland*, 119.

16. Ibid., 119–20.

17. e.g. TNA:PRO E32/112, m. 3, listing the oaks felled in 1345.

18. Leckhampstead: 600 pigs, 695 acres (1:1.16); Stowe: 540 pigs, 630 acres (1:1.17).

19. Rackham, *Ancient Woodland*, 179; cf. Stenton, *Anglo-Saxon England*, 684; Elvey, *Luffield Priory Charters*, I, 16.

20. Bartlett, *England under the Norman and Angevin Kings*, 170.

21. Page, 'Extent of Whittlewood Forest', 29–30.

22. Davis *et al.*, *Regesta Regum Anglo-Normannorum*, II, no. 1671.

23. Allen Brown *et al.*, *History of the King's Works*, II, 1002, 1006; *Pipe Roll 17 Henry II* (Pipe Roll Soc., 16, 1893), 45.

24. *Pipe Roll 24 Henry II* (Pipe Roll Soc., 27, 1906), 49; *Pipe Roll 25 Henry II* (Pipe Roll Soc., 28, 1907), 60–1; *Pipe Roll 26 Henry II* (Pipe Roll Soc., 29, 1908), 82; *Pipe Roll 27 Henry II* (Pipe Roll Soc., 30, 1909), 67; *Pipe Roll 28 Henry II* (Pipe Roll Soc., 31, 1910), 129; *Pipe Roll 29 Henry II* (Pipe Roll Soc., 32, 1911), 118–19.

25. Allen Brown *et al.*, *History of the King's Works*, II, 742–4, 1002–3.

26. Stamper, 'Woods and parks', 140–1.

27. Baker, *County of Northampton*, II, 341; Hall, 'Woodland landscapes', 44.

28. *CR 1251–3*, 414.

29. e.g. *CR 1256–9*, 131.

30. Stamper, 'Woods and parks', 133, 145.

31. TNA:PRO E32/114, m. 1.

32. *CCR 1288–96*, 234.

33. Turner, *Select Pleas*, 124.

34. TNA:PRO SC6/1089/17, m. 10d.

35. NRO Map 4210.

36. Gover *et al.*, *Place-names of Northamptonshire*, 105; Allen Brown *et al.*, *History of the King's Works*, II, 1006.

37. *CPR 1247–58*, 198.

38. Hall, 'Woodland landscapes', 44.

39. Gelling, 'Place-names of Milton Keynes', 45.

40. Pettit, *Royal Forests*, 49 n.81; *VCH, Northamptonshire*, II, 348.

41. *CLR 1226–40*, 286.

42. *CPR 1370–4*, 354.

43. Page, 'Extent of Whittlewood Forest', 32.

44. *CR 1227–31*, 346; *CR 1231–4*, 406.

45. Gover *et al.*, *Place-names of Northamptonshire*, 44, 101–2; Hall, 'Woodland landscapes', 36–7.

46. Stamper, 'Woods and parks', 130–2; Hall, 'Woodland landscapes', 36.

47. *CPR 1354–8*, 484.

48. *CPR 1247–58*, 406.

49. Page and Jones, 'Whittlewood project', 16–17.

50. Elvey, *Luffield Priory Charters*, I, 117–18.

51. TNA:PRO E32/115, m. 2.

52. Rackham, *Ancient Woodland*, 155; *CFR 1272–1307*, 116–17.

53. Page, 'Extent of Whittlewood Forest', 29–32.

54. *VCH, Northamptonshire*, V, 305, 418.

55. Page, 'Extent of Whittlewood Forest', 31–2.

56. Ibid., 29–31.

57. TNA:PRO E32/115, m. 2.

58. Page, 'Extent of Whittlewood Forest', 23.

59. Ibid., 25, 28.

60. Ibid., 27–8, 34.

61. Ibid., 28–9.

62. Young, *Royal Forests*, 147–8.

63. Page and Jones, 'Whittlewood interim report 2000–1', 14–15.

64. Jones and Page, 'Whittlewood interim report 2003–4', 41.

65. *CIPM*, II, no. 49. For *locatores*, see Roberts, 'Nucleation and dispersion', 66.

66. Elvey, *Luffield Priory Charters*, I, 269.

67. Young, *Royal Forests*, 109.

68. See the regard and eyre rolls: TNA:PRO E32/2, m. 10 (1250), 64 (1250), 66 (1253), 69 (1255), 72, m. 8 (1272), 76, m. 6 (1286), 108 (1345), 115 (1348), 249, mm. 6–6d, 17 (early 13th century). See also Raftis, *Assart Data*, 97–149.

69. TNA:PRO E32/249, m. 6d; NRO, Map 2948.

70. *CIM*, I, no. 1111.

71. TNA:PRO DL43/8/6A, fos. 28v, 30v.

72. Jones, 'Luffield Priory grange', 129–31.

73. Elvey, *Luffield Priory Charters*, I, 162.

74. TNA:PRO E32/64, m. 5; Page and Jones, 'Whittlewood interim report 2000–1', 14–15.

75. TNA:PRO E32/115; NRO, Map 4210.

76. TNA:PRO E32/249, m. 6d.

77. For a list of forest lodges and their keepers in the eighteenth century, see *Eighth Report*, 9.

78. *CPR 1281–92*, 497.

79. *CPR 1301–7*, 229; *CCR 1279–88*, 220, 403.

80. TNA:PRO E32/75, m. 15.
81. TNA:PRO E32/2, m. 1.
82. Illingworth and Caley, *RH*, II, 340; *CIPM*, XII, no. 355; XVII, no. 45.
83. TNA:PRO E32/2, m. 1.
84. Birrell, 'Peasant deer poachers'.
85. TNA:PRO E32/70, m. 2.
86. TNA:PRO E32/249, mm. 9–9d, 17–18d; E32/2, mm. 1–3; E32/70, mm. 1–2; E32/72, m. 9; E32/76, mm. 14–15; E32/112, m. 2.
87. TNA:PRO E32/76, m. 14d; Birrell, 'Forest law', 154–5.
88. Birrell, 'Peasant deer poachers', 88.
89. TNA:PRO E32/70, m. 1.
90. Birrell, 'Forest law', 155–6.
91. Turner, *Select Pleas*, 123–4.
92. WAM 27783, m. 1.
93. Foard, 'Rockingham Forest'; *VCH, Staffordshire*, V, 62–3; *VCH, Gloucestershire*, V, 326–30, 337–40, 346.
94. TNA:PRO E179/155/31, mm. 9–10, 12–14; WAM 27783.
95. TNA:PRO E32/112, m. 3.

96. *CCR 1302–7*, 408.
97. *VCH, Northamptonshire*, V, 318.
98. Ibid., 319.
99. TNA:PRO SC2/195/25, m. 1.
100. Jones and Page, 'Whittlewood interim report 2003–4', 41.
101. *VCH, Northamptonshire*, I, 304.
102. Salter, *Oseney Abbey*, V, no. 757; Illingworth and Caley, *RH*, II, 341.
103. Elvey, *Luffield Priory Charters*, II, 420; TNA: PRO SC6/949/2, m. 1.
104. TNA:PRO DL29/324/5312, m. 2.
105. TNA:PRO SC2/155/19, m. 1; NRO TC 104, fo. 106v.
106. TNA:PRO DL29/324/5306, m. 2.
107. TNA:PRO SC2/195/25, m. 1; BRO D96/21/1.
108. Clark, *Leckhampstead dog*; Kowaleski, 'Hide and leather trade', 58.
109. Birrell, 'Peasant craftsmen'.
110. Birrell, 'Forest law', 150.
111. TNA:PRO E179/155/31, m. 9.
112. Neeson, *Commoners*.
113. Linnell, *Old Oak*, 3.

Notes to Chapter 7: Farming the Forest

1. TNA:PRO C134/50/30; Campbell, *Seigniorial Agriculture*, 80–3.
2. Lewis *et al.*, *Village, Hamlet and Field*, 135–6, 140–2.
3. Jones, 'Signatures in the soil', 165–6, 174–5, 179.
4. Bailey, *English Manor*.
5. Illingworth and Caley, *RH*, II, 338–41; Kosminsky, *Studies*, 90; Campbell, *Seigniorial Agriculture*, 56–8.
6. Page and Jones, 'Whittlewood interim report 2002–3', 32–5.
7. Page and Jones, 'Excavation of a medieval manor'.
8. *VCH, Northamptonshire*, V, 132–3.
9. TNA:PRO C134/50/30; SC6/949/2; Langdon, 'Watermills and windmills', 431–2; Langdon, *Mills*, 26–31, 34–7.
10. TNA:PRO SC6/1089/17, m. 9.
11. *CLR 1240–5*, 31, 217; *CLR 1245–51*, 82–3; *CLR 1251–60*, 415.
12. TNA:PRO C133/28/19; C133/25/3; C133/80/6.
13. Campbell, *Seigniorial Agriculture*, 68.
14. *CIPM*, III, no. 175; *RH*, II, 835.
15. BL Harleian Ch 86A44.

16. TNA:PRO DL43/8/6A; *VCH, Northamptonshire*, V, 224.
17. TNA:PRO C133/80/6.
18. TNA:PRO C135/6; WAM,27783.
19. TNA:PRO SC6/1089/16, m. 12; SC6/1089/17, m. 6d.
20. TNA:PRO SC6/1089/17, m. 9.
21. TNA:PRO SC6/1089/17, m. 6d; SC6/1089/18.
22. Campbell, *Seigniorial Agriculture*, 257, 262–3.
23. Elvey, *Luffield Priory Charters*, II, 86–7.
24. TNA:PRO SC6/1123/4, m. 3d.
25. Elvey, *Luffield Priory Charters*, II, 45–6.
26. TNA:PRO E32/66, m. 4.
27. TNA:PRO C133/25/3.
28. TNA:PRO C135/47/8.
29. Campbell, *Seigniorial Agriculture*, 12–13, 177, 191–3.
30. Jones, 'Signatures in the soil', 167, 183–4; TNA: PRO DL29/324/5306, m. 2.
31. TNA:PRO SC6/1089/17, m. 9.
32. WAM 27783; TNA:PRO SC6/1089/6, m. 3d; SC6/1089/16, m. 11.
33. TNA:PRO SC6/1089/17, m. 6d; SC6/1089/18; SC6/1123/4, m. 3d.
34. Jones, 'Luffield Priory grange', 137.

35. Elvey, *Luffield Priory Charters*, I, 174–5.
36. NRO Map 5692; Latham and Howlett, *Dictionary of Medieval Latin*, I, 1011.
37. Campbell *et al.*, *Medieval Capital*, 76–7.
38. *CIPM*, II, no. 279; TNA:PRO C135/6.
39. TNA:PRO C133/80/6; C133/100/1; C134/50/30; C134/90/16.
40. TNA:PRO SC6/1123/4, mm. 3d–4d.
41. Campbell, *Seigniorial Agriculture*, 232–4.
42. *Nonarum Inquisitiones*, 330.
43. TNA:PRO C133/80/6; C134/90/16; C133/28/19; C135/6; C135/47/8.
44. King, 'East midlands', 214–16; Campbell, *Seigniorial Agriculture*, 301–2.
45. TNA:PRO DL29/324/5306, mm. 1–1d.
46. Campbell, *Seigniorial Agriculture*, 286.
47. TNA:PRO DL29/324/5311, m. 1d.
48. TNA:PRO DL29/324/5311, 5312; DL29/325/5316, 5317, 5318, 5319, 5321.
49. TNA:PRO SC6/1089/16, m. 11; Campbell, *Seigniorial Agriculture*, 111, 120.
50. TNA:PRO SC6/1123/4, m. 3d; Campbell, *Seigniorial Agriculture*, 118, 120.
51. Elvey, *Luffield Priory Charters*, II, 46; TNA: PRO JUST1/720/1; Dyer, 'Goats', 30.
52. Pettit, *Royal Forests*, 153.
53. *Eighth Report*, 5.
54. Illingworth and Caley, *RH*, I, 33.
55. TNA:PRO E32/305A, m. 4.
56. *CPR 1247–58*, 406.
57. *CPR 1247–58*, 198.
58. Elvey, *Luffield Priory Charters*, I, 162.
59. TNA:PRO DL43/8/6A; C135/47/8.
60. TNA:PRO C135/6; C133/100/1.
61. TNA:PRO SC6/1089/17, m. 9.
62. TNA:PRO DL29/324/5311.
63. Elvey, *Luffield Priory Charters*, II, 438.
64. BLO Oseney Rolls 94.
65. TNA:PRO JUST1/720/1.
66. TNA:PRO SC6/1089/6, 16, 17, 18; SC6/1123/4; DL29/324/5303, 5304, 5306, 5311, 5312; DL29/325/5316, 5317, 5318, 5319, 5321; Elvey, *Luffield Priory Charters*, II, 46.
67. Campbell, *Seigniorial Agriculture*, 286; Dyer, *Age of Transition*, 72–3.
68. Langdon, *Horses, Oxen*, 108–11; TNA:PRO SC6/1123/4, m. 3d; DL29/324/5311, m. 2d.
69. Chibnall, *Early Taxation Returns*, 39–41.
70. TNA:PRO E32/249, mm. 6–6d.
71. Turner, *Select Pleas*, 123–4.
72. NCO 4084, mm. 4d, 7, 8; 4085, mm. 7, 11.
73. WAM 27772; NRO XYZ 1390, mm. 5, 15.
74. NCO 4084–5.
75. NRO XYZ 1390, m. 12.
76. NCO 4084, mm. 4, 5, 8.
77. WAM 27769.
78. TNA:PRO DL29/324/5311, m. 1.
79. Chibnall, *Early Taxation Returns*, 39–41.
80. TNA:PRO SC6/1089/17, m. 9.
81. NRO XYZ 1390, m. 24.
82. TNA:PRO JUST1/60, m. 5d.
83. NCO 4086, m. 28.
84. TNA:PRO DL42/115, fo. 16v; BRO D104/73.
85. TNA:PRO DL43/8/6A, fos. 12–13v, 45–51.
86. Jenkins, *Snelshall Priory*, no. 215.
87. BRO D104/73.
88. Langdon, *Mills*, 283–7.
89. TNA:PRO SC6/1123/4, m. 3; *VCH, Northamptonshire*, V, 314–16.
90. Dyer, 'Market towns', 25.
91. Ibid., 20.
92. NRO E(B) 221–30; BRO B/BUC6/1/1.
93. TNA:PRO E179/155/31, mm. 9–10, 12–14, 20.
94. Brewer *et al.*, *Letters and Papers* XII, i, 456; Shagan, 'Rumours', 37–8.
95. *VCH, Northamptonshire*, V, 198–207; NRO Map 4210.
96. Britnell, 'Stony Stratford'; Letters *et al.*, *Gazetteer*, I, 65.
97. TNA:PRO DL29/324/5303, m. 1; 5306, m. 1.
98. Jones and Page, 'Whittlewood interim report 2003–4', 41; NRO Map 4210.
99. Jones and Page, 'Whittlewood interim report 2001–2', 17; NCO 4084, m. 3.
100. CP40 database, IHR, London.
101. TNA:PRO SC12/13/38; BL, Add Ch 75994.
102. TNA:PRO E179/155/31, m. 13.
103. TNA:PRO DL29/324/5306, m. 2; Harris, *Register*, 75.
104. e.g. *CR 1242–7*, 100, 166, 298, 401; *CR 1261–4*, 337.
105. Lewis *et al.*, *Village, Hamlet and Field*, 145; Hall, *Open Fields*, 95–6; NRO Map 4210; TNA:PRO DL43/8/6A.

Notes to Chapter 8: Medieval Villagescapes

1. NRO Map 4210; Map 842; Map 358; Map 5692; BL, Map K7 TAB 10.
2. Woodfield *et al.*, *Historic buildings surveys*.
3. Barnwell, *Medieval churches*.
4. Lewis *et al.*, *Village, Hamlet and Field*, 49–60, 103, 110–12.
5. RCHME, *South-west Northamptonshire*, 110; Taylor, *Village and Farmstead*, 172.
6. Jones, 'Luffield Priory grange'.
7. NRO Map 4210; RCHME, *South-west Northamptonshire*, 169.
8. *VCH, Northamptonshire*, V, 210–11.
9. Page, 'Destroyed by the Temples', 190–4.
10. RCHME, *South-west Northamptonshire*, 121; *VCH, Northamptonshire*, V, 292.
11. BRO D22/22/5; BL, Map K7 TAB 10.
12. Roberts, *Making of the English Village*, 26–9.
13. Illingworth and Caley, *RH*, II, 340.
14. *VCH, Oxfordshire*, I, 421–2.
15. Illingworth and Caley, *RH*, II, 835.
16. Page and Jones, 'Whittlewood interim report 2002–3', 32–6.
17. RCHME, *South-west Northamptonshire*, 109–10; *VCH, Northamptonshire*, V, 226; Page and Jones, 'Whittlewood interim report 2000–1', 13–14; NRO Map 4210.
18. Aerial photograph, English Heritage, SP 6638/4.
19. Brown, *Lamport*.
20. Davis, *Rotuli Grosseteste*, 183; Franklin, *Minsters and parishes*, 302.
21. Jones and Page, 'Whittlewood interim report 2001–2', 20–4.
22. NCO 4467.
23. NCO 4085, m. 9.
24. *VCH, Northamptonshire*, V, 291–2, 296–7; TNA:PRO C133/80/6; C133/100/1; C134/50/30; C134/90/16.
25. Page and Jones, 'Whittlewood interim report 2002–3', 27–32.
26. Aerial photograph, English Heritage, SP 7337/20.
27. Aerial photograph, English Heritage, SP 7337/1.
28. Jones and Page, 'Whittlewood interim report 2003–4', 37–42.
29. Ibid., 41.
30. Gover *et al.*, *Place-names of Northamptonshire*, 108.
31. BRO D22/22/5; *VCH, Buckinghamshire*, IV, 187–8.
32. RCHME, *South-west Northamptonshire*, 110.
33. NRO Map 5692; RCHME, *South-west Northamptonshire*, 170; *VCH, Northamptonshire*, V, 415.
34. RCHME, *South-west Northamptonshire*, 171–2; Aerial photograph, English Heritage, SP 7537/1/384.
35. Courtney, 'Between two forests', 43–50.
36. Aerial photographs, English Heritage, SP 7142/7; RAF VAP CPE/UK/1926, 3235–6, 5235–6.
37. Jones, 'Luffield Priory grange', 127–9.
38. Platt, *Monastic Grange*, 16–48.
39. Mynard, 'Passenham'; Aerial photograph, English Heritage, SP 7839/1/244.
40. *VCH, Northamptonshire*, V, 214.
41. Page and Jones, 'Whittlewood interim report 2000–1', 13–14.
42. BRO D22/22/5.
43. Woodfield *et al.*, *Historic buildings surveys*, I.
44. TNA:PRO C133/100/1.
45. TNA:PRO C134/50/30; C134/90/16.
46. TNA:PRO C133/25/3.
47. Aerial photograph, English Heritage, SP 7237/5.
48. *CIPM*, XI, no. 113; XV, no. 809; *CIM*, IV, no. 12.
49. HL Stowe Papers, STTM Box 2 (4); *VCH, Northamptonshire*, V, 226–7.
50. TNA:PRO C132/6/1; C133/28/19.
51. Aerial photographs, English Heritage, SP 7337/20, 7139/4.
52. *VCH, Northamptonshire*, V, 435; Pevsner and Williamson, *Buckinghamshire*, 129.
53. Bell *et al.*, *Church of St Martin*.
54. Proudfoot, 'Extension of parish churches'.
55. Morris, *Churches in the Landscape*, 277.
56. Barnwell, 'The laity, the clergy'.
57. Barnwell, *Medieval churches*, 7.
58. Wade-Martins, *Launditch Hundred*, 87–8.
59. *VCH, Northamptonshire*, V, 326.
60. This dating and the architectural details that follow are taken from Barnwell, *Medieval churches*.
61. Salter, *Newington Longeville Charters*, no. 16.
62. Brown and Roberts, *Passenham*, 188, 196–7; Jones, 'Ghostly mentor'.
63. For the location of other churches within hillforts, see Kidd, 'Hillforts and churches'; Morris, *Churches in the Landscape*, 272.

64. Baker, *County of Northampton*, II, 90.
65. Dyer, 'English peasant buildings', 139; Astill, 'Rural settlement', 50–4.
66. e.g. Oosthuizen, 'Unravelling the morphology', 58–60.
67. TNA:PRO C47/12/7.
68. *CCR 1307–13*, 152.
69. Illlingworth and Caley, *RH*, II, 340–1.
70. Brown, *Lamport*; Illingworth and Caley, *RH*, II, 341; RCHME, *South-west Northamptonshire*, 110.
71. Contrast the evidence from Whittlewood with that from Milton Keynes, e.g. Ivens *et al.*, *Tattenhoe and Westbury*; Mynard *et al.*, *Great Linford*.
72. For recently published excavations of tofts, see Ford and Preston, 'Medieval occupation at The Orchard'; Hardy, 'Excavation of a medieval cottage'; Thorne, 'Medieval tenement at Deene End'; Jones and Chapman, 'Medieval tene-

ment at College Street'; Browning and Higgins, 'Excavations of a medieval toft and croft'; Pine, 'Excavations of a medieval settlement'; Jones and Rátkai, 'Excavations at no. 15'; Mortimer, 'Village development'.
73. Woodfield *et al.*, *Historic buildings surveys*, I, III, XI.
74. The same ground plan has been found by Hardy, 'Excavation of a medieval cottage', 377–8.
75. Woodfield *et al.*, *Historic buildings surveys*, V/VI.
76. Ivens, *Archaeological evaluation of Broadlands*.
77. Dyer, *Standards of Living*, 157–60.
78. Astill, 'Rural settlement', 50.
79. Foard, 'Rockingham Forest', 92.
80. RCHME, *South-west Northamptonshire*, 118–19, 169.
81. RCHME, *South-west Northamptonshire*, 71, 81–3, 135–6, 139–41.

Notes to Chapter 9: Ends: Village Decline and Desertion

1. Beresford, *Lost Villages*; Beresford and Hurst, *Deserted Medieval Villages*.
2. Dyer, 'Peasants and farmers', 72.
3. Williamson, *Shaping Medieval Landscapes*, 1–5.
4. Pesez and Le Roy Ladurie, 'Le cas français', 138 ('it is very difficult to kill a village').
5. cf. Campbell, *Seigniorial Agriculture*, 402–5; Dyer, *Making a Living*, 235.
6. Kershaw, 'Agrarian crisis', 96, 102–8.
7. Smith, 'Human resources', 190–6.
8. Campbell, *Seigniorial Agriculture*, 375–85.
9. Thirsk, *Alternative Agriculture*, 7–20.
10. Dyer, 'Peasants and farmers', 74.
11. Lewis *et al.*, *Village, Hamlet and Field*, 164.
12. *Nonarum Inquisitiones*, 330.
13. Elvey, *Luffield Priory Charters*, II, 108–9.
14. Brown, *Lamport*.
15. Page, 'Destroyed by the Temples', 196.
16. TNA:PRO E179/155/109.
17. Page and Jones, 'Whittlewood interim report 2002–3', 32–5.
18. Woodfield *et al.*, *Historic buildings surveys*, V/VI.
19. BRO PR130/28/1.
20. Illingworth and Caley, *RH*, II, 835 (40 tenants in 1279); TNA:PRO E179/161/9, m. 5d (21 taxpayers in 1327, but 60 per cent of the population may have been too poor to pay, as

suggested in Carpenter, *Struggle for Mastery*, 59); TNA:PRO E179/161/39, m. 10 (60 taxpayers in 1377 over the age of 14, with an average household size of about 2.5, as suggested in Russell, *British Medieval Population*, 26–7).
21. Woodfield *et al.*, *Historic buildings surveys*, V/VI.
22. Beresford, *Lost Villages*, 158–63; Hoskins, *Making of the English Landscape*, 120–3; Taylor, *Village and Farmstead*, 167–72.
23. Dyer, *Hanbury*, 52–8; Dyer, *Age of Transition*, 227–8.
24. Taylor, *Village and Farmstead*, 171.
25. Horrox, *Black Death*, 299; Miles and Rowley, 'Tusmore'; Taylor, *Village and Farmstead*, 171.
26. *VCH, Northamptonshire*, V, 208, 227–8, 290, 314–22; Barnwell, *Medieval churches*, 14.
27. Page and Jones, 'Whittlewood interim report 2002–3', 27–31.
28. Beresford, *Lost Villages*, 247–60.
29. *VCH, Northamptonshire*, V, 425.
30. Jones and Page, 'Whittlewood interim report 2001–2', 24.
31. TNA:PRO E179/155/31, m. 9; E179/155/159, m. 9; Allison *et al.*, *Deserted Villages of Northamptonshire*, 31–48.
32. e.g. NRO XYZ 1390, mm. 3, 10; WAM 27770; NRO Map 4210.

33. Jones and Page, 'Whittlewood interim report 2001–2', 20.
34. Woodfield *et al.*, *Historic buildings surveys*, I.
35. TNA:PRO E179/77/65–6.
36. Elvey, *Luffield Priory Charters*, II, 427.
37. Woodfield *et al.*, *Historic buildings surveys*, XI.
38. Jones and Page, 'Whittlewood interim report 2003–4', 41.
39. e.g. NRO XYZ 1390, mm. 2–2d, 19.
40. NRO Spencer roll 112; Page, 'Destroyed by the Temples', 198–200.
41. Beresford, *Lost Villages*, 257–61; Taylor, *Village and Farmstead*, 171–2; Dyer, *Age of Transition*, 66–75.
42. *VCH, Northamptonshire*, V, 302.
43. TNA:PRO E32/2, m. 1; Illingworth and Caley, *RH*, II, 340.
44. *CIPM*, XII, no. 355; XVII, nos. 45–6; XX, no. 751.
45. Elvey, *Luffield Priory Charters*, I, 171–4, 177; II, 432, 434; Jones, 'Luffield Priory grange', 127–9, 137–8.
46. Taylor, *Village and Farmstead*, 171.
47. Beresford, *Lost Villages*, 84, 87.
48. Wrightson, *Earthly Necessities*, 55, 102–4.
49. NRO Map 4210; Map 5692; Map 842.
50. Leadam, *Domesday of Inclosures*, I, 204; II, 576–7; *VCH, Northamptonshire*, V, 100, 102; Page and Jones, 'Whittlewood interim report 2002–3', 27–32.
51. Leadam, *Domesday of Inclosures*, I, 285–6.
52. *VCH, Northamptonshire*, V, 210–11.
53. Leadam, *Domesday of Inclosures*, I, 197–8; II, 574–5.
54. BRO D22/22/5.
55. *VCH, Northamptonshire*, V, 127–8, 134–5.
56. Page, 'Destroyed by the Temples', 195–6; Barnwell, *Medieval churches*, 17.
57. Page, 'Destroyed by the Temples', 198–202.
58. Page and Jones, 'Whittlewood interim report 2002–3', 32; *VCH, Northamptonshire*, V, 210–11; TNA:PRO DL43/8/6A, fo. 52v.
59. Taylor, *Village and Farmstead*, 171–2.
60. Page, 'Destroyed by the Temples', 200.
61. TNA:PRO DL43/8/6A, fos. 2v, 5v; DL42/115, fo. 17.
62. TNA:PRO SC6/HenVIII/6033, m. 3; BRO, D22/9/1.
63. Elvey, *Luffield Priory Charters*, II, 420; BRO, D22/22/5.
64. Page and Jones, 'Whittlewood interim report 2000–1', 12, 14–15.
65. BRO D96/21/1.
66. NRO Spencer roll 112.
67. Jones and Page, 'Whittlewood interim report 2001–2', 18–19.
68. Leadam, *Domesday of Inclosures*, I, 285; Page, 'Destroyed by the Temples', 198–200.
69. *VCH, Northamptonshire*, V, 224.
70. *CPR 1550–3*, 104.
71. Jones and Page, 'Whittlewood interim report 2001–2', 19.
72. TNA:PRO E310/20/100. The wood was grubbed up and the land ploughed again in the 1630s: NRO YZ 614.
73. BL Add MS 32091, fo. 254.
74. NRO XYZ 1391, m. 2; Map 4210.
75. Beaver, '"Bragging and daring words"', 151.

Notes to Chapter 10: Implications and Wider Perspectives

1. e.g. Beresford and Hurst, *Deserted Medieval Villages*.
2. Maitland, *Domesday Book and Beyond*, 38–9.
3. Britnell, *Britain and Ireland*, 7–27.
4. e.g. Hall and Martin, 'Brixworth'; Hall, 'Field surveys'; Croft and Mynard, *Changing Landscape*.
5. Jones and Page, 'Characterizing rural settlement', 74.
6. Foard, 'Rockingham Forest', 46–9; Bellamy, 'Anglo-Saxon dispersed sites', 33–4; Schumer, *Wychwood*, 13.
7. Hooke, *Kingdom of Hwicce*, 14–15.
8. Gelling and Cole, *Landscape of Place-names*, 310–12.
9. Discussion of names in *-feld* follows Gelling, *Place-names in the Landscape*, 235–45.
10. Gelling and Cole, *Landscape of Place-names*, 276, 278.
11. Taylor, *Village and Farmstead*.
12. Hamerow, *Early Medieval Settlements*, 104.
13. Losco-Bradley and Kinsley, *Catholme*, 123–9.
14. Taylor, *Village and Farmstead*, 128–9.
15. e.g. Finberg, *Roman and Saxon Withington*.
16. Hadley, 'Multiple estates'; Corcos, *Affinities and Antecedents*, 48–96.
17. *VCH, Northamptonshire*, 208, 289–90.

18. e.g. Brown and Taylor, 'Chellington'.
19. Dyer, 'Power and conflict'.
20. Birrell, 'Forest and chase', 45.
21. Hoskins, *Devon*, 47.
22. Warner, *Greens*, 9–13; Williamson, 'North-west Essex'.
23. e.g. Warner, *Greens*; Dunsford and Harris, 'Colonization of the wasteland'; Taylor, 'Dispersed settlement in nucleated areas'.
24. Ibid.; Brown and Taylor, 'Origins of dispersed settlement'.
25. e.g. Dyer, 'Dispersed settlements in medieval England'; Dyer, 'Villages and non-villages'; Roberts and Wrathmell, 'Dispersed settlement in England'.
26. Brown and Foard, 'Saxon landscape', 75–7.
27. Shaw, 'Discovery of Saxon sites'; Shaw, 'Higham Ferrers'; Parry *Raunds*.
28. Lewis *et al.*, *Village, Hamlet and Field*, 198–200.
29. Hall, 'Late Saxon countryside'; Brown and Foard, 'Saxon landscape'.
30. Schelling, *Strategy of Conflict*.
31. Taylor, 'Nucleated settlement', 53–5.
32. Brown and Foard, 'Saxon landscape'; Williamson, *Shaping Medieval Landscapes*; Lewis *et al.*, *Village, Hamlet and Field*.
33. Roberts and Wrathmell, *Region and Place*, 143–6; Taylor, 'Nucleated settlement', 53–5; Lewis *et al.*, *Village, Hamlet and Field*, 198–9.
34. For an introduction to these ideas, see Lewin, *Complexity*.
35. Williamson, *Shaping Medieval Landscapes*, 182.

Bibliography

Aldred, D. and Dyer, C. (1991) 'A medieval Cotswold village: Roel, Gloucestershire', *Transactions of the Bristol and Gloucestershire Archaeological Society* **109**, 139–70.

Allen Brown, R., Colvin, H. M. and Taylor, A. J. (1963) *The History of the King's Works: The Middle Ages*, 2 vols, London.

Allison, K. J., Beresford, M. W. and Hurst, J. G. (1966) *The Deserted Villages of Northamptonshire*, Leicester.

Astill, G. (1988) 'Rural settlement: the toft and the croft', in *The Countryside of Medieval England*, eds G. Astill and A. Grant, Oxford, 36–61.

Aston, M. and Gerrard, C. (1999) '"Unique, traditional and charming": the Shapwick project, Somerset', *Antiquaries Journal* **79**, 1–58.

Bailey, K. (1994) 'Early Anglo-Saxon territorial organization in Buckinghamshire and its neighbours', *Records of Buckinghamshire* **36**, 129–43.

Bailey, M. (2002) *The English Manor c. 1200–c. 1500*, Manchester.

Baker, A. R. H. and Butlin, R. A. eds (1973) *Studies of Field Systems in the British Isles*, Cambridge.

Baker, G. (1822–41) *The History and Antiquities of the County of Northampton*, 2 vols, London.

Barnwell, P. (2004) 'The laity, the clergy and the divine presence: the use of space in smaller churches of the eleventh and twelfth centuries', *Journal of the British Archaeological Association* **157**, 41–60.

Barnwell, P. (2004) *The Whittlewood project: notes on the medieval churches*, unpublished report.

Bartlett, R. (2000) *England under the Norman and Angevin Kings 1075–1225*, Oxford.

Bassett, S. (1989) 'In search of the origins of Anglo-Saxon kingdoms', in *The Origins of Anglo-Saxon Kingdoms*, ed. S. Bassett, Leicester, 3–27.

Beaver, D. (2001) '"Bragging and daring words": honour, property and the symbolism of the hunt in Stowe, 1590–1642', in *Negotiating Power in Early Modern Society: Order, Hierarchy and Subordination in Britain and Ireland*, eds M. J. Braddick and J. Walter, Cambridge, 149–65.

Beckett, J. (1994) *The Rise and Fall of the Grenvilles, Dukes of Buckingham and Chandos, 1710 to 1921*, Manchester.

Bell, R. D., Beresford, M. W. *et al.* (1987) *Wharram: A Study of Settlement on the Yorkshire Wolds, III, The Church of St Martin*, Society for Medieval Archaeology Monograph Series no. 11.

Bellamy, B. (1994) 'Anglo-Saxon dispersed sites and woodland at Geddington in Rockingham Forest, Northamptonshire', *Landscape History* **16**, 31–8.

Beresford, M. W. (1954; repr. 1998) *The Lost Villages of England*, Stroud.

Beresford, M. W. and Hurst, J. G. eds (1971) *Deserted Medieval Villages*, London.

Bevington, M. *et al.* (1997) *Stowe Landscape Gardens*, The National Trust.

Birrell, J. (1969) 'Peasant craftsmen in the medieval forest', *Agricultural History Review* **17**, 91–107.

Birrell, J. (1988) 'Forest law and the peasantry in the later thirteenth century', in *Thirteenth Century England II*, eds P. R. Coss and S. D. Lloyd, Woodbridge, 149–63.

Birrell, J. (1990–1) 'The forest and the chase in medieval Staffordshire', *Staffordshire Studies* **3**, 23–50.

Birrell, J. (1996) 'Peasant deer poachers in the medieval forest', in *Progress and Problems in Medieval England*, eds R. Britnell and J. Hatcher, Cambridge, 68–88.

Bishop, M. (n.d.) *An archaeological resource assessment for medieval Nottinghamshire*, unpublished report, East Midlands Archaeological Research Framework.

Blair, J. (1988) 'Introduction: from minster to parish church', in *Minsters and Parish Churches: The Local Church in Transition 950–1200*, ed. J. Blair, Oxford University Committee for Archaeology Monograph no. 17, 1–19.

Blair, J. (1994) *Anglo-Saxon Oxfordshire*, Stroud.

Bolton, D. (1994) 'Buckinghamshire', in *English County Histories: A Guide*, eds C. R. J. Currie and C. P. Lewis, Stroud, 54–61.

Bradley, R. (1987) 'Time regained: the creation of continuity', *Journal of the British Archaeological Association* **140**, 1–17.

Branch, N.P., Green, M., Silva, B., Swindle, G.E. and Turton, E. (2003) *Whittlewood project: preliminary results of the environmental archaeological investigations*, unpublished report, Royal Holloway University of London.

Brewer, J.S., Gairdner, J., Brodie, R.H. *et al.* eds (1862–1932) *Letters and Papers, Foreign and Domestic, of the Reign of Henry VIII*, 21 vols and addenda, HMSO.

Bridges, J. (1791) *The History and Antiquities of Northamptonshire*, 2 vols, Oxford.

Britnell, R. (1977) 'The origins of Stony Stratford', *Records of Buckinghamshire* **20**, 451–3.

Britnell, R. (2004) *Britain and Ireland 1050–1530: Economy and Society*, Oxford.

Brown, A. and Taylor, C. (1989) 'The origins of dispersed settlement: some results from fieldwork in Bedfordshire', *Landscape History* **11**, 61–81.

Brown, A. and Taylor, C. (1999) 'Chellington field survey', *Bedfordshire Archaeology* **23**, 98–110.

Brown, A.G. and Meadows, I. (1996–7) 'Environmental analysis of a Neolithic/early Bronze Age palaeochannel of the river Nene at Turnells Mill Lane, Wellingborough, Northamptonshire', *Northamptonshire Archaeology* **27**, 185–91.

Brown, F. and Taylor, C. (1978) 'Settlement and land use in Northamptonshire: a comparison between the Iron Age and the Middle Ages', in *Lowland Iron Age Communities in Europe*, eds B.Cunliffe and T.Rowley, BAR International Series Supplementary 48, 77–89.

Brown, G. (2005) *Earthwork survey at Lamport, Buckinghamshire*, unpublished report.

Brown, O.F. and Roberts, G.J. (1973) *Passenham: The History of a Forest Village*, Chichester.

Brown, T. and Foard, G. (1998) 'The Saxon landscape: a regional perspective', in *The Archaeology of Landscape*, eds P.Everson and T.Williamson, Manchester, 67–94.

Browning, J. and Higgins, T. (2003) 'Excavations of a medieval toft and croft at Cropston Road, Anstey, Leicestershire', *Transactions of the Leicestershire Archaeological and Historical Society* **77**, 65–81.

Campbell, B.M.S. (2000) *English Seigniorial Agriculture 1250–1450*, Cambridge.

Campbell, B.M.S., Galloway, J.A., Keene, D. and Murphy, M. (1993) *A Medieval Capital and its Grain Supply: Agrarian Production and Distribution in the London Region c. 1300*, Historical Geography Research Series 30.

Campbell, J. ed. (1982) *The Anglo-Saxons*, Oxford.

Carpenter, D. (2003) *The Struggle for Mastery: Britain 1066–1284*, London.

Chapman, A. (1995) 'Crick', *South Midlands Archaeology* **25**, 37–9.

Chibnall, A.C. ed. (1966) *Early Taxation Returns: Taxation of Personal Property in 1332 and Later*, Buckinghamshire Record Society 14.

Clark, K. (2002) *The Leckhampstead dog*, unpublished report.

Clarke, G.B. (1967) 'The history of Stowe, I: ancient and medieval Stowe', *The Stoic* **132**, 210–16.

Coates, R. (1999) 'New light from old wicks: the progeny of Latin vicus', *Nomina* **22**, 75–116.

Cooper, N. and Priest, V. (2003) 'Sampling a medieval village in a day: the "Big Dig" investigation at Great Easton, Leicestershire', *MSRG Annual Report* **18**, 53–6.

Corcos, N. (2002) *The Affinities and Antecedents of Medieval Settlement: Topographical Perspectives from Three of the Somerset Hundreds*, BAR British Series 337.

Courtney, P. (2003) 'Between two forests: the social and topographic evolution of medieval Anstey', *Transactions of the Leicestershire Archaeological and Historical Society* **77**, 35–64.

Croft, R.A. and Mynard, D.C. eds (1993) *The Changing Landscape of Milton Keynes*, Buckinghamshire Archaeological Society Monograph Series 5.

Dark, P. (2000) *The Environment of Britain in the First Millennium AD*, London.

Davies, W. ed. (2003) *From the Vikings to the Normans*, Oxford.

Davis, F.N. ed. (1913) *Rotuli Roberti Grosseteste, Episcopi Lincolniensis, 1235–53*, Canterbury and York Society 10.

Davis, H.W.C. *et al.* eds (1913–69) *Regesta Regum Anglo-Normannorum 1066–1154*, 4 vols, Oxford.

Davis, R.H.C. (1982) 'Alfred and Guthrum's frontier', *English Historical Review* **97**, 803–10.

Douglas, D.C. and Greenaway, G.W. eds (1981) *English Historical Documents*, II, *1042–1189*, 2nd edn, London.

Dumville, D. (1992) 'The Treaty of Alfred and Guthrum', in D.Dumville, *Wessex and England from Alfred to Edgar*, Woodbridge, 1–27.

Dunsford, H.M. and Harris, S.J. (2003) 'Colonization of the wasteland in County Durham, 1100–1400', *Economic History Review* **56**, 34–56.

Dyer, C. (1989) *Standards of Living in the Later Middle Ages: Social Change in England c. 1200–1520*, Cambridge.

Dyer, C. (1991) *Hanbury: Settlement and Society in a Woodland Landscape*, Leicester.

Dyer, C. (1994) *Everyday Life in Medieval England*, London.

Dyer, C. (1994) 'Dispersed settlements in medieval England: a case study of Pendock, Worcestershire', in C. Dyer, *Everyday Life in Medieval England*, London, 47–76.

Dyer, C. (1994) 'English peasant buildings in the later Middle Ages (1200–1500)', in C. Dyer, *Everyday Life in Medieval England*, London, 133–65.

Dyer, C. (1994) 'Power and conflict in the medieval English village', in C. Dyer, *Everyday Life in Medieval England*, London, 1–11.

Dyer, C. (1996) 'Market towns and the countryside in late medieval England', *Canadian Journal of History* **31**, 17–35.

Dyer, C. (1997) 'Peasants and farmers: rural settlements and landscapes in an age of transition', in *The Age of Transition: The Archaeology of English Culture 1400–1600*, eds D. Gaimster and P. Stamper, Society for Medieval Archaeology Monograph Series 15, 61–76.

Dyer, C. (1999) 'The Medieval Settlement Research Group Whittlewood project', *MSRG Annual Report* **14**, 16–17.

Dyer, C. (2002) *Making a Living in the Middle Ages: The People of Britain 850–1520*, London.

Dyer, C. (2002) 'Mapping rural England', *Rural History Today* **3**, 5–7.

Dyer, C. (2002) 'Villages and non-villages in the medieval Cotswolds', *Transactions of the Bristol and Gloucestershire Archaeological Society* **120**, 11–35.

Dyer, C. (2004) 'Alternative agriculture: goats in medieval England', in *People, Landscape and Alternative Agriculture*, ed. R. W. Hoyle, British Agricultural History Society, 20–38.

Dyer, C. (2005) *An Age of Transition? Economy and Society in England in the Later Middle Ages*, Oxford.

Eighth Report of the Commissioners Appointed to Enquire into the State and Condition of the Woods, Forests, and Land Revenues of the Crown, London (1792).

Elvey, G. R. ed. (1968–75) *Luffield Priory Charters*, 2 vols, Northamptonshire Record Society 22 and 26.

Evans, J. G. (1975) *The Environment of Early Man in the British Isles*, London.

Evans, J. G., Limbrey, S., Máté, I. and Mount, R. (1993) 'An environmental history of the upper Kennet valley, Wiltshire, for the last 10,000 years', *Proceedings of the Prehistoric Society* **59**, 139–95.

Everitt, A. (1985) 'Country, county and town: patterns of regional evolution in England', in A. Everitt, *Landscape and Community in England*, London, 11–40.

Faith, R. (1997) *The English Peasantry and the Growth of Lordship*, Leicester.

Fenwick, C. ed. (1998–2001) *The Poll Taxes of 1377, 1379 and 1381*, 2 vols, Records of Social and Economic History, 27, 29.

Finberg, H. P. R. (1959) *Roman and Saxon Withington: A Study in Continuity*, Leicester.

Finch, J. (2004) '"Grass, grass, grass": fox-hunting and the creation of the modern landscape', *Landscapes* **5.2**, 41–52.

Foard, G. (1978) 'Systematic fieldwalking and the investigation of Saxon settlement in Northamptonshire', *World Archaeology* **9**, 357–74.

Foard, G. (1985) 'The administrative organization of Northamptonshire in the Saxon period', *Anglo-Saxon Studies in Archaeology and History* **4**, 185–222.

Foard, G. (2001) 'Medieval woodland, agriculture and industry in Rockingham Forest, Northamptonshire', *Medieval Archaeology* **45**, 41–95.

Ford, S. and Preston, S. (2002) 'Medieval occupation at The Orchard, Brighthampton', *Oxoniensia* **67**, 287–312.

Foster, P. J. (1998) *Changes in the landscape: an archaeological study of the clay uplands in the Brigstock area of Northamptonshire*, unpublished BA dissertation, University of Sheffield.

Foster, P. J. (1998–9) 'Late Iron Age/early Roman Northamptonshire: a study in the use of ceramic analysis to investigate social, economic and landscape changes', *Northamptonshire Archaeology* **28**, 129–35.

Fowler, P. (2000) *Landscape Plotted and Pieced: Landscape History and Local Archaeology in Fyfield and Overton, Wiltshire*, Society of Antiquaries, London.

Fox, H. S. A. (1981) 'Approaches to the adoption of the midland system', in *The Origins of Open-Field Agriculture*, ed. T. Rowley, London, 64–111.

Fox, H. S. A. (1989) 'The people of the wolds in English settlement history', in *The Rural Settlements of Medieval England*, eds M. Aston, D. Austin and C. Dyer, Oxford, 77–101.

Franklin, M. J. (1982) *Minsters and parishes: Northamptonshire studies*, unpublished PhD thesis, University of Cambridge.

Friendship-Taylor, R. M. (1999) 'Piddington', *South Midlands Archaeology* **29**, 27–8.

Fyfe, R. M., Brown, A. G. and Coles, B. J. (2003) 'Mesolithic to Bronze Age vegetation change and human activity in the Exe valley, Devon, UK', *Proceedings of the Prehistoric Society* **69**, 161–81.

Gaffney, V. and Tingle, M. (1989) *The Maddle Farm Project: An Integrated Survey of Prehistoric and Roman Landscapes on the Berkshire Downs*, BAR British Series 200.

Gelling, M. (1953–4) *The Place-names of Oxfordshire*, 2 vols, Cambridge.

Gelling, M. (1982) 'Some meanings of Stôw', in *The Early Church in Western Britain and Ireland*, ed. S. M. Pearce, BAR British Series 102, 187–96.

Gelling, M. (1984) *Place-names in the Landscape*, London.

Gelling, M. (1993) 'Place-names of the Milton Keynes area', in *The Changing Landscape of Milton Keynes*, eds R. A. Croft and D. Mynard, Buckinghamshire Archaeological Society Monograph Series 5, 45–7.

Gelling, M. and Cole, A. (2000) *The Landscape of Place-names*, Stamford.

Gerrard, C. (1997) 'Misplaced faith? Medieval pottery and fieldwalking', *Medieval Ceramics* 21, 61–72.

Gilbert, J. M. (1979) *Hunting and Hunting Reserves in Medieval Scotland*, Edinburgh.

Gover, J. E. B., Mawer, A. and Stenton, F. M. (1933) *The Place-names of Northamptonshire*, Cambridge.

Gray, H. L. (1915) *English Field Systems*, Cambridge, Mass.

Green, H. S. (1974) 'Early Bronze Age burial, territory, and population in Milton Keynes, Buckinghamshire, and the Great Ouse valley', *Archaeological Journal* 131, 75–139.

Green, H. S. (1976) 'The excavation of a late Neolithic settlement at Stacey Bushes, Milton Keynes, and its significance', in *Settlement and Economy in the Third and Second Millennia BC*, eds C. Burgess and R. Miket, BAR British Series 33, 11–27.

Grimes, W. F. (1960) *Excavations of Defence Sites 1939–1945*, I, HMSO.

Hadley, D. (1996) 'Multiple estates and the origins of the manorial structure of the northern Danelaw', *Journal of Historical Geography* 22, 3–15.

Hall, D. (1981) 'The origins of open-field agriculture: the archaeological fieldwork evidence', in *The Origins of Open-Field Agriculture*, ed. T. Rowley, London, 22–38.

Hall, D. (1985) 'Survey work in eastern England', in *Archaeological Field Survey in Britain and Abroad*, eds S. Macready and F. H. Thompson, Society of Antiquaries, London, 25–44.

Hall, D. (1988) 'The late Saxon countryside: villages and their fields', in *Anglo-Saxon Settlements*, ed. D. Hooke, Oxford, 99–122.

Hall, D. (1991) 'Field surveys in Bedfordshire', *Bedfordshire Archaeology* 19, 51–6.

Hall, D. (1995) *The Open Fields of Northamptonshire*, Northamptonshire Record Society 38.

Hall, D. (2001) 'The woodland landscapes of southern Northamptonshire', *Northamptonshire Past and Present* 54, 33–46.

Hall, D. and Coles, J. (1994) *Fenland Survey: An Essay in Landscape and Persistence*, London.

Hall, D. and Martin, P. (1979) 'Brixworth, Northamptonshire: an intensive field survey', *Journal of the British Archaeological Association* 132, 1–6.

Hamerow, H. (1991) 'Settlement mobility and the "middle Saxon shift": rural settlements and settlement patterns in Anglo-Saxon England', *Anglo-Saxon England* 20, 1–17.

Hamerow, H. (2002) *Early Medieval Settlements: The Archaeology of Rural Communities in North-West Europe 400–900*, Oxford.

Hardy, A. (2000) 'The excavation of a medieval cottage and associated agricultural features at Manor Farm, Old Grimsbury, Banbury', *Oxoniensia* 65, 345–80.

Harris, M. D. ed. (1935) *The Register of the Guild of the Holy Trinity, St Mary, St John the Baptist, and St Katherine of Coventry*, Dugdale Society 13.

Harrison, S. (2002) 'Open fields and earlier landscapes: six parishes in south-east Cambridgeshire', *Landscapes* 3.1, 35–54.

Harvey, M. (1981) 'The origin of planned field systems in Holderness, Yorkshire', in *The Origins of Open-Field Agriculture*, ed. T. Rowley, London, 184–201.

Harvey, P. D. A. (1989) 'Initiative and authority in settlement change', in *The Rural Settlements of Medieval England*, eds M. Aston, D. Austin and C. Dyer, Oxford, 31–43.

Healy, F., Heaton, M. and Lobb, S. J. (1992) 'Excavations of a Mesolithic site at Thatcham, Berkshire', *Proceedings of the Prehistoric Society* 58, 41–76.

Hesse, M. (2000) 'Field systems in south-west Cambridgeshire: Abington Pigotts, Litlington and the Mile Ditches', *Proceedings of the Cambridge Antiquarian Society* 89, 49–58.

Hey, G. (2004) *Yarnton: Saxon and Medieval Settlement and Landscape*, Oxford.

Higham, N. (2004) *A Frontier Landscape: The North-west in the Middle Ages*, Macclesfield.

Hinton, D. (1997) 'The "Scole-Dickleburgh field system" examined', *Landscape History* 19, 5–13.

Homans, G. C. (1941) *English Villagers of the Thirteenth Century*, Cambridge, Mass.

Hooke, D. (1985) *The Anglo-Saxon Landscape: The Kingdom of the Hwicce*, Manchester.

Hooke, D. (1989) 'Early medieval estate and settlement patterns: the documentary evidence', in *The Rural Settlements of Medieval England*, eds M. Aston, D. Austin and C. Dyer, Oxford, 9–30.

Hooke, D. (1992) 'Early units of government in Herefordshire and Shropshire', *Anglo-Saxon Studies in Archaeology and History* **5**, 47–64.

Hooke, D. (1998) *The Landscape of Anglo-Saxon England*, Leicester.

Horrox, R. ed. (1994) *The Black Death*, Manchester.

Hoskins, W. G. (1954) *Devon*, London.

Hoskins, W. G. (1955; repr. 1970) *The Making of the English Landscape*, London.

Hughes, G. (1998) *The excavation of an Iron Age settlement at Covert Farm (DIRFT East), Crick, Northamptonshire: post-excavation assessment and updated research design*, unpublished report, Birmingham University Field Archaeology Unit.

Illingworth, W. and Caley J. ed. (1812–18) *Rotuli Hundredorum*, 2 vols, Record Commission.

Ingle, C. (1993–4) 'The quernstones from Hunsbury hillfort, Northamptonshire', *Northamptonshire Archaeology* **25**, 21–33.

Innes, J. B. and Blackford, J. J. (2003) 'The ecology of late Mesolithic woodland disturbances: model testing with fungal spore assemblage data', *Journal of Archaeological Science* **30**, 185–94.

Ivens, R. (n.d.) *Archaeological evaluation of Broadlands, Leckhampstead Road, Akeley, Buckinghamshire*, unpublished report.

Ivens, R., Busby, P. and Shepherd, N. (1995) *Tattenhoe and Westbury: Two Deserted Medieval Settlements in Milton Keynes*, Buckinghamshire Archaeological Society Monograph Series 8.

Jackson, D. (1993–4) 'Iron Age and Anglo-Saxon settlement and activity around the Hunsbury hillfort', *Northamptonshire Archaeology* **25**, 35–46.

Jackson, D. and Dix, B. (1988) 'Late Iron Age and Roman settlement at Weekley, Northants', *Northamptonshire Archaeology* **21**, 41–93.

James, E. (2001) *Britain in the First Millennium*, London.

Jenkins, J. G. ed. (1945) *The Cartulary of Snelshall Priory*, Buckinghamshire Record Society 9.

Jones, C. and Chapman, A. (2003) 'A medieval tenement at College Street, Higham Ferrers, Northamptonshire', *Northamptonshire Archaeology* **31**, 125–35.

Jones, G. (2000) 'Ghostly mentor, teacher of mysteries: Bartholomew, Guthlac, and the apostle's cult in early medieval England', in *Medieval Monastic Education*, eds G. Ferzoco and C. Muessig, Leicester, 136–52.

Jones, L. and Rátkai, S. (2000) 'Excavations at no. 15, The Green, Kings Norton, 1992', *Transactions of the Birmingham and Warwickshire Archaeological Society* **104**, 101–21.

Jones, R. (2002) 'The Luffield Priory grange at Monksbarn, Whittlebury, Northants', *Northamptonshire Archaeology* **30**, 126–39.

Jones, R. (2004) 'Signatures in the soil: the use of ceramic manure scatters in the identification of medieval arable farming regimes', *Archaeological Journal* **161**, 159–88.

Jones, R. and Page, M. (2001) 'Medieval settlements and landscapes in the Whittlewood area: interim report 2001–2', *MSRG Annual Report* **16**, 15–25.

Jones, R. and Page, M. (2003) 'Medieval settlements and landscapes in the Whittlewood area: interim report 2003–4', *MSRG Annual Report* **18**, 37–45.

Jones, R. and Page, M. (2003) 'Characterizing rural settlement and landscape: Whittlewood Forest in the Middle Ages', *Medieval Archaeology* **47**, 53–83.

Kershaw, I. (1976) 'The great famine and agrarian crisis in England 1315–1322', in *Peasants, Knights and Heretics: Studies in Medieval English Social History*, ed. R. H. Hilton, Cambridge, 85–132.

Kidd, S. (2004) 'Hillforts and churches: a coincidence of locations?', *Records of Buckinghamshire* **44**, 105–9.

King, E. (1991) 'Farming practices and techniques: the east midlands', in *The Agrarian History of England and Wales, III, 1348–1500*, ed. E. Miller, Cambridge, 210–22.

Kitson, P. R. (2002) 'How Anglo-Saxon personal names work', *Nomina* **25**, 91–131.

Klingelhöfer, E. (1992) *Manor, Vill and Hundred: The Development of Rural Institutions in Early Medieval Hampshire*, Toronto.

Knight, D. (1984) *Late Bronze Age and Iron Age Settlement in the Nene and Great Ouse Basins*, BAR British Series 130.

Kosminsky, E. A. (1956) *Studies in the Agrarian History of England in the Thirteenth Century*, trans. R. Kirsch, ed. R. H. Hilton, Oxford.

Kowaleski, M. (1990) 'Town and country in late medieval England: the hide and leather trade', in *Work in Towns 850–1850*, eds P. J. Corfield and D. J. Keene, Leicester, 57–73.

Kron, G. (2000) 'Roman ley-farming', *Journal of Roman Archaeology* **13**, 277–87.

Langdon, J. (1986) *Horses, Oxen and Technological Innovation: The Use of Draught Animals in English Farming from 1066–1500*, Cambridge.

Langdon, J. (1991) 'Watermills and windmills in the west midlands, 1086–1500', *Economic History Review* **44**, 424–44.

Langdon, J. (2004) *Mills in the Medieval Economy: England 1300–1540*, Oxford.

Latham, R.E. and Howlett, D.R. (1975–97) *Dictionary of Medieval Latin from British Sources, I, A-L*, Oxford.

Leadam, I.S. ed. (1897) *The Domesday of Inclosures 1517–1518*, 2 vols, London.

Letters, S. *et al.* (2003) *Gazetteer of Markets and Fairs in England and Wales to 1516*, 2 vols, List and Index Society Special Series 32–3.

Lewin, R. (1993) *Complexity: Life on the Edge of Chaos*, London.

Lewis, C. and Mitchell-Fox, P. (1993) 'The Leverhulme medieval settlements and landscapes project: report on site selection for future fieldwork in the east midlands', *MSRG Annual Report* **8**, 27–35.

Lewis, C., Mitchell-Fox, P. and Dyer, C. (1997; 2nd edn 2001) *Village, Hamlet and Field: Changing Medieval Settlements in Central England*, Macclesfield.

Liddle, P. (n.d.) *An archaeological resource assessment for Anglo-Saxon Leicestershire and Rutland*, unpublished report, East Midlands Archaeological Research Framework.

Linnell, J.E. (1932) *Old Oak: The Story of a Forest Village*, London.

Lipscomb, G. (1831–47) *The History and Antiquities of the County of Buckingham*, 4 vols, London.

Losco-Bradley, S. and Kinsley, G. (2002) *Catholme: An Anglo-Saxon Settlement on the Trent Gravels in Staffordshire*, Nottingham.

Loyn, H.R. (1984) *The Governance of Anglo-Saxon England 500–1087*, London.

Maitland, F.W. (1897; repr. 1960) *Domesday Book and Beyond*, London.

Malim, T. (2000) 'The ritual landscape of the Neolithic and Bronze Age along the middle and lower Ouse valley', in *Prehistoric, Roman, and Post-Roman Landscapes of the Great Ouse Valley*, ed. M. Dawson, CBA Research Report, 119, 57–88.

Marshall, G. (1995) *Bourbon Fields: Roman pottery and kiln waste recovered from a watching brief across the Bourbon Fields*, unpublished report, The National Trust, Stowe Landscape Gardens, 8.

Martin, P. and Hall, D. (1980) 'Brixworth, Northamptonshire: new evidence for early prehistoric settlement and agriculture', *Bedfordshire Archaeological Journal* **14**, 5–14.

Mastoris, S. and Groves, S. eds (1997) *Sherwood Forest in 1609: A Crown Survey by Richard Bankes*, Thoroton Society Record Series 40.

Mawer, A. and Stenton, F.M. (1925) *The Place-names of Buckinghamshire*, Cambridge.

Meadows, I. (1995) 'Wollaston', *South Midlands Archaeology* **25**, 41–5.

Meaney, A.L. (1997) 'Hundred meeting-places in the Cambridge region', in *Names, Places and People*, eds A.R. Rumble and A.D. Mills, Stamford, 195–240.

Meek, J. (1996–7) 'An Iron Age and Romano-British settlement site at Potterspury', *Northamptonshire Archaeology* **27**, 193–7.

Meek, J. (1997) *An archaeological evaluation of the Salcey Deanshanger mains duplication pipeline, stage 3*, unpublished report, University of Leicester Archaeological Services.

Mellars, P. (1976) 'Fire ecology, animal populations and man: a study of some ecological relationships in prehistory', *Proceedings of the Prehistoric Society* **42**, 15–45.

Miles, D. and Rowley, T. (1976) 'Tusmore deserted village', *Oxoniensia* **41**, 309–15.

Millett, M. (1983) 'Excavations at Cowdery's Down, Basingstoke, Hampshire, 1978–81', *Archaeological Journal* **140**, 151–279.

Morris, R. (1997) *Churches in the Landscape*, London.

Mortimer, R. (2000) 'Village development and ceramic sequence: the middle to late Saxon village at Lordship Lane, Cottenham, Cambridgeshire', *Proceedings of the Cambridge Antiquarian Society* **89**, 5–33.

Mynard, D.C. (1968) 'Passenham', *Wolverton and District Archaeological Society Journal* **1**, 12–13.

Mynard, D.C., Zeepvat, R.J. and Williams, R.J. (1992) *Excavations at Great Linford, 1974–80*, Buckinghamshire Archaeological Society Monograph Series 3.

Neal, D.S. (1989) 'The Stanwick villa, Northants: an interim report on the excavations of 1984–8', *Britannia* **20**, 149–68.

Neeson, J.M. (1993) *Commoners: Common Right, Enclosure and Social Change in England, 1700–1820*, Cambridge.

Nonarum Inquisitiones (1807) Record Commission.

Northamptonshire Archaeology (2002) *A43 Towcester to M40 dualling project: Northamptonshire and Oxfordshire post-excavation assessment and updated project design*, unpublished report.

Oosthuizen, S. (1997) 'Medieval settlement relocation in west Cambridgeshire: three case-studies', *Landscape History* **19**, 43–55.

Oosthuizen, S. (1997) 'Prehistoric fields into medieval furlongs? Evidence from Caxton, Cambridgeshire', *Proceedings of the Cambridge Antiquarian Society* **86**, 145–52.

Oosthuizen, S. (1998) 'The origins of Cambridgeshire', *Antiquaries Journal* **78**, 85–109.

Oosthuizen, S. (2002) 'Ancient greens in "midland" landscapes: Barrington, south Cambridgeshire', *Medieval Archaeology* **46**, 110–15.

Oosthuizen, S. (2002) 'Unravelling the morphology of Litlington, south Cambridgeshire', *Proceedings of the Cambridge Antiquarian Society* **91**, 55–61.

Oosthuizen, S. (2003) 'The roots of the common fields: linking prehistoric and medieval field systems in west Cambridgeshire', *Landscapes* **4.1**, 40–64.

Ovenden-Wilson, S. M. (1997) *Grange Park, Northamptonshire*, unpublished report, Geophysical Surveys of Bradford.

Page, M. (2003) 'The extent of Whittlewood Forest and the impact of disafforestation in the later Middle Ages', *Northamptonshire Past and Present* **56**, 22–34.

Page, M. (2005) 'Destroyed by the Temples: the deserted medieval village of Stowe', *Records of Buckinghamshire* **45**, 189–204.

Page, M. and Jones, R. (2000) 'The Whittlewood project interim report 2000–1', *MSRG Annual Report* **15**, 10–18.

Page, M. and Jones, R. (2003) 'The Whittlewood project interim report 2002–3', *MSRG Annual Report* **18**, 27–36.

Page, M. and Jones, R. (2004) 'The Whittlewood project: excavation of a medieval manor at Wicken, 2004', *MSRG Annual Report* **19**, 24–7.

Parker Pearson, M. (1993) *Bronze Age Britain*, London.

Parry, S. (2006) *Raunds Area Survey: An Archaeological Study of the Landscape of Raunds, Northamptonshire, 1985–94*, Oxford.

Pesez, J.-M. and Le Roy Ladurie, E. (1965) 'Le cas français: vue d'ensemble', in *Villages Désertés et Histoire Économique*, ed. F. Braudel, Paris, 127–252.

Pettit, P. A. J. (1968) *The Royal Forests of Northamptonshire: A Study in their Economy, 1558–1714*, Northamptonshire Record Society 23.

Pevsner, N. and Cherry, B. (1994) *Northamptonshire*, 2nd edn, London.

Pevsner, N. and Williamson, E. (1994) *Buckinghamshire*, 2nd edn, London.

Phillips, G. (n.d.) *An archaeological resource assessment of the Mesolithic in Northamptonshire*, unpublished report, East Midlands Archaeological Research Framework.

Phythian-Adams, C. (1978) *Continuity, Fields and Fission: The Making of a Midland Parish*, Leicester.

Phythian-Adams, C. (1993) 'Introduction: an agenda for English local history', in *Societies, Cultures and Kinship, 1580–1850: Cultural Provinces and English Local History*, ed. C. Phythian-Adams, Leicester, 1–23.

Pine, J. (2003) 'Excavation of a medieval settlement, late Saxon features and a Bronze Age cremation cemetery at Loughton, Milton Keynes', *Records of Buckinghamshire* **43**, 77–126.

Platt, C. (1969) *The Monastic Grange in Medieval England: A Reassessment*, London.

Poole, A. L. (1955) *Domesday Book to Magna Carta 1087–1216*, 2nd edn, Oxford.

Powlesland, D. (1990) *The Anglo-Saxon village at West Heslerton, North Yorkshire*, unpublished report.

Proudfoot, L. J. (1983) 'The extension of parish churches in medieval Warwickshire', *Journal of Historical Geography* **9**, 231–46.

Quinnell, H. (1991) 'The villa and temple at Cosgrove, Northamptonshire', *Northamptonshire Archaeology* **23**, 4–66.

Rackham, O. (1980) *Ancient Woodland: Its History, Vegetation and Uses in England*, London.

Rackham, O. (1986) *The History of the Countryside*, London.

Raftis, J. A. (1974) *Assart Data and Land Values: Two Studies in the East Midlands 1200–1350*, Toronto.

RCHME (1982) *An Inventory of the Historical Monuments in the County of Northampton, IV, South-west Northamptonshire*, HMSO.

Reed, M. (1979) *The Buckinghamshire Landscape*, London.

Reed, M. (1981) 'Seventeenth-century Stowe', *Huntington Library Quarterly* **44**, 189–203.

Reynolds, S. (1984) *Kingdoms and Communities in Western Europe, 900–1300*, Oxford.

Riley, H. (2001) *Stowe Park, Stowe, Buckinghamshire: Survey Report*, English Heritage.

Rippon, S. (2000) 'Landscapes in transition: the later Roman and early medieval periods', in *Landscape: The Richest Historical Record*, ed. D. Hooke, Society for Landscape Studies Supplementary Series 1, 47–61.

Rippon, S. (2000) *The Transformation of Coastal Wetlands: Exploitation and Management of Marshland Landscapes in North-west Europe during the Roman and Medieval Periods*, Oxford.

Rippon, S. (2004) *Historic Landscape Analysis: Deciphering the Countryside*, CBA Practical Handbook, 16.

Rivet, A.L.F. and Smith, C. (1979) *The Place-names of Roman Britain*, London.

Roberts, B.K. (1977) *Rural Settlement in Britain*, London.

Roberts, B.K. (1985) 'Village patterns and forms: some models for discussion', in *Medieval Villages*, ed. D. Hooke, Oxford, 7–25.

Roberts, B.K. (1987) *The Making of the English Village: A Study in Historical Geography*, Harlow.

Roberts, B.K. (1989) 'Nucleation and dispersion: distribution maps as a research tool', in *The Rural Settlements of Medieval England*, eds M. Aston, D. Austin and C. Dyer, Oxford, 59–75.

Roberts, B.K. and Wrathmell, S. (1998) 'Dispersed settlement in England: a national view', in *The Archaeology of Landscape*, eds P. Everson and T. Williamson, Manchester, 95–116.

Roberts, B.K. and Wrathmell, S. (2000) *An Atlas of Rural Settlement in England*, English Heritage.

Roberts, B.K. and Wrathmell, S. (2002) *Region and Place: A Study of English Rural Settlement*, English Heritage.

Russell, J.C. (1948) *British Medieval Population*, Albuquerque.

Salter, H.E. ed. (1921) *Newington Longeville Charters*, Oxfordshire Record Society 3.

Salter, H.E. ed. (1935) *The Cartulary of Oseney Abbey*, V, Oxford Historical Society 98.

Schelling, T.C. (1960) *The Strategy of Conflict*, London.

Schumer, B. (1984) *The Evolution of Wychwood to 1400: Pioneers, Frontiers and Forests*, Leicester.

Seebohm, F. (1883) *The English Village Community*, 2nd edn, London.

Shagan, E.H. (2001) 'Rumours and popular politics in the reign of Henry VIII', in *The Politics of the Excluded, c. 1500–1850*, ed. T. Harris, Basingstoke, 30–66.

Shaw, M. (1981) 'Saxon and earlier settlement at Higham Ferrers, Northamptonshire', *MSRG Annual Report* **6**, 15–19.

Shaw, M. (1993) 'The discovery of Saxon sites below fieldwalking scatters: settlement evidence at Brixworth and Upton, Northamptonshire', *Northamptonshire Archaeology* **25**, 77–92.

Sheahan, J.J. (1862) *History and Topography of Buckinghamshire*, London.

Simmons, I.G. (1996) *The Environmental Impact of Later Mesolithic Cultures: The Creation of Moorland Landscape in England and Wales*, Edinburgh.

Smith, R.M. (1988) 'Human resources', in *The Countryside of Medieval England*, eds G. Astill and A. Grant, Oxford, 188–212.

Stafford, P. (1985) *The East Midlands in the Early Middle Ages*, Leicester.

Stamper, P. (1988) 'Woods and parks', in *The Countryside of Medieval England*, eds G. Astill and A. Grant, Oxford, 128–48.

Stamper, P. (1994) 'Northamptonshire', in *English County Histories: A Guide*, eds C.R.J. Currie and C.P. Lewis, Stroud, 291–301.

Steane, J.M. (1974) *The Northamptonshire Landscape*, London.

Steedman, K. (1994) 'Excavation of a site at Riby Crossroads, Lincolnshire', *Archaeological Journal* **151**, 212–306.

Stenton, F.M. (1971) *Anglo-Saxon England*, 3rd edn, Oxford.

Sumbler, M.G. (1996) *British Regional Geology: London and the Thames Valley*, 4th edn, HMSO.

Swanton, M.J. ed. (1996) *The Anglo-Saxon Chronicle*, London.

Taylor, C. (1967) 'Whiteparish', *Wiltshire Archaeological Magazine* **62**, 79–102.

Taylor, C. (1977) 'Polyfocal settlement and the English village', *Medieval Archaeology* **21**, 189–93.

Taylor, C. (1983) *Village and Farmstead: A History of Rural Settlement in England*, London.

Taylor, C. (1995) 'Dispersed settlement in nucleated areas', *Landscape History* **17**, 27–34.

Taylor, C. (2002) 'Nucleated settlement: a view from the frontier', *Landscape History* **24**, 53–71.

Taylor, G. (2003) 'An early to middle Saxon settlement at Quarrington, Lincolnshire', *Antiquaries Journal* **83**, 231–80.

Taylor, S. and Dix, B. (1985) 'Iron Age and Roman settlement at Ashley, Northants', *Northamptonshire Archaeology* **20**, 87–112.

Thirsk, J. (1964) 'The common fields', *Past and Present* **29**, 3–29.

Thirsk, J. (1997) *Alternative Agriculture: A History from the Black Death to the Present Day*, Oxford.

Thirsk, J. ed. (2000) *Rural England: An Illustrated History of the Landscape*, Oxford.

Thomas, A. (1998) *Grange Park, Courteenhall, Northamptonshire: archaeological evaluation*, unpublished report, Cotswold Archaeological Trust.

Thomas, A. and Enright, D. (2003) 'Excavation of an Iron Age settlement at Wilby Way, Great Doddington', *Northamptonshire Archaeology* **31**, 15–70.

Thorne, A. (2003) 'A medieval tenement at Deene End, Weldon, Northamptonshire', *Northamptonshire Archaeology* **31**, 105–23.

Thorpe, H. (1964) 'Rural settlement', in *The British Isles: A Systematic Geography*, eds J. W. Watson and J. B. Sissons, London, 358–79.

Toulmin Smith, L. ed. (1906–10) *The Itinerary of John Leland*, 5 vols, London.

Turner, G. J. ed. (1899) *Select Pleas of the Forest*, Selden Society 13.

Upex, S. G. (2002) 'Landscape continuity and the fossilization of Roman fields', *Archaeological Journal* **159**, 77–108.

Van de Noort, R. (2004) *The Humber Wetlands: The Archaeology of a Dynamic Landscape*, Macclesfield.

Vaughan-Williams, A. (2005) *Whittlewood: assessment of the archaeobotanical remains*, unpublished report, Royal Holloway University of London.

Wade-Martins, P. (1980) *Village Sites in Launditch Hundred*, East Anglian Archaeology Report, 10.

Wainwright, A. (1990) *Fallow deer park: excavation of a Roman pottery kiln north of Stowe School sports ground*, unpublished report, The National Trust, Stowe Landscape Gardens, 45.

Walker, G. (1992) *Towcester retail development, Northamptonshire: report on the results of an archaeological evaluation*, unpublished report, Cotswold Archaeological Trust.

Warner, P. (1987) *Greens, Commons and Clayland Colonization: The Origins and Development of Greenside Settlement in East Suffolk*, Leicester.

Warner, P. (1996) *The Origins of Suffolk*, Manchester.

Waterbolk, H. T. (1995) 'Patterns of the peasant landscape', *Proceedings of the Prehistoric Society* **61**, 1–36.

Watts, V. ed. (2004) *The Cambridge Dictionary of English Place-names*, Cambridge.

Whitelock, D. ed. (1979) *English Historical Documents, I, c. 500–1042*, 2nd edn, London.

Williams, R. J. (1993) *Pennyland and Hartigans: Two Iron Age and Saxon Sites in Milton Keynes*, Buckinghamshire Archaeological Society Monograph Series 4.

Williams, R. J. and Zeepvat, R. J. (1994) *Bancroft: A Late Bronze Age/Iron Age Settlement, Roman Villa and Temple-Mausoleum*, 2 vols, Buckinghamshire Archaeological Society Monograph Series 7.

Williamson, T. (1986) 'The development of settlement in north-west Essex: the results of a recent field survey', *Essex Archaeology and History* **17**, 120–32.

Williamson, T. (1998) 'The "Scole-Dickleburgh field system" revisited', *Landscape History* **20**, 19–28.

Williamson, T. (2003) *Shaping Medieval Landscapes: Settlement, Society, Environment*, Macclesfield.

Willis, B. (1755) *The History and Antiquities of the Town, Hundred and Deanry of Buckingham*, London.

Woodfield, P., Conlon, R. and de Broise, A. (2005) *Whittlewood project: historic buildings surveys*, 12 vols, unpublished report.

Wright, L. W. (2003) 'Woodland continuity and change: ancient woodland in eastern Hertfordshire', *Landscape History* **25**, 67–78.

Wrightson, K. (2000) *Earthly Necessities: Economic Lives in Early Modern Britain, 1470–1570*, London.

Young, C. R. (1979) *The Royal Forests of Medieval England*, Leicester.

Index

Numbers in italics refer to pages showing figures